Books of Merit

Almost THERE

The Family Vacation Then and Now

Curtis Gillespie

THOMAS ALLEN PUBLISHERS
TORONTO

Library and Archives Canada Cataloguing in Publication

Gillespie, Curtis, 1960–
        Almost there : the family vacation, then and now / Curtis Gillespie.

ISBN 978-0-88762-938-9

1. Family vacations—Humor.   2. Gillespie, Curtis, 1960– —Family.
I. Title.

GV182.8.G54   2012   306.4'8125   C2011-908272-1

Editor: Janice Zawerbny
Cover design: Michel Vrana
Cover images: Folded Map: Jami Garrison / dreamstime.com; Vintage neon: Darla Hallmark /
    dreamstime.com; Retro Diner Interior: jgroup / istockphoto.com; Sunny Beach: Trout55 /
    istockphoto.com; Canola Road Sunset: Ben Goode / dreamstime.com; Toy Car: Michel Vrana

Published by Thomas Allen Publishers,
a division of Thomas Allen & Son Limited,
390 Steelcase Road East,
Markham, Ontario L3R 1G2 Canada

www.thomasallen.ca

ONTARIO ARTS COUNCIL
CONSEIL DES ARTS DE L'ONTARIO

Canada Council
for the Arts

The publisher gratefully acknowledges the support of
The Ontario Arts Council for its publishing program.

We acknowledge the support of the Canada Council for the Arts, which
last year invested $20.1 million in writing and publishing throughout Canada.

We acknowledge the Government of Ontario through the Ontario
Media Development Corporation's Ontario Book Initiative.

We acknowledge the financial support of the Government of Canada
through the Canada Book Fund for our publishing activities.

11 12 13 14 15   5 4 3 2 1

Text printed on a 100% PCW recycled stock

Printed and bound in Canada

This book is dedicated to my mother, Pat Gillespie,
for reasons too numerous to itemize (all of them good).

The perceived importance of family bonding to the construction of a happy family . . . situates the family at the centre of tourism and tourism as a potentially core component in the healthy maintenance of the happy family. The good parent, within this construct, is someone who ensures the well-being of the family through the provision of holiday opportunities for the family that allow the unit to bond together away from the distractions of the everyday.

— Neil Carr

Associate Professor, Department of Tourism,
University of Otago, New Zealand
Children's and Families' Holiday Experiences

There's no such thing as fun for the whole family.

—Jerry Seinfeld

Contents

1

The Memory Well

IN THE SUMMER of 1973, my parents announced our family was going to take a trip. A *trip*, mind you. They didn't use the word *vacation* because, I suspect, it implied things they weren't willing to commit to, such as our safety and comfort. The plan was that in mid-December eight of us—mother, father, and six children aged three to thirteen, five boys and one girl—were going to pile in our faux-wood-panelled Ford Country Squire station wagon and drive through the middle of the continent from Calgary to Mexico City, then turn around and come back along the west coast. Six weeks. Eight thousand kilometres. Through the high snowy passes of Montana and Utah. The emptiness of Arizona. The heat of the central Mexican desert. I still find this next fact hard to square with a memory of sane and loving parents, but once we got past Utah we were going to *camp*. Every night in a three-room eighty-pole oilskin canvas cave that when rolled up was roughly the size and weight of a small refrigerator. It took four of us two hours to put up and almost as long to take down, and had once caused my father to suffer a perforated hernia. I loved that tent, but I hated it, too.

We set off on a cold and gloomy December morning. The canvas tent and most of our luggage was roped to the roof of the car and covered with a tarp. The trip started as every trip did, whether it was to the local mall or Mexico City—a jostling for seats, superior position, bragging rights. No single seat was really that much better than any other, but we fought over them because they were something to fight over; usually the fighting was nothing but shoving and pushing, though often it escalated into rabbit punches, eye pokes, head butts, and nut chops. The monarch's throne was the space between the middle row of forward-facing seats and the set of facing jump seats at the back; the throne wasn't very comfortable, but there was room enough for just one child, which made it the only spot really worth having (and this was long before the days when seat belts were mandatory; in fact, I don't remember if that old wagon even *had* seat belts). At thirteen, as the oldest child, I believed myself entitled to the throne, but I was slow getting to the car and when I tried to rough up my brother Keith for the spot, he and my brother Bruce ganged up on me and gave me a double nipple twist. I ended up in the jump seats with my sister, Janine. Sitting perpendicular to the direction in which the car was moving always made me feel queasy. I hated the jump seats.

We were smart enough kids, the six of us (though not nearly as smart as we thought we were), but we had zero notion that by travelling in this way in 1973 we were personifying the zenith of a significant historical trend. In fact, we were living in the last great gasp of the family car trip as a major North American cultural expression, an expression crank-started into life fifty years earlier by the introduction of automobile travel as a recreational pursuit and brought into full flower after the Second World War when the buying power of the middle class increased such that cars were widely available and families could afford them. Families could also afford to *take* a vacation; prior to the war, workers' rights began to crystallize, and legislated paid vacation time, once unheard of, was becoming commonplace. The combination of paid holidays and being able to purchase a station wagon one could load to the roof (and above) was, in many ways, the starting line of what we now understand as the family vacation.

Which was what we were up to, even though, as mentioned, we were probably already living in the latter stages of the automobile trip as the predominant family vacation mode. It was history itself we were taking part in, though it was hardly history of a Hegelian stamp, since you might say the jury is still out on whether the automobile will ultimately be seen as progressive in humanity's run. Not that we'd have known, or cared, anything about Hegel, history, progress, or the zenith of the automobile trip; we just figured we were going on a really long drive. My hope, though (no matter where history comes down on oil and the automobile), is that there will always be room for the road trip in the family vacation. It's so rich in possibility. I know that driving to Mexico and back created something larger than a simple collection of experiences and destinations for our family; it created memories and moments so strong, so singular, that we saw our family as unique. It gave us a vision of the larger family project at work, particularly upon reflection in later years, of course. There wasn't much conscious articulation of it when we were all sitting around watching TV a few months later, as if twelve-year-old Bruce said to nine-year-old Conor, "Hey, that trip really helped me understand and put into words the nature of our family dynamic, don't you agree?" Yet, at some level, it did precisely that; spending six weeks in a car driving to Mexico and back became a key component in the shared baseline knowledge of what we were as a unit, of how we related to one another, of how we were moving together through time—reflections that have stayed with us as a family decades later.

Orvar Löfgren, in *On Holiday*, wrote about making a discovery one day, as an adult, down in his basement, where he found "an old holiday album, which I produced as a twelve-year-old. It describes a family trip across Sweden and starts with a pasted-in map where the route is carefully drawn. Snapshots, admission tickets, hotel labels, and picture postcards document each step, along with the author's running commentary. It documents a vacation *and* shows the project 'our family,' an institution that became very visible during those summer months of intensive interaction."

I love that notion of the family as a *project*, suggesting as it does that it takes time, that it involves construction, that it requires thought and craft, that it speaks to an ongoing evolution. The family as project helps create a family that can talk, be together, and travel together. Whether we realize it or not, our family vacations are key building blocks in the creation of a family, of a "project."

Whatever piece of the family project Mexico was meant to be, however, all we knew, as kids, was that we were heading towards an intensely foreign place known to us mostly through the cliff divers of Acapulco we saw Saturday afternoons on *The Wide World of Sports*. My delicious nightmares leading up to the day of departure were of scorpions, rattlesnakes, and getting lost in the empty, wobbly-hot Mexican desert.

As we pulled out of our cold, gaunt northwest Calgary suburb, my mother lit a cigarette, turned around and did a head count to avoid a repeat of a trip to Edmonton a year earlier when we were an hour down the highway before realizing we'd left two-year-old Matt at home playing in the basement. The goal for the first day of our trip was to make it at least as far as central Montana. Seven or eight hours of total driving would be a good start. We'd been driving for half an hour, approximately six-tenths of one percent into the journey there, when Bruce, eleven months younger than me, shouted from the middle seats. "Pass me a comic book," he said. "An *Archie*."

I reached into the huge cardboard box between my feet. Our mother had spent the previous three months collecting thousands of comics and puzzle books to help occupy us during the slog ahead. She'd kept them locked in a closet leading up to our journey, under the not unreasonable premise that there'd be no point to having them in the car if we'd already read them all. Bruce and I had tried to break into the closet a month earlier. Somehow Mom found out and we were sent to confession at St. Luke's daily for two weeks. Every one of us had been anxious to dig into the stacks. I pulled out an *Archie* for Bruce and held it aloft to show him who controlled the means of distribution.

"Give it to me, you loser," he said.

I flung it at his head as hard as I could, the pages flapping like the wings of a buckshot-filled bird. He ducked, picked up his comic, and started reading. I looked back at the box. So many comics! It was a stroke of genius on my mother's part to have hoarded them. I riffled through the stacks and found a *Spider-Man*, my favourite.

Ten minutes later, I was in trouble. I'd been concentrating too hard, reading too close, with the comic too near my face, and this, combined with the side seating and the relative cold of the back seats, brought the car sickness up from the bottom of my stomach to where it pressed against my windpipe. I swallowed hard to keep it down, but a tiny spurt of burning liquid came into the back of my throat.

"We have to stop," I said thinly.

My sister, seated across from me, looked up from her comic.

"We have to stop," I repeated.

"Dad! Curt's gonna hurl! Stop the car!"

My mother looked back. "Oh, for heaven's sake," she said. "Just stop reading for a few minutes. You'll be fine."

"We just left the goddamn house," said my father. "Why didn't you throw up before you got in the car?"

Janine clambered a bit up onto her seat, and then with no fanfare my throat opened. The contents of my stomach splashed into the middle of the comic box, covering the entire library in partially digested Froot Loops and Cap'n Crunch. Janine put her hand to her mouth and nose, and watched my sickness run itself out across my chest and pants.

"Oh, gross!" she said, scrambling across the throne into the middle row of seats. "He puked! He puked right into the box of comics. They're covered. All of them!"

My father pulled over. Everybody piled out onto the side of the highway. We were still less than an hour from home. My mother stood with her arms crossed, smoking a cigarette with great melancholy as she watched my father create a minor ecological calamity by hurling the entire swampy box of bloated comics into the snow-filled ditch. There was no such a thing as the *environment* back then. My mother dropped her cigarette on the ground and extinguished it with the toe of her boot. Her months of hoarding and protecting and planning were ruined. Everybody hated me. On the way back to the car, my brother Conor punched me in the kidneys from behind, doubling me over. "Loser," he said.

"You'll all have to find something else to do in the car now," my mother said. "And it's a long way to Mexico City and back."

Nobody would sit with me in the jump seats, where the smell of vomit would stay sharp for days afterwards. I had to strip down to my underwear, but my father refused me a change of clothing on the grounds that my duffel bag was on the roof rack buried somewhere under that canvas tent, and there was no goddamn way he was untying that goddamn tent an hour into our trip. I hated that tent. My father hadn't had a cigarette in three years, but he was smoking again two hours into the trip. As we neared the U.S. border I sat alone in the back, despised by everyone, myself included. The U.S. border guard said nothing about the naked shivering boy hugging his knees to his chest in the back of the station wagon, but I could see him peering at me when we pulled away. I think he wrote down our license plate number. It was, indeed, a long way to Mexico City and back. And that *Spider-Man* was the last comic book I ever read.

*

The family vacation and the *idea* of the family vacation have always held considerable interest for me, a fascination that has to do, I suppose, with an abiding curiosity about families in general, how they form and disband, how they communicate or don't, how they operate or don't. I've written about family from the day I started writing and will continue to do so, I'm sure, until I lay that pen down, and you can't think about the family without thinking about the family vacation; I can't, at any rate. Families are obviously infinitely and uniquely complex, which means their vacations are likely to be the same.

I'm fortunate enough to recall the family vacations of my childhood with actual fondness, and although these memories are no doubt rimed with nostalgia (as every happy childhood is), there was an objective love and goodwill at the core of my upbringing. Which is why this book will perhaps not resonate with those who grew up in less-than-nurturing environments (although I hope it does) and who were forced to go on trips with people they felt no affection towards. Happy families are not the most fertile writerly soil, for as Tolstoy so famously wrote in *Anna Karenina*, "Happy families are all alike; every unhappy family is unhappy in its own way." But if I can be so presumptuous as to reframe Tolstoy's words, I would say that every happy family will vacation in its own unique way (ready as they are to share any and all experiences together), whereas unhappy families are all alike on vacation (turned inward and anxious to be elsewhere). At the risk of sounding naive, I happen to think that families are not always or necessarily the seething angst-ridden prisons of alienation that art and the therapy industry typically make them out to be, but that sometimes they are both a stimulus and framing device for understanding and intimacy and unity . . . sometimes even on vacation.

The family vacation as I have experienced it, and as I view it symbolically and metaphorically, makes me smile. Am I lucky? Yes. Am I deluded? Possibly. For this, I can only blame my parents, who raised six children in a spirit of love and patience, even if they spanked us, grounded us, and failed to push me hard enough as a child to become the professional soccer player I know I could have become with even just the occasional dose of belligerent sports-parent hectoring. I grew up in a small house jammed to the rafters with human beings, not just because we were a family of eight, but because our parents were well-liked by our friends, which meant there were always an extra couple of bodies hanging around at any given moment. Ours was a disorganized, fun, energetic household, and as you'd guess, our vacations were about the same. The further my wife, Cathy, and I advance into raising our two daughters, the more astonished I am by what my parents achieved: the raising of six children, all of whom still like one another, none of whom have ever been in jail, and all of whom are, if not well-adjusted, at least not mis-anthropically maladjusted. I once told a poet friend of mine that my mother used to read to us at the dinner table after supper on many nights. Sometimes it was *The Hobbit*. A couple times she might have even read Shakespeare; I know my dad liked Shakespeare, even though he didn't finish high school (my dad, not Shakespeare). My poet friend has never let this family detail go, and to this day shakes his beard and goes on about how my family was, in fact, the most dis-torted of all because we got along and exited our childhoods with minimal emotional scar tissue.

Growing up, I had garden-variety teenage concerns—girls fasci-nated and terrified me, I didn't have my own bedroom or privacy of any sort, I was short and pudgy, my roster of friends was not that long or reliable, school sucked. But my family life, far from exacerbating these problems or alienating me further, in fact saved me from getting swallowed up by whatever troubles I had. And whenever we went on vacation, I can truly report that I went with a spirit of excitement and anticipation (which would usually prove to be warranted), not dread or opposition. That's not to say that every vacation was a peak experience or one fantastic and warm family outing after another. Hardly. I was often underwhelmed with our destination. I was frequently driven to violence by the immature antics of my siblings in the car (which I obviously never instigated). I was frequently carsick. We spent a lot of our vacation capital visiting relatives. But despite all this, going on holidays with my family was never something I rebelled against. It was, most of the time, a hell of a lot of fun.

When you stop to think about it, though (which I often have, sometimes in the middle of a family vacation moment going pear-shaped all around us), going on vacation with your entire family is hardly the way to guarantee that you will have, in the first place, a good vacation, or, in the second, a happy—or even a monosyllabically communicative—family upon your return. In fact, I'm sure we can all recall examples of family vacations that seemed to conclude not just as periods away from home but as harbingers that the family itself was aboard the *Titanic* and all that was left to do was to get pickled and wait for the iceberg.

This, luckily, was a rare experience for me, because I have always believed the family vacation was about so much more than the activity or destination. Certainly, the family vacations we took in my childhood were enjoyable for the most part, even usually great fun and adventure, but they have also been central to my ability to recollect memories of growing up, of what it was like to be part of my family, and to form conclusions and understandings about the nature of the family structure. They also helped me, and still help me, understand who I am. Memory is the wheel on which we are forever turning the raw material of our experience, and the family vacation supplies a great deal of that raw material. From that memory wheel comes insight. And because these times in our lives are so amplified—these family vacations when we are separated from the structure and distraction of daily life—they bear great meaning and influence.

The family vacation is a deep well; it's one of the best tools we have to interpret our past and present, and peek into our future. The kids, a tent and sleeping bags, some sunscreen, the open road—just another road trip, you say? Hardly. The meaning of our memories can and will shift, alter, and morph, but memory will always be an instrument we use to define our families, ourselves, our relationships. There are many situations and moments we use to create the movie in our heads of what our family is, of what "family" is, but the clearest often come from the family vacation. It's specific in its time frame and is often conducted in sharp contrast with our daily lives, which means our senses and attention are heightened. The family vacation is a way to bank family memories, to colour in what might otherwise be broad outlines. As Julia Harrison writes in her book, *Being a Tourist: Finding Meaning in Pleasure Travel*, "All those who travel for pleasure, no matter what name they apply to themselves . . . unfailingly want to gather valuable and enduring memories."

Furthermore, the family vacation is a highly fluid socio-cultural institution. As the culture in which families exist has changed, so the vacation has adapted to fit or reflect that culture. The family vacation, in both structure and meaning, has evolved as society has evolved, although one or two seismic shifts in the nature of the family vacation have, I think it's fair to say, moved the needle on the broader culture. How families choose to vacation is a clear expression of who we are, and the nature of the family vacation tends to reflect, and sometimes even predict, societal change.

The family vacation, then, is central to how individuals and families define themselves, how families form, and most particularly how these intensified periods in the life of a family continue through the years to replenish our individual and shared memory pools. "Family memories offer us a way to make sense of our family history," writes Susan Sessions Rugh in her book *Are We There Yet?* Vacations are significant events in the lives of adults *and* children: we remember them keenly for good reason—because they help tell us who we are and how we fit into our family. The vacations I went on with my family when I was growing up may have been fun, but they were also much more than *fun*; the nuance and richness of what it all meant has only gradually been revealed through adulthood and the raising of children. I understand much better now that the manner and quality of vacation a family experiences together are a symbol for many things besides a trip's stated raison d'être (which is frequently interesting enough in and of itself, of course). It can also be viewed theoretically, moving into the philosophical sandbox of thinkers like the French philosopher Jean Baudrillard and his ideas around the interpretation of experience, which are relevant to how we interpret the experience of the family vacation. To boil a dozen works of philosophy down to a few sentences (which I am only too happy to do), Baudrillard says we live in an ongoing state of "hyper-reality," that we utilize and then inevitably begin to *prefer* representations of reality rather than reality itself, and that the human condition is so impossibly overwhelming that our experiences can't help but devolve into mere encounters with simulations of reality—simulacra, he calls them—encounters that we end up preferring to reality. We'd rather visit New York–New York hotel in Las Vegas than actually take on New York's crime, grime, and complexity; we'd rather consume pornography than deal with the complications of real sex; we feel stronger emotional ties to characters on TV than we do to the flawed and inconsistent people in our own lives. And so on.

Sounds odd, I know, but once you've visited Disney's various themed experiences, been to a dude ranch, or seen the "island" Royal Caribbean built to replicate a real tropical island, you might think Baudrillard is on to something. This is a counterpoint to what Orvar Löfgren calls the stance of the "anti-tourist" and the obsession with locating "authentic" experience, or that of the "post-tourist" who has given up trying to find new and authentic experiences, and has joined in with the throng going to Disneyland, knowing it's fake but taking their fun with a heavy dose of irony. There is no such thing as inauthentic experience for the post-tourist, because even an encounter with an utterly fabricated site—a fake island, say, or Disney's Swiss Family Robinson tree house (a fake of a fake, since it was a fictional experience and the "tree" holding the tree house is made of steel, concrete, and stucco)—will nevertheless yield insights into contemporary culture.

Authenticity comes up again and again in travel and leisure literature, but what, precisely, do we understand by the word *authenticity*, anyway, as it relates to our travel experience? There's no easy answer for that, and much depends on what you're looking for in the first place. We all know that a "tourist trap" is something contrived and manufactured and best avoided, but what if we are *looking* for tourist traps? What if we like tourist traps? Don't we then want to find the most authentic tourist trap? Of course, there are times when even being sure of what you want won't help you find it, given that much of today's marketing is not just manipulative or misleading (we expect that) but blatantly fraudulent. Recently in both Spain and my home province of Alberta tourism marketing bodies were found to be using photos of exotic locations to stand in for home base. Alberta used a beach in Northumberland, England, of all places, to represent Alberta's natural beauty; Spain used a photo of a deserted Bahamas beach to stand in for its crowded Costa Brava.

So the question *What does it mean for a family to go on vacation?* is certainly not as simple as it might first appear. We want our children, and ourselves as parents, to have as much access as possible to what we view as authentic, real, genuine experiences and places, however we define that, though we also want our children to gradually be exposed to the world's complexity, part of which is undeniably the way in which our leisure is manipulated by corporate interests. We want our children to touch and know the world as it is, but we also want to keep them physically safe and allow their emotional innocence to exfoliate naturally rather than have it torn away painfully and too early. These tensions are constantly at play, so to speak, in the family vacation. Furthermore, since we're on the subject, if perhaps we are unfortunate enough to lack "authentic" connections with one another in the first place, then what's the point of seeking authentic experiences on a family vacation? Or can one help create the other? We need to ask these probing questions of family travel because the answers say so much about who we are and how we find the shared experience that allows us to communicate inside the family compact.

Why *do* families travel? Are parents trying to create bonds they are failing to make elsewhere? Are we broadening our children, or setting them up for dissatisfaction with their lives back at home? What is the value of travelling together as opposed to staying home together? Do we truly believe we are providing our children with valuable experiences, or just *exposing* them to the world so as to provide a baseline for future individual explorations? Or is it just about having fun? There is research being conducted today around the role of the family vacation in the creation of the family unit overall, and one of the terms in use for the family vacation is the "memory-making process." The family vacation, as we can see, is an ongoing memory-creation operation that's never going to be straightforward:

It involves taking a multifarious and usually ill-disciplined unit—the family—sending it on a logistically complex mission—the vacation—and asking it to secure a poorly defined and highly subjective outcome—"fun."

That doesn't sound so hard, does it?

*

Our first major stop on our Mexico-or-bust trip was Salt Lake City, where my parents wanted us to see the Mormons and the Tabernacle Choir. Why they did, I'm not sure. Perhaps it had something to do with the catholic and Catholic nature of our upbringing. My mother was, and still is, a devout Roman Catholic. My father respected my mother's faith, but he was an avowed agnostic who used to stand in the bathroom on Sunday mornings, church day, with shaving foam on his face and his razor in his hand and answer our theological queries with things like, "How the hell am I supposed to know if there's a God. Go ask your mother."

Or it could have been the profligate nature of the procreative impulse on display in Salt Lake City; my mother might have reckoned it would do us good to see that Irish Catholics weren't the only people that bred like bacteria. My mother was pregnant for forty-five of the first sixty-four months of her marriage, and on the day of my sister Janine's birth my mother was a twenty-six-year-old woman with five preschoolers in the house. Much later in life I remarked to my friend Rich, who was also a friend of the family, how astounding it was to me that my parents hadn't killed off one or two of us out of frustration and simple expedience. "How do you know they didn't?" he said.

Salt Lake City was a place of great mystery to us, and its shrouded, misty December climate seemed suited to that feeling. I had trouble imagining who would want to live near a salt lake: what was the point of that? We toured the Tabernacle Choir, and Brigham Young University, and learned about the pilgrimage to find religious freedom. It made an impression, to be sure, but then our mother told us that some Mormons believed a man could have more than one wife. We kids absorbed that as best we could, and one or two of us simply looked our father's way for help as to how we might interpret this. He said nothing, just offered his characteristic sly grin and then raised his eyebrows suggestively. My mother slapped him on the shoulder. We piled into the car and got back on the road.

In 1924, the renowned British essayist and travel writer Hillaire Belloc (who once walked across the western United States to visit his future wife) wrote a piece entitled *The Road*. "The Road is one of the great human institutions because it is fundamental to social existence," he wrote. "The Road moves and controls all history."

Belloc may have written those words nearly ninety years ago with some confidence, but he could hardly have known how prescient they were, particularly in relation to North American history. His thoughts on the connection between man and road coincided with something of a sea change in the national psyche which allowed the common person to believe that travel for leisure purposes was not just possible, but morally acceptable. Elmer Davis summed it up in 1932 when he wrote that the "pioneer conditions that made indolence suspect and leisure unknown discouraged the habit of traveling for pleasure . . . till good roads were general. There was not enough fun in it to make it worth while . . . Then suddenly, the automobile came within reach of every one. There were immense distances to be covered and a machine capable of covering them."

Davis was broadly correct, but I think his words have particular resonance for someone from the western part of North America; in our own early family travels we had farther to go to get somewhere. It was that simple. On the wide and endless prairie where I was raised and still live you could drive for hours and hours, stop, get out of your car, look around, and be hard pressed not to conclude that you'd forgotten to put the car in gear back home. I have no doubt that in choosing to go to Mexico and back in 1973, my parents were not just trying to do something different and unusual for their children, but also that they simply had no choice but to go far away in order for us to see something far different. The almost genetic need to cover vast distances has, to my observer's eye, less purchase on the subconscious of the eastern North American because history and geography have conspired to create a denser, more tightly concentrated web of sights and destinations worth seeing in the east. Within two hours' drive of Washington, DC, you can, for instance, reach most of the sites central to America's formation. Within two hours' drive of Edmonton you can reach places that look about the same as what you'd find if you drove two minutes from Edmonton; there is precious little of historical interest within two hours' drive of my home, unless you are a student of the fur trade, Native history, or the North-West Mounted Police, and even less of geographical interest, unless you are an aficionado of the prairie landscape (luckily I happen to find all of the above quite compelling).

But none of this was of any consequence to the middle class until the automobile became widely available. John Rae, writing in 1971, concurred with Elmer Davis on the middle-class leap to the automobile. In *The Road and the Car in American Life*, Rae tells us that it wasn't until the advent of an automobile readily accessible for nearly every class of citizen that the notion of an actual "vacation" for all was thinkable. Travel for the purposes of pleasure and recreation was a novelty as the 1920s dawned; by the 1930s it was not novel at all, largely due to the affordability, mobility, and control the automobile gave those without a summer house in the Hamptons to escape the pressures of the Upper East Side. Going on a vacation with the family was suddenly not just possible, but convenient and affordable, although the trickle-down effect for the masses didn't hit until after the Second World War.

It was a trend that would not stop for decades and which only began to abate with the advent of cheap air travel and the gasoline crises of the 1970s. In 1971, the year Rae published *The Road and the Car in American Life* (and when my parents were probably subconsciously hatching the idea for our epic family car trip), he reported that nine out of ten families took their family vacations in a car via the highway. It's important to point out—because it's crucial to understanding the evolution of the family vacation—that the development of the American automobile industry was from the start pursued by people with a mass market in mind; this was the opposite of the European auto industry. Manufacturers in Britain and Germany pursued auto development as a purview of the wealthy. Henry Ford, conversely, expressly stated that his dream was to create "a car for the great multitude." His dream came true. Even in dire circumstances, car ownership was possible; in *The Grapes of Wrath* the Joads may have had to escape to California during the Depression, but they were able to do so in a car.

There may have been times along the way to Mexico that we looked like a bunch of Okies, too, with eight of us jammed into that wagon and with most of our earthly possessions roped to the roof.

*

It was in 1956 that President Dwight D. Eisenhower signed into law the Federal Aid Highway Act, which was the plan to change the highway system from one of semi-anarchic toll road state construction to a federally controlled Interstate Highway system. It was essentially from that point forward that the family car trip became the vacation idiom of the average family; the creation of the Interstate

corresponded with increased postwar economic power (more families could afford cars), increased industry advances (cars could go
faster and were safer), and increased amenities along the way (more
motels, gas stations, and restaurants, not to mention better tourism
facilities to handle the travellers). In short, Ike built the highways
when people were willing and able to travel on them in great numbers (although the Interstate was, as many a book has noted, hardly
an unqualified success: maintenance and repair was radically under-
funded; critics felt freeways leading into cities cut off and therefore
quarantined low-income areas from upscale neighbourhoods; there
was widespread corruption in the highway construction industry).
In 1955, Los Angelenos protesting against Eisenhower's plan labelled
the increased auto pollution *smog*, which was the first time the word
had been applied to carbon emissions in America (the word was
first recorded in 1905 in London, England, to describe a mixture of
smoke and *fog*).

The massive upgrade in the highway system brought change
everywhere. The motel industry developed in lockstep with the
travelling population, becoming more convenient and consumer-
friendly, attracting families with children-stay-free offers, swimming
pools, free breakfasts for children under certain ages, playgrounds.
Fast-food outlets changed to accommodate family car travel, as well,
perhaps the most iconic example being the A&W drive-in, a car-
friendly approach that was rapidly adopted by numerous chains and
independents.

Of course, the car and its corollary industries were everywhere.
During this period, one-sixth of all Americans produced, sold, serviced, or drove motorized vehicles for their livelihood, and certainly
this was the case in Canada, as well, which has always featured the
auto industry as a huge component of its economy. In fact, it was
even the basis of our *household* economy. My father ran his own business, Calgary Glass and Trim, and although he repaired and recov-

ered furniture now and then, his biggest customers, by a wide margin, were the car dealerships in town. Most of his business revolved around car-windshield repair, seat-cover repair, and (here's a nostalgia item) vinyl-roof repair—the *canopy*, the *halo*, and, my favourite, the glorious *landau*, which was a covering of the rear third or so of the roof, designed to make it appear as though it were a convertible. He regularly removed and applied these vinyl roofs, and I can so easily winch up from my memory the smell of the glue he used, a smell that delivers me whole to my youth and my father's workshop.

My siblings and I often spent time in his workshop helping him— or so we thought—although I wish now I'd gone more often. In retrospect, it feels as though in pulling off those vinyl roofs we were also peeling away some of the symbols of the auto industry's excesses, even that my father was, in fact, part of an industry soon to have the lid yanked off its trash can full of problems. Car travel might well have reached its peak in the sixties and seventies, which meant that just before the oil embargo of 1973 the family vacation was the epicentre of the North American family's love affair with the car, that moment when romance, cost, and efficiency met and group-hugged, an embrace that lasted until mass air travel, OPEC, and the environment broke up the party. Susan Sessions Rugh, in her book *Are We There Yet?*, termed this period—roughly from the end of the Second World War to the mid-seventies—the "golden age" of the American vacation.

All of which means that the family vacation as a common notion, even as a kind of universal expectation, could be said to have started with the advent of mass automobile travel on American highways. An efficient means of transportation, which was also cheap, became available through large-scale production to the bulging lower and middle classes. After the Second World War, when North America was flush with confidence and economic growth, roadways sprung up to provide corridors on which to use these vehicles. Suddenly, and it almost *was* sudden, millions of families could afford to travel as a *family*. Travel they did, and so did we.

*

By the time we got to Arizona, the car was beginning to feel more like a space capsule we'd been trapped in for months as opposed to a means to an end, as if the trip was not about seeing the world, but was simply a way to spend six weeks sitting in the car. My parents had done their research, though. They knew the kind of thing we'd like, and they knew about the Meteor Crater just outside Flagstaff. As we drove to it, they pumped us up. We were incredulous. *An outer-space meteor hit the earth? The crater's a mile wide and six hundred feet deep?! It hit fifty thousand years ago?!!* When we pulled into the parking lot, the six of us kids, especially us four oldest boys, were so hyped we sprinted to the edge of the crater. My mom and dad ran after us, leaving Matt and Janine straggling behind in the middle of the parking lot.

"Hey," my dad shouted. "Hold up, you little brats!"

They were terrified, I'm sure, that we were just going to go careening over the lip of the cliffside. Had we visited the Meteor Crater on our way *back* from Mexico City instead of our way down—in other words, after another month's worth of driving, fighting, throwing up, getting lost on Mexican back roads, and an incident with a whip—perhaps they'd have egged us on. *Yeah, there's a great swimming pool right over the lip, you guys. Just jump right in.*

Half an hour after we'd arrived at the Meteor Crater, my mother and sister were strolling around the crater's rim, enjoying the heat, the brilliant sunshine, simply being out of the car. She'd sent my father off with the five boys. Mom and Janine stopped at one of the designated viewing areas and peered into the 600-foot-deep crater, taking in its awesome scope, perhaps recalling what she'd told us all earlier, that the impact explosion was 150 times greater than Hiroshima.

"Hey, look," said Janine, pointing to the distant centre of the crater. "There are people down there."

My mother peered deep into the crater. Her radar must have gone off, because she slotted a quarter into the viewing telescope and trained it towards the centre of the crater, half a mile away. Seconds later, she let it drop. "Gerry!! Gerry. Oh my God! Gerrrry. Helpp!"

My father came running over from the interpretive centre, where he'd been occupied showing Matt a display about the crater's mineral-debris field. He'd assumed that when we left him, it was to head back to where our mother was.

We were quite happy, the four of us, me, Bruce, Keith, and Conor. There weren't any fences once you got past the formal viewing area, and it really hadn't been that hard a climb down to the crater floor, though some tricky descent work had been required. There seemed no reason not to explore the crater. After all, what was the point of visiting the thing if you couldn't go to the middle? I wanted to stand there and look up and out. Who wants to be on the periphery?

The four of us didn't eat that night. After the rescue, which necessitated an emergency scrambling of half the Crater staff on duty that day, we drove away in humiliated silence. As the oldest, I got the blame. I always got the blame. I hated being the oldest. Everybody else got to play the younger-sibling card, and my parents fell for it every time.

"I swear," I said in the car. "I swear I didn't know there was quicksand at the bottom. I swear, Mom. Do you think we'd have gone down there if we knew that?"

The logic of my argument didn't sway her. "Quicksand!" she kept repeating. "I mean, quicksand. Didn't you see the signs?! They were everywhere. What if you'd stepped in it? Disappeared?!"

"You know," said Bruce. "That's actually a myth. You don't sink in quicksand."

My mother turned around and glared at us, lips tight. It may have been the angriest I had ever seen her . . . to that point (the qualifier being necessary since we still had 80 percent of the trip remaining). But to this day I insist that I did not see a single warning sign as we crossed the lip or clambered down the cliff face. Okay, yes, we saw them at the middle of the crater, but by then we were already there, and the ground felt solid enough, so what would have been the point of turning back then? What a waste of effort that would have been.

Mom and Dad, and Janine and Matt, ate KFC that night in Flagstaff, and the smell of it—the thirteen secret spices, the fries, the gravy—was almost too much to bear. It wasn't right. It was unfair. We pointed out that it was, technically speaking, child abuse to starve your children.

"We're so hungry," we said. "We have to eat. You can't not feed us. We're going to die."

"Good," said Janine.

"I don't care if you're hungry," said my mother. "You should have thought about how hungry you were when you were walking through that quicksand."

"I wasn't hungry then," said Keith.

My mom shot us a look that made us shut up. Who could blame her? She was probably wishing we'd found the quicksand. We spent the night in agony, stomachs growling, the scent of KFC everywhere. I have not eaten KFC since.

*

The early seventies was a tricky time to be making a trip like the one my parents had orchestrated for us. I doubt they would have set about planning it had it been even a few months later, given that it was in mid-October of 1973 that OPEC announced it was ceasing oil shipments to countries that supported Israel in the Yom Kippur War, which meant the United States, Canada, most of western Europe, and Japan. OPEC also used their power to begin hiking the price of oil, so not only was gas in short supply, it cost more. Gas was about 30 cents a gallon in January of 1973 and had tripled by year's end.

This was no small burden for my parents; my father's business was steady but unspectacular, and my mother had only recently returned to part-time work. We were not exactly poor, but my mother shopped for cheap cuts of meat and had a friend at the bakery who put aside half a dozen loaves of day-old bread a couple times a week. We lived in a small bungalow in the Calgary suburbs, and I recently brought about dropped jaws and bulging eyes in our two teenage daughters, Jessica and Grace, when I told them I did not have my own bedroom until I left home for university.

The oil crisis had an impact, albeit a minor one, on our trip, but it had a much greater effect on car travel in general for many years to come—and therefore on the family vacation. In fact, it's fair to say that the fall of 1973 may have been the last time when a family could look upon the cross-country car trip with virtually no guilt or worries other than those of individual family logistics. Following the autumn of 1973, the world of oil security has never been the same; these pressures increased throughout the seventies and early eighties, with another oil crisis in 1979 brought about by the fall of the Shah of Iran. There has also been a radical increase in the number of cars on the road, which has had an impact on traffic safety (which has been negatively affected even further by deteriorating highway infrastructure). The rise of environmental awareness has also changed the thinking of many families who otherwise might have hit the road for a few weeks to see where the wheel turned.

By the time we'd left on our trip in early December 1973 there were some gas lineups and the speed limit had dropped to 55 mph;

this was perhaps the first time since the end of the Second World War, nearly a full generation, that there was an inkling that an automobile trip was anything less than the most convenient and carefree way for a middle- or lower-middle-class family to take a vacation.

In many ways, the golden age of the gas-powered automobile is not only over, but died a long time ago; we've just yet to fully accept the inevitable. Of course, we are still reliant in many key ways on the car, but less so than we were a decade ago, a trend that will be even more pronounced a decade from now. And who knows if alternative fuel sources for cars, such as batteries or hydrogen, will allow us to fully recapture our traveller's imagination. Even the automobile industry's core incubator group—young teenage men—are increasingly getting their thrills from different places, such as electronics and other technology. A 2004 story in the *Los Angeles Times* revealed that in the decade from 1992 to 2002, the percentage of males aged sixteen and seventeen getting their driver's licenses dropped from 52 percent to 43 percent.

The sixties and early seventies—through the automotive confluence of the cost, safety, environmental innocence, and overall convenience—may well have been the apex of the family car vacation. This mode of vacation has become less predominant since then, given the rise in cost of gasoline, the rise in insurance rates, the introduction of mass air travel, the increased cost of lodging and food along the roadway, the deteriorating state of the highways, all combined with what has become an often crushing sense of crowdedness on the roads. Sometimes it seems as if, against all logic, there are more people moving than stationary. *Who are all these people?* I often ask myself now while driving on teeming highways. *And where are they in such a rush to get to?* A long drive on the highway used to be a pleasure; now it has the air of a chore.

This sense of congestion is not solely about the number of cars on the highway, but is also related to the hassle it has become in many major urban centres to actually get *to* the highway. By 2000, almost 80 percent of the population in Canada and the United States lived in urban areas, and of that number close to two-thirds lived in the suburbs, meaning that fully 50 percent of us live in a suburban environment. Suburbs have metastasized to monstrous degrees. More and more commuters live farther and farther out from the urban core, and use the suburban freeway system to get to work and get home. It has become a trial to *find* the open road, let alone travel along it. Travelling from one major city to another, particularly along the eastern seaboard, is not so much a highway drive as a series of hops between vast suburban links and ring road freeways.

All these factors speak to why the family vacation as expressed through the long-distance car trip already has an air of nostalgia to it, a *Leave It to Beaver* smell of a long-gone world we now choose to romanticize, but which we would have trouble re-creating even if we wanted to. Robert Sullivan, the author of *Cross Country*, predicted the demise of such trips in an article he wrote recently in the *Los Angeles Times*. The summer driving trip, meaning the "pack the kids in the car and set out for the West or the East or possibly the Grand Canyon trip," is under threat. "It's been endangered before," he wrote, "especially during the first energy crises in 1973 and 1979, when people spent good portions of their vacation lined up at the gas station." But today, referring mostly to the crowded attractions and highways, he concludes, "The death of the car-bound family vacation feels real to me."

I know I've considered attempting a re-creation of the Mexico trip my parents took their children on, but the truth is that it would be impossible to re-create even if we decided to try it. The vehicles of today, for one, are simply that much more comfortable, and I can assure you that a significant portion of the antics we got up to in the car were due to sheer discomfort. And we simply couldn't allow our children to not wear seat belts, the lack of which was central to the free-for-all that ruled our car on the way to Mexico. There are more people on the roads today, more people at the sights worth seeing, simply more people period. And at the sights worth seeing, the level of bureaucratic people management has altered the nature of the family vacation experience, so that events and encounters are now more sanitized, more packaged—pre-experienced, as it were—so that we are too often informed beforehand, by aggressively cheerful "interpreters," what we are supposed to feel and understand and take away. Of course, today we would have our own experiences, unique to us, memorable episodes in tune with our times. Of that I have no doubt, and it would be a good thing. But to consider the continental car trip as a way to reconnect with what our parents did for us is to indulge, I fear, in a kind of nostalgic and fruitless search. Such reconnection must, it feels to me, be performed through memory, not mimicry.

*

In exploring the nature and history of the family vacation—how it's evolved, what it means, how it shapes us—it's fair to say that I've researched principally those areas that seem most applicable to my life and time. My take on the family vacation will also be less than comprehensive for two other reasons: First, the family vacation is still, as already alluded to, a relatively new phenomenon. Second, there is a shortage of data on the subject. The tourism studies field has grown in the last couple of decades, to be sure, which is understandable, given that tourism is such a vast global enterprise. But even as late as 1985, John Jakle opened his book, *The Tourist*, by saying, "I present this book as an argument for renewed scholarly interest in tourism." Jakle has lived up to his end of the bargain: He has also written scholarly studies of the motel, the gas station, and the roadside fast-food restaurant.

The need for *renewed interest* is peculiar, though perhaps it has begun to happen since Jakle published his book in 1985. The level of tourist activity certainly warrants it. In 1999, Orvar Löfgren reported that 7 percent of the world's total workforce was employed in the tourism industry by the mid-1990s, an industry in which $3.4 trillion is spent every year. By 2020, Löfgren noted, it is expected that 1.6 billion of the planet's 7.8 billion people will take a trip abroad. These would appear to be significant numbers, but even as recently as 2003, research on the subject appeared to be lagging. Nancy Chesworth, a Canadian academic, wrote in the *International Journal of Consumer Studies* that, "A review of the literature on the impact of the family vacation experience in the fields of consumer issues, tourism, hospitality, home economics, family studies, psychology and sociology indicates little research reported to date. Furthermore, there has been little published in this area of study in the last decade. This seems unusual considering the high degree of importance placed on families and on vacations by societies around the world." In addition, she found a lack of research on the impact of the family vacation on single-parent families, marital relationships, gender differences in terms of vacation choices and satisfaction, individual family members, the positive and negative impacts on children (including academic achievement and sociability), children's reaction to holiday experiences, and the well-functioning family versus the mildly or seriously dysfunctional family.

Pretty much everything, in other words.

It's perplexing that there are not think tanks and university departments specializing in the family vacation. If there is one, I wasn't able to find it. As Jakle wrote in 1985, "The study of tourism, like the study of recreation generally, has not been recognized by most professions as a respectable field for scholarly inquiry. Apart from the bias against leisure inherent in the work ethic, the supposed superficiality of touristic experience has weighed against serious study."

In the course of my research, I did find a book called *The Nuclear Family Vacation*, which initially elicited the satisfaction of finally having found something directly related to my own research, until I read the jacket and discovered that it was about a husband-and-wife team touring the world's nuclear weapons production sites. There was also Christie Mellor's *The Three-Martini Family Vacation: A Field Guide to Intrepid Parenting*, which I confess I did not read, primarily because I had already long ago endorsed what seemed to be its central thesis. There are academic books devoted to the family vacation; Neil Carr's *Children's and Families' Holiday Experiences*, and Susan Session Rugh's *Are We There Yet?* Rugh notes that the family vacation "fits squarely into the study of the history of tourism" but that the literature has focused on "authentic experience" without taking into account how family travel could alter that experience.

As for arts and culture, there have been many investigations into the family vacation over the years. A fine minor-chord road-trip story is Alice Munro's "Miles City, Montana," and although it's not particularly heartwarming, Munro does capture, with her standard impeccable prose and insight, some of the strange pressures of being car-bound for long periods of time. We will, of course, always have the subtly realistic adventures of the Griswold family in the National Lampoon *Vacation* series. The creator of those films, John Hughes, who also made films such as *Ferris Bueller's Day Off*, *Home Alone*, and *Planes, Trains and Automobiles*, got one of his first breaks writing satirically about the family vacation. His story, "Vacation 58," not only ended up securing his employment with National Lampoon, but it became the inspiration for the first *Vacation* movie. *Vacation 58* is a funny saga of one family's road trip to Disneyland in 1958, replete with the station wagon, the cross-country drive from Michigan to California, an aunt dying en route, a father falling asleep at the wheel, a father driving off a cliff, a father robbing a motel, a father forgetting the dog tied to the bumper and then driving off, a father running from the law, a father pulling into Disneyland to find it closed for repairs, and a father snapping and hunting down, then shooting, Walt Disney.

Chevy Chase did seem ideally suited for the role. Yet despite the cornball comedy of both the story and the movie, the inherent satire did have a serious point to make, which, for me, is that "arrival" is overvalued and that a more measured approach to the journey itself is of value.

Possibly there is a shortage of fine writing on the subject because most of our artistically gifted and creative writers are simply too busy writing stories of misfit outsiders coping with alienation, loss, sexual jealousy, and the betrayals of their past. Perhaps writers and artists just can't be bothered with the family vacation's perceived and sometimes real sentimental overtones. But here's a question: If you really do enjoy going on vacation with your family, and you really do think it makes you closer as a family, and if you really do think it's important to say so, then is that sentimental? Why can this not be meaningful? Is it because drama constitutes art and happiness lacks drama? Maybe it's just that most of our talented artists, writers, and thinkers were unlucky enough to have parents who didn't take them on family vacations, thereby consigning them as children to summer holidays consisting of nothing but sitting in their rooms with the door closed reading book after book after book, ruining their eyesight, and dreaming of the day when they could escape their non-vacationing families, and get busy writing searing accounts of misfit outsiders coping with alienation, loss, sexual jealousy, and the betrayals of their past.

What all this adds up to is that, despite the fact that tourism is a huge part of the global economy, despite the fact that a high percentage, possibly even the majority, of this tourism is conducted by families, and despite the fact that family vacations are part of the core matter of self-definition of both the individual and the family unit, there has been disproportionately little serious study or art about the family vacation. This gap is surprising, since the family vacation is not peripheral but central to our understanding of the family construct. Recently, one or two researchers have begun looking at the family vacation from this point of view, such as the husband-and-wife team Sarah and Joel Agate, who conducted much of their research while at Clemson University in South Carolina. Their work is principally rooted in American history, but it's revealing nonetheless. Speaking at the Vacation Matters summit in Seattle in 2009, they noted in a joint presentation that there was no historically significant record of the family vacation prior to the American Civil War. Families simply did not take vacations, for a variety of reasons, the most obvious being that most people were either poor or slaves. Not only that, there was a relative lack of focus on vacationing as a family, even among families who could afford it, largely due in the United States and to a lesser degree in Canada to what we might call a Puritanical hangover. People mistrusted the very idea of leisure, since there was a country to build and wilderness to tame and colonial barriers to overcome. Diligence was next to Godliness, and the Puritans of both the pre– and post–Civil War era were beholden to both. What chance, in this atmosphere, did the family vacation have of emerging, let alone thriving? The upper class travelled as families, but that didn't really count: their whole life was a vacation.

After the Civil War, a middle class began to emerge, the Reconstruction Era ensued, prosperity increased, travel increased, and new modes of transportation emerged, which allowed for some, but not much, family travel. Around the turn of the twentieth century the still rather embryonic middle class saw the earliest signs of labour rights—meaning, among many other things, legislated holidays—and this had an inevitable trickle-down effect to the working class. African-Americans were seeing small gains in prosperity. Immigrants were settling and adapting.

By the time the First World War ended, the working class witnessed entrenched time off actually getting passed as legislation, though this was still often only expressed as the maximum number of working hours per week. Still, it was the thin edge of the wedge and it wasn't long until vacation time was a concept and a reality that both worker and employer saw as the norm. When the Depression hit, it was, ironically, becoming more common for the family vacation to be seen as, if not a universal right, then at least a common expectation. Just prior to the Second World War, in fact, a recommendation for mandatory paid vacation for all workers was put before the US Senate. It failed, but it did create a sense of widespread acceptance that "the vacation," paid or unpaid still to be determined, was something a worker could reasonably expect.

Of course, the family vacation has through time often been an expression of a society's vision of itself. In the immediate post–Second World War era there was a newly felt freedom, the expansiveness of victory, and a relative level of affluence, all of which brought about a vacation mode wherein families of nearly every stripe piled into the big station wagon and travelled enormous distances, staying in motels, often driving halfway across the country simply because they could.

Yet the conservative, rather uniform nature of the family vacation during this period was also in many ways a reflection of the conformity of the time as exemplified by McCarthyism, and by a society shaken by the Kennedy assassination and shattered by Vietnam. The family vacation was also slowed, oddly, by feminism. As women increased their agency, went back to work, and had children according to their own desire to do so—developments that may have slowed the family vacation but which sped the development of our species—it became harder for a family to coordinate long vacations. Not only that, the Agates noted, the sexual revolution made it less fashionable for women to advocate for family togetherness.

And then came mass middle-class air travel. The increasing ease and declining cost of air travel made the international family vacation a much more likely possibility in the seventies and early eighties, and although mass air travel may have hampered the car trip, it positively killed the Atlantic-crossing industry. The phoenix that rose from those ashes was the cruise industry. They had to do *something* with all those ships. The cruise industry began with obsolete luxury liners, but soon enough it saw the value of catering to families. Today, there might be no aspect of the tourism industry more constructed around the family vacation, and increasingly the intergenerational family vacation, than the cruise industry. (And I'll speak more to the historical details of both mass middle-class air travel and the cruise industry further on.) It took a century—roughly from 1850 to 1950—for the family vacation to go from being the exclusive purview of the wealthy to becoming, as Orvar Löfgren called it, a fully democratized institution. It's now taken half that time again for the family vacation to become such an accepted cultural institution that no one even imagines today that it might have been our grandparents who fought for mandatory holiday time.

The social and anthropological history of the family vacation is evolving, too. One of the themes I want to explore throughout the book is that of safety versus experience. Although strongly shaped by personal observation, my belief is that the family vacations children grow up to remember fondly and/or vividly and which become part of family lore (and which therefore help us define ourselves, our families, and our place within those families) are achieved only by wrapping both arms around something we can't embrace; namely, abandon. A disregard for outcome, if you will. You must plan for the unplannable, and the best way to care is to not care, to—at the risk of being sued—not prize safety over experience. Bear with me.

We baby boomers and immediate post baby boomers are obsessed with preparation, mapping, detail, specialization. Our culture wants certainty, guarantees, a return on our investment. And it appears we are now applying these approaches to the family vacation. Well-planned, organized, safe, a sound investment—we'll get our money's worth and the activities will warrant the effort—but predictable, homogenous, *managed*. The Disney Cruise?! Is this what we want from the family vacation? It's the holiday equivalent of the gated community . . . and sometimes we holiday *in* a gated community. But don't we want grist for family lore? Adventure? Fun? Danger? Hair-raising experiences served up by blithely oblivious parents? Will we find that on a Disney cruise? Franz Kafka once wrote that you needn't frantically chase the world in order to find it, since it would "present itself to you for its unmasking" even if you chose to just sit at your desk and be utterly still and silent. And so it is with the family vacation . . . well, except for the sitting-still part. Simply the act of being together will open the world up to you and allow you to define it through family—the world that is your family will unmask itself with or *without* grand plans, with or *without* great sights and peak experiences. The value created by the family vacation, its long-term familial meaning, will not necessarily reside in whether you got on all the rides you wanted to at Disneyland, or whether you got the table by the window every night on the cruise. Observing and existing in each moment together—accepting instead of grasping, as Kafka is essentially saying—is the fertile soil from which memories and meaning will grow. Abandon. Risk. Accept. Of course, you will be forgiven if you choose not to put your faith in Franz Kafka as the patron saint of the family vacation, given that his most famous story is about a man who wakes up one morning as a giant cockroach.

*

The road trip is an institution that has sometimes resulted in parents wishing they could be committed to one, and it's hard to predict how it will evolve. There are the obvious environmental issues, although that is less about the vehicle than what's fuelling it. Whether it's hydrogen, battery power, even biomass fuel, families will still need ways to get from one place to another on their holidays. A more environmentally friendly fuel source might well fuel a resurgence in the road trip. The bigger question for me around the future of the road trip might be the creation of individual solitudes within the vehicle. Now that children have iPods, MP3s, iPads, and most significantly, movie centres that fold down out of the ceiling or the headrest in front of them, there is simply less chance for spontaneous interaction, less opportunity for something to happen, good or bad. Spending ten hours in a car will result in tedium somewhere along the way, and so whatever you can do to alleviate that can't be a bad thing. It's just that creating an impermeable bubble around each and every one of us may not be the answer. That bubble of distraction will occupy our children, to be sure, but it also signals to them that the journey is to be endured rather than considered.

Perhaps that's why I can say we knew, even as kids, that our Mexico trip was significant. We didn't have the words, but we understood it had meaning from the day we left until the day we arrived back home; especially once we were back home. Furthermore, *home* eventually became a fluid continuum rather than a specific physical structure, since that trip was part of what helped us understand that wherever we gathered as a family was our home, and that the support and togetherness we shared as a family was also our home.

Not that there weren't times I would have loved to have escaped that car. And I know I wasn't the only one. At one stretch my father drove seventeen hours. Halfway through that day, Keith turned from his spot in the throne and with no warning, delivered a wrecking-ball head butt directly onto my unsuspecting skull. I was briefly dazed and left with a throbbing headache for the next couple of days.

"What!" I half-shouted, trying to scramble back to retaliate, before my father shouted back at us to stop horsing around.

"He head-butted me . . . for no reason!"

"I've got a reason," he said.

"I don't give a damn about who did what," said my father. "Stop horsing around. Do you want me to stop the car?"

I glared at Keith. "You're dead. What'd you do that for?"

"Because I wish I had a comic to read right now," he said.

Even though there were no comics to read, we made it through that day, and the days that followed in which there was still so much to come. There was Keith finding a dead baby hammerhead shark on the beach at Mazatlán, which he somehow persuaded my parents, and the American border guards, and the Canadian border guards, to let him bring home for show-and-tell at school, even though it had rotted badly by the time we got to Calgary. And then there was Mom, jumping up off her towel on the beach at Puerto Vallarta, shrieking at the top of her lungs, utterly hysterical, because she saw sharks in the water.

"Where?" said my dad, staring out over the water once we were all ashore.

"There," she said, pointing. "Right there! See them?!"

My dad gazed out. "Pat," he said. "Those are dolphins."

She didn't say anything more, but sometimes I've wondered, given the stresses involved in that trip, if she wasn't screaming out of giddy hopefulness instead of terror. Who would have blamed her? Which was why it was so mystifying to me when my parents turned around less than a year later to buy a ratty old school bus and convert it into a long-haul recreational vehicle.

But I'll come to that.

2

The Great Outdoors

THE GILLESPIE FAMILY of 4232 Dalhart Road, circa 1975, was not poor in the strictest sense of the word: the family's six children were clothed, fed, and in school. Still, we didn't have wads of cash to throw around for frivolous expenditures like the latest toys, new ball gloves, haircuts, food. We ate out about once every four years. It was all about hand-me-downs, do-it-your-selves, and "I don't care if you don't want to use your brother's old hockey equipment, and I don't care that you think it smells like an armpit. If you don't want it you can walk down the street and see if there are any other families that might want to adopt you." I'm speaking hypothetically, of course; none of us played much competitive hockey. My mother and father were, however, parents of epic patience and resourcefulness who could have, and probably should have, been running the country; it would have been easier on them and better for the country. Ours was a small house for a family of four, let alone eight; for most of my teen years, my "bedroom" was a corner of the basement that I turned into a room by hanging a bed-sheet from the rafters; it was a cross between a Moroccan yurt and the set of *Midnight Express*, depending on the state in which I kept it. As for privacy, well, that was like some foreign custom we'd heard about, but couldn't imagine experiencing.

Our relative lack of affluence growing up was no hardship I recognized, resented, or even gave much thought, but it did mean that our early family vacations were usually low-budget. Or no budget. This meant camping, even though it has to be said, up front in the interests of full disclosure, that we were not one of those families deeply in touch with nature, who hiked regularly, who got out into the woods and mountains at every opportunity. Yes, we did the occasional hike, and we made it up to Banff National Park every now and then. But we were not the outdoorsy types. There were various reasons for this, chief among them that my mother liked plumbing. Communing with nature at that level never appealed to her much, and frankly it didn't much to me, either. Whenever we hit a campground that had running water and indoor plumbing, she always seemed to cheer up and view camping as not so bad, really. I've since done my share of long hikes and roughing it in the bush, but I would still pick a decently equipped campground over the backwoods experience any day. I don't know what that makes me, but what it does not make me is an outdoorsman.

We never journeyed too far away on our short camping trips around Alberta. We camped at Elbow Falls, just outside Calgary, or at Gull Lake, north of Red Deer. These were short trips, but in my memory they were some distance from home, journeys we had to plan for, pack up for, bring the tent, and generally just be organized about (to the degree that we were ever organized). I don't think we camped much at these spots after I was about ten or twelve years old, but our early trips remain evocative for me, a true removal from home and our life there. Part of it was that we called it "a vacation," which instantly gave it a meaning it wouldn't have otherwise had. We had so little money when I was in elementary school that I'm sure my parents called camping at Gull Lake a "vacation" so that we could at least tell our friends we'd done something over the summer break.

But looking back, it seems clear to me now that what made our early camping trips worth remembering was the tent, the same one we would eventually take to Mexico; it may have been a beast, but it was a magical beast. The thing was gigantic and like no other tent I'd seen before or since. There were different rooms, caverns, corners, places to hide, folds from which to leap out and frighten a sibling, a hundred different smells, a separate room for the kids, a "living room," our parents' room, a front awning that always acted as a kind of water basin when it rained. It was both a curse and a temple, the kind of tent that for some reason my imagination wants to give a trapdoor leading to the underworld. A lack of plumbing may have prevented us from camping more, but the primary reason had to be the tent. Yes, it may have been a child's portal, but it was also so daunting a proposition to set it up that I think my dad had to gird himself for days and weeks beforehand just to get in the proper mindset. It was so monstrously heavy and bulky and finicky that it made any trip—one night or ten—something that required full emotional commitment, not to mention a few days of Marine Corps physical preparation. Remember, we're talking 1970 here. This was not a tent made of the lightweight waterproof fabrics of today, with their hollow, high-strength aluminum poles. Putting up one of today's tents is a breezy five-minute stroll compared to the full-pack, army-boot, abusive-drill-sergeant swampy day-hike that was the erecting of that tent. It was not just a nightmare to put up, but I'm sure once it was up my father never slept, consumed as he must have been by nightmares of having to take it down. There were hundreds of poles of differing lengths, none of them attached by the interior elastic of today's tents. They were heavy suckers, too, capable of braining you if one dropped on your head during decamping. Thick skin-shredding twine, attached to the four corners of the eternally useless rain guard, had to be regularly uncoiled and recoiled from many metres away. The tent itself was made of oiled canvas that through years of wear and tear had lost most of its ability to repel water but none of its ability to stain your clothes, leave streaks on your skin, integrate and return odour, and resist folding. It was a solid material, probably an eighth of an inch thick, and was so stiff that folding it, and keeping it folded, was like trying to fold thick rubber; you could do it, but unless you literally stood on it until the moment it was roped, it would spring back into some new, shapeless and utterly demoralizing version of itself. It was a kind of freestyle fabric origami, though by the time we'd been at it for an hour or so, it veered closer to Noh drama, a silent, haunting tale of frustration (and repression, surely, given my father couldn't swear nearly to the degree I'm sure he wanted to, with six impressionable children looking to him as a role model).

Yes, our tent was a portal to a different experience, a family experience, but putting that beast up and deconstructing it afterwards was always a kind of test, a passage of a different sort, one in which our patience, and particularly my father's, was taken to the limits of human endurance. You might think I'm joking, but I'm not. Compressed into its so-called "packed" state, it would have easily crushed a small dog or disabled a young child had it toppled from the roof of the station wagon.

Our camping trips today, with our two girls, are a mixture of the farce of yesteryear and the discomfort of an aging body lying on a rocky surface with crawling ants. We do insist on camping occasionally, and it often turns out to be fun, but as often as not, it's more of an exercise in "teaching our children" something outdoorsy (what that is, precisely, I'm not sure). This was compounded in recent years by tossing a deaf dog with bladder problems into the mix, and into the tent—a small and light tent, I should add. Who says we can't learn from the past?

*

Given that camping has long been, and still is, a vacation choice for so many families, it's somewhat surprising that the formal history of camping is not that long. You'd think that camping out would have been something started pretty much the minute we dragged our knuckles off the ground and learned to walk upright. I suppose the difference is that when you didn't really have any other options but to live outdoors you couldn't really call it camping. Neanderthal man did not come home from a hard week of hunting and gathering to suggest to his wife and the little Neanderthals that they should get out of that smelly, dank cave and trek a few miles across the Serengeti (which you may be surprised to learn was not then known as the Serengeti) so as to pitch a mastodon-hide tent and roast meat over an open fire for a few days. That wasn't a holiday, that was daily living. I can hear it now: *"Dad, you said we were going to do something fun. That's not fun. We might as well just stay home. That sucks."* At which point the Neanderthal dad, in time-honoured tradition, would have responded that that was just as fine with him and he'd be perfectly happy to stay home and get some work done on the cave painting, only to witness the intervention of the mother, urging family unity, reiterating that the family that vacations together evolves together. (It occurs to me as I write this that it's entirely possible our original family tent was, in fact, not canvas but a mastodon hide, passed down from generation to generation, and evolutionary adaptation to evolutionary adaptation, absorbing every smell across the millennia, until it finally arrived at a garage sale where my father immediately recognized it as the only campsite dwelling fit for his children.)

Camping as we know it today only became a leisure pursuit once people had leisure to use, so perhaps it's no surprise then that camping did not come into being as a pursuit until the decade or so prior to the First World War. The founder of so-called recreational camping—as opposed to the Cro-Magnon or Civil War survival variety—is generally acknowledged to be Thomas Hiram Holding. He wrote the original *Campers Handbook* in 1908, and many have written about how his understanding of how to live in the outdoors came from having crossed the plains of the United States with his parents in 1853. He was also a dedicated bicyclist and often rode and camped around the UK, and in fact wrote a book entitled *Cycle and Camp in Connemara*. Historians have said that it was this very trip that led Holding to create the Association of Cycle Campers in 1901, which had thirteen original members. It was the inaugural meeting of that association that led to the founding of what is today called the Camping and Caravanning Club.

Holding had hit upon something. Just five years later his organization had over five hundred members and modern camping was effectively born. Camping clubs sprang up all over the UK, and there was soon a breakaway club, led by Holding, that ditched cycling and devoted itself strictly to camping, though they did rejoin a few years later, only to then join with another group in 1910, all of which was then singly known as the National Camping Club. That membership was listed at 820 campers in its initial year.

Real world events soon intervened, of course, but after the First World War, camping picked up again as a leisure pursuit. It's worth remembering that camping at that time was essentially a novelty pursuit of the wealthy; the lower and middle classes still did not possess organized or formalized workers' power or rights, and such things as paid days off were still to come. So although camping, as the leisure pursuit we might recognize today, was formally initiated during these *fin-de-siècle* years, it was not a particularly radical movement. The lower and middle classes didn't own cars or land on which to camp. North American camping at this time was almost certainly of the pioneering or homesteading variety, borne of necessity rather than leisure or desire to get back to the land.

In the years between the wars, camping continued to grow in popularity. One of the principal camping clubs of the UK at the time, the Camping Club of Great Britain and Ireland, had Sir Robert Baden-Powell—the man who started the Boy Scouts—as its president. The Second World War interrupted the growth of camping, although in Britain many sought to escape German bombing by going to the countryside; fascinatingly, this very well may have been one of the progenitors of camping as a family pursuit (although most fathers were off at war). Mothers and their children, wanting to escape the horror and danger, fled to the countryside; many of them had to camp because they were not wealthy enough to own second homes.

In the years following the Second World War, camping truly began to grow, particularly as a family pursuit. By this time, workers' rights were becoming more entrenched and, helped by the rise of the automobile, the good highway system, and many thousands of new campsites in the national parks, camping exploded as a cheap and accessible family pursuit. By the 1960s, it would be no exaggeration to say that the family camping trip—piling into the car, tent on the roof, hitting the open highway, finding a national park, setting up camp, and hanging out for a week—became the norm for the lower- and middle-class family vacation. (Caravans and trailers experienced rapid gains in popularity during this time, as well, but I'll discuss those further on.)

That was then, but what of now? Martin Hogue, writing for the *Design Observer* in 2009, noted that the Kampgrounds of America—the KOA to most of us—had five million visitors at its sites across North America, and that there were 113,000 federally managed campsites in the United States and 166,000 campsites in various state parks, as well as a virtually uncountable number in private facilities. But, writes Hogue, modern camping displays a strange contradiction, in that it is "defined and serviced by an increasingly sophisticated range of utilities and conveniences, and yet marketed to perpetuate the cherished American ideal of the backwoods camp." In other words, we like to think we're roughing it, but, really, we're not. There was certainly no sophistication to our camping in the mastodon-hide tent, however; it was anarchy, pretty much like every day at home—a scramble for cereal at the picnic table, a frenzied rush to get a wiener on a stick for dinner. And there's no sophistication in our camping today with Jess and Grace; there's a primitive cast to our dinners, eased only by the presence of a slosh of wine in a cheap plastic cup.

But what Hogue is talking about is part of the larger narrative of today's vacations, including family vacations, a phenomenon that I think is increasingly peculiar to our era and to relatively rich and cocooned westernized populations. We want authenticity, but we also desire comfort and security, which, again, reflects the matrix of safety versus experience. Camping sits at the intersection of the competing desires for safety and experience; it offers a gateway to the natural world, to a simpler existence, to a better understanding of and sympathy towards the planet and our fellow creatures— all fine and desirable things—yet so many of us want all this but with good plumbing and WiFi. Most of us, myself included, have become, in some way or another, acolytes worshipping at the altar of Gear. We want great gear, high-end gear, the best gear. Water-proofed, Velcroed, leathered, Gore-Texed, and micro-layered to within an inch of our lives, we set off into the wilderness in our SUVs and ATVs for an authentic back-to-nature experience . . . and if something bad happens, well, hopefully we'll still be within cell range. If not, the GPS locator will help the rescuers to find us. We remain shocked when, every year, someone dies after getting lost in the backwoods or attacked by a cougar or skiing on an out-of-bounds slope. Well, that's what's *supposed* to happen in nature. Life in the natural world is nasty, brutish, and short, and the surprise is that it doesn't happen more often.

But it doesn't happen more often because we've tamed it to our will for the most part. Which is why camping, particularly as a family exercise, can be fun and inexpensive—the reasons for its popularity with families—but which most of the time cannot really be classed as an authentic journey into the natural world. At least not the way *we* camp; I think my daughter Jessica would revolt if she had to spend more than a day away from her hair straightener. Hogue notes ironically that a "campsite" in any major park today ain't what it used to be. "Each 'lone' campsite," he writes, "functions as a stage upon which cultural fantasies can be performed in full view of an audience of fellow campers interested in much the same 'wilderness' experience. Who in the camping community has not experienced a degree of gear envy at the sight, on a neighbouring camp, of a brand new Primus Gravity II EasyFuel stove (with piezo ignition), a Sierra Designs tent, or a Marmot sleeping bag?" KOA rents out permanently parked Airstream trailers, which means "campers" don't even have to bring any equipment.

Little wonder then that the things we used to have to do just to stay alive when camping—find wood, chop it, draw water, clear a site, hunt for food—are now, says Hogue, nothing but a series of "almost spiritual rituals intended to reconnect the camper with what has been largely lost." Now, instead of clearing a site, chopping wood, and finding water, we show up at a campsite, park the car, pitch lightweight tents, grab some food at the camp store, hook up our electricity, light up the propane stove, and set up our patio chairs.

In other words, we're just playing at it.

Not that there's anything inherently wrong or immoral about that, though it's interesting to remember that campgrounds were originally created to protect nature from campers as much as campers from nature. It's ironic that so many of these sites we consider "outdoorsy" actually serve to separate us from nature. Many of today's larger campsites have conveniences such as water taps, electrical outlets, toilets and showers, all of which make "nature" something of an abstraction. We're separated from a visceral sense of its power and mystery. Hogue relates a sad incident, reported in the wider media, that occurred in June 2010, in Arkansas, where a flash flood at a large campground led to numerous deaths, including six children under the age of seven, all of which underscored "crucial historical shifts within the culture of camping itself: an increasing lack of awareness of potential danger, and an implicit trust in the protective confines of . . . the campsite and the resources at hand."

So what's a family to do? Take the children on a safe back-to-nature holiday, where there is no or minimal risk (though, as the Arkansas disaster illustrates, there is still *some* risk), or do we seek out something as close to nature as possible, a worthwhile goal in a digital age that increasingly distances children from the natural world they might not even know they occupy. It's no accident that a considerable amount of advertising in today's media universe trumpets the desire to get back to nature or participate in the natural world. Vehicle advertising and naming, for example: Tahoe. Outback. Ram. Mustang. Sierra. Highlander. Tacoma. Yukon. Outlander. Cougar. Bighorn. Lynx. Sequoia. Tracker. Trail Blazer. Most of these gas guzzlers are as close to being celebrations of the natural world as Three Mile Island. The inherent contradiction and complexity of camping and the family vacation is that it's getting harder and harder to actually get back to nature these days, which means it's becoming harder to locate an authentic natural experience for our children, all while recognizing the additional contradiction that the only path most of us can use to seek out such an experience is to pile the family into an SUV or a van and drive in our environmentally unsound vehicles to find a place where the environment has largely been tamed for our consumption. An additional layer of irony lies in the fact that when we camped back then (as well as when we camp today), we as often as not used the car *itself* as part of our camping equipment, tying ropes to it for the tent and/or an awning, dropping the back gate on the station wagon as an extra table, opening the door and playing the radio for entertainment. When our family camped at Gull Lake, the station wagon was almost as much a part of our camping experience as the beast tent.

It all raises the question, in retrospect as much as in the present, of what precisely it is we're achieving when we "camp," particularly in the highly organized sites described above, replete with water, showers, electricity, toilets, and check-ins with map distribution? Are we telling our children that *this* is nature? The only real difference between that type of camping and staying at home is a worse sleep and no cable TV. It might just be better to watch the Nature Channel on TV with the kids and a bowl of popcorn.

I jest. But only partly, because we do continue to cherish and demand our conveniences and gadgets, and this is, obviously and disturbingly, more the case with today's children than with previous generations (not that they are to blame since it's us, their parents, who are their prime facilitators in this regard). Still, the trend towards convenience in camping was established long before the Internet, long before the cellphone, before television even (for many of my younger readers, this period—Before Television—is what your teachers mean when they talk about "pre-history"). In the 1920s, Denver's Overland Park was among the first campgrounds in the US to focus on a range of civilizing services; the Overland became the model for the KOA, which, to anyone who camped in the seventies, was as pervasive as tight jeans and bad haircuts. KOA was the Starbucks of campgrounds. This was part of its appeal to parents, my own included, who had enough to worry about without fretting over the unknown campgrounds they were taking themselves, and us, into. This would explain, I suppose, why we drove four thousand kilometres—one way—to stay in a KOA campground in Mexico City. KOA ruled the campground world at the time; it started with but a single campground in 1961 and by 1979 it had 829 campgrounds across North America. KOA had individual owner/operators, supposedly to put a personal touch on the service, though in our case, in Mexico City, it led to "personal touches" we could have done without.

The oil crisis may have been ongoing at the time, but I can safely say that none of us children were aware of it. It's possible my parents took note of these world events, and it's also possible they relayed them, but for that to have made an impact on us would have meant listening to them. Certainly I do not recall ever being unable to gas up during any of our stops, and once we hit Mexico City just before Christmas, you'd have been hard pressed to say the oil crisis was putting the squeeze on vehicle usage. Quite the opposite. We'd never seen traffic like it. Driving from the middle of Mexico City, from Chapultepec Park, say, to our KOA campground fifteen miles outside the city centre, seemed to take almost as long as it had to drive from Calgary to Mexico City. The snaking endless line of cars, six lanes regularly converging into three, the choking pollution caught in Mexico City's unlucky inversion basin, the sheer number of people—we'd never seen anything on this scale. We'd also never camped outside a city of twelve million people. At times the KOA felt as crowded as walking through the city itself. Row after row of tents. It was a tented village, though this was hardly a negative thing. Some of the memories of playing in that campground are stronger than the time we actually spent in Mexico City.

That KOA campground no longer exists, or at least it's no longer in the hands of the KOA. Whoever owns it now has, I'm sure, or I hope, relaxed the draconian laws of the place. They shut down things early. They closed bathrooms at ten o'clock at night. They shut off the water taps at 10:05. They turned off the electricity at 10:10. They closed the office and went home at 10:15. They locked the gate so no one could break in . . . but no one could get out, either. Basically, it was a jail without the humane conditions. Not that we especially noticed at first, as long as you weren't thirsty or had to go to the bathroom late at night. They said it was a safety issue, which was fair enough, given that we were in a huge city in a third-world country and had *gringo* written all over our pasty faces. Only as our time there progressed did it start to feel oppressive. Still, we reasoned, we were nearly through with Mexico City, and from there it was off to the coast, to Acapulco, to see the cliff divers. Us boys were beside ourselves with excitement. Okay, Mexico City was one of the world's great cities, a place with lampposts older than our country, the repository of an entire civilization. That was interesting, vaguely, but an hour away there were cliff divers!

Our last night in Mexico City was full of anticipation, for a variety of reasons, I think. One was the cliff divers. The other was the ocean and beachcombing, which we were all looking forward to after three weeks of driving through the desert. The sense of moment was also pitched because the day we left Mexico City meant it was the day we turned around. Even as kids I think we understood that we were on a very peculiar grand adventure and that as of the next day we'd be heading for home.

We wanted to make the most of our last night in the tent city and we played hard, exploring far and wide throughout the vast grounds. Late that night, before the water got shut off, Matt decided he was thirsty as we ran back to our tent. He put his lips to the nearest tap and took a drink, despite his brothers telling him not to. "You're not supposed to, Matt," we said. "You'll get Mount Zooma's revenge."

We didn't know the term, and had only heard our parents use it in relation to warnings not to drink water that hadn't been boiled first. I can't speak for my siblings, but I had no idea what the term referred to, other than that it meant bad things. Matt ignored us, we kept playing, and he didn't seem the worse for it.

In the canvas cave at bedtime, my parents laid their own sleeping bags out in their room; the second, larger, room was held as the "living room"; the third room was where the kids slept. Our sleeping bags were laid out in a row, six of them, like coffins at a mass funeral. We crawled in as Dad shone the flashlight at us. He said good-night, and then said what he always said before he left us alone. "No horsing around. It's time for bed." We horsed around for a while and then fell asleep, but it wasn't long before the inevitable came. Matt was in his sleeping bag between Bruce and Conor, and when Mount Zooma exploded, the eruption forever changed the lives of the people in that tent, of those who escaped and those who didn't. Matt threw up as he woke up and instinctively turned to one side. It was fate, that was all. Conor or Bruce. One clean, one forever scarred. Who says life isn't random?

Matt turned Bruce's way.

Unluckily, Bruce tends to sleep on his back, face up. Well, he used to. I don't know what position he sleeps in today. Or if he sleeps at all. And though Matt was at least a foot shorter than Bruce, somehow he'd managed to arrange himself such that their heads were side by side. A further piece of ill fate was that Bruce also tended to snore a bit, even as a young teenager, and consequently he usually had his mouth open.

Who knows what Bruce was dreaming about at that moment, but he was violently yanked from sleep. Everybody in the tent was up in a flash, listening to Bruce choke and swallow and cough, and to Matt moan. The rest of us were horrified, laughing at first, but then so truly sympathetic to the awful thing that had just happened to Bruce (and Matt was none too happy, either), that we didn't laugh at Bruce or tease him or taunt him until well into the next day. We couldn't really see much, either, because it was dark, after all, and we were camping in a tourist holding compound without any of the necessities for sustaining human life. Dad and Mom came scurrying into our room of the tent, with Dad jiggling his big flashlight. He trained it on Bruce and Matt, and we saw in stark relief what had just happened. Bruce looked like a wax figure left in a steam room.

The nature versus nurture debate has long raged in psychological circles, and I'm not here to come down on one side or the other, but you can't tell me something like that doesn't somehow shape a person. Bruce grew up to be a high school teacher, and to all outward appearances seems a normal and balanced person, but, let's face it, the jury's still out, and if he dropped off the edge tomorrow into a life of crime and addiction, I know what I'm blaming.

My mother sprang into action, immediately trotting out her greatest gift, her empathy. She tried to make Bruce feel better and attended to Matt.

"Gerry," she said to my father. "Look at this. Oh my God. Poor things. Go get some water so we can at least clean Bruce off, and they can all get back to sleep."

My dad stood there, looked at his watch.

My mom looked back to him. "What?"

"It's two in the morning."

"So . . ."

"No water. It's shut off."

"But don't we have any?"

My father shook his head. "I was going to boil some more in the morning before we left for Acapulco."

The full horror of it hit us all, but none more than Bruce. "You mean I can't even wash off?!"

"Oh, that's just so gross," emphasized Janine. "I think I'm going to be sick."

My mother helped Bruce clean off as best he could. It wasn't until the morning, though, until the full light of day arrived, that we were able to see just what Bruce had endured. His face was a strange hue, almost orangey-peach, like he'd used too much fake-tan cream. His hair was stiff and coarse, pre-punk, sticking out in forty different directions. Nobody used hair gel back then, but, again in reference to the nature versus nurture debate, I don't think it's any coincidence that Bruce today is the one amongst the six of us kids who pays the most attention to his hair and overall physical appearance. He has, for a male high school teacher, an unusually keen interest in hair products and facial cleansers.

We left Mexico City later that morning, after Bruce had cleaned up and Matt had thrown up another couple of times (into a plastic bag; nobody would go within five feet of him). We were turning for home, but first we had most of North America to travel back through, only this time we were headed up the length of the west coast, to Acapulco, Mazatlán, Puerto Vallarta, San Diego, and Los Angeles, before turning back inland to go through Vegas and back up the eastern edge of the Rockies, through Montana, and finally back to Alberta. A few days later, after a visit to Acapulco to see the cliff divers (which turned out to be a colossal disappointment as the various Mexicans present refused to dive off the cliffs for us, and because our mom wouldn't let us out of arm's length when we wanted to look for divers), we continued back north. We decided to stop in Guadalajara, for a much-needed rest. My parents decided to open their wallets for a motel. It was almost New Year's, and I think they thought beds and a swimming pool would help take the edge off the collective trauma of Mount Zooma. They were right ... for the most part.

KOA, incidentally, was sold in 2001 to Interactive Corp., which also manages Ticketmaster, Expedia, and hotels.com, a fact that makes it even clearer that camping is now a radically different thing than in generations past. It's one piece of recreation for the masses, one writer noted, which can "be bundled along with other forms of entertainment." Online planning and preparation for camping has become the norm. The government of Alberta recently introduced a provincewide campsite reservation system that has proven enormously popular; a necessity, in fact, for securing a campsite during busy times.

Yet this, along with all the other mod cons mentioned earlier, is not camping in the way that I understand it, or want to understand it. I speak not as an experienced naturalist, but as a modern urbanite who nevertheless longs for the (admittedly occasional) genuine immersion into nature's unfettered beauty, an immersion unpolluted by humanity's presence, except for my own, of course. I fear my children will lose access to those places, and moreover, that they will lose access to understanding how fragile our lives are, and are meant to be, in the natural cycle. Perhaps camping, as I think of it, is not even about nature at all (at least not "nature" in the way that we commonly understand it—as something to appreciate and revel in). Perhaps it's about trial and difficulty and resistance. Camping isn't *supposed* to be easy. It's not meant to be frictionless. Isn't that, at some level, what we're trying to achieve when we want to take the kids camping? I know it's the case that when we camp, one of the objectives is to remove Jess and Grace from the convenience and fluidity of their daily lives, to the point where we need to get that fire started or we don't eat. The removal of physical obstacles is, I would say, counter to the point of camping as a family. You want to make it hard. Some of my best camping memories involve when it was hard, such as when Cathy and I camped in northern Alberta and forgot our axe. We made fires the old native way, just laying logs in a firepit like spokes on a wheel, pushing them in as they burned. There was no other solution. Of course, this was also the camping trip in which Cathy swore that fish were attracted to mini-marshmallows, which led to a few dozen coloured blobs floating into shore as every fish in the lake assiduously turned up their gills at the little morsels.

I suppose in the end camping as a family vacation, or even as a short family activity over a weekend, is for me more about creating a set of conditions than it is about communing with nature, though I have nothing against communing with nature and will always happily accept it as a secondary benefit. After all, a thirty-foot fir tree in my backyard is more or less the same as a thirty-foot fir tree in the forests of Alberta's wild and unpopulated eastern slopes. There is something appealing, however, about leaving the city and leaving all those people behind, but is it possible that in so doing we are in fact trying to teach our children a different lesson: that not everything gets handed to you on a silver platter . . . and that sometimes what gets handed to you is something you're going to have to eat off a tin plate crusted over with last night's baked beans. And that WiFi, hot showers, and central heating are wonders of modern convenience and fortunate birth circumstances, not inalienable human rights.

My friend, the poet Tim Bowling, says one of the things he most cherishes about living in Edmonton, with its harsh winters, is that he likes to be reminded every now and then that nature has the power to kill you if you make the wrong decision. That, it strikes me, is about as good a lesson as you could hope to give your family by going camping. What could be more fun than that?

*

The cottage and the organized camp are also significant expressions of the outdoors family vacation, and both have developed in significant ways in the last generation. The "cottage" has been an aspect of the family vacation for centuries, and I only put it in quotation marks because it has taken on so many different guises over time. The upper class have always sought refuge in second homes in the country or at the waterside, but that trend has shifted, to be sure, with the post–Second World War economic strength of the middle class. Now, many middle-class families own holiday homes, whether they be cottages, condos, farms, time-shares.

As for "camp," that formalized institution run by any number of church, youth and not-for-profit groups, they are now starting to move into more of a family concept. In the old days, parents used summer camp as a mental health and marriage regeneration tool (*Let's get rid of these irritating mini-humans for a week to see if we can still recognize one another*), but parents today are increasingly attending "camp" with their children, which from where I'm sitting has to be stressful for all of them. The sketchy camp days of old are not what they used to be. When you go to the American Camp Association website, for instance, and do a search on the types of camps available, your options are broken down into sixty-five specialized camp options, such as golf, hiking, tennis, aviation, clowning, and, of course, religious study. There are "targeted focus" areas, which include Academic Camp, Equestrian Camp, Grief/Bereavement Camp, Sports Camp, Visual and Performing Arts Camp, Weight Loss Camp, and Wilderness Trip Camp. "Specialty Camps" included camps for the "Gifted and Talented" and for "Inclusion and Mainstreaming," a category for which I was not able to find a definition (but which I am assuming has to do with youths who are struggling with their sexuality or gender identity). As you fill out the various categories of camps you are interested in, there is a button to identify if you wish to attend these camps as a family, but curiously it's not listed as "Family" but "Family Sessions," which is, I suppose, as good a sign as any that what we're really talking about here is not camping with the family, but something more like group therapy.

To be fair, a detailed look through the hundreds of summer camps available in Canada and the US will reveal that there are many straightforward camping and adventure–style experiences available for families, though the vast majority are guided and/or staffed.

As mentioned, the cottage (or its equivalent) is also a significant feature of many family vacations though it tends towards a more static, single-site, repetitive experience, which is hardly all bad. Often factored into the cottage summertime family vacation is the "coming and going" effect, with the working parent usually only at the lake for part of the vacation, while the other parent stays at the lake with the kids the entire time. The "cottage" represents many things to children, of course, but it's also a powerful and nostalgic symbol for adults, a symbol of innocence and coming-of-age from their past and in the children's present.

"Cottage cultures," writes Orvar Löfgren, "develop a strange mix of the ephemeral and the long-term. Summer life allows relaxed improvisations—you can make do with simple solutions, cheap materials, temporary arrangements—and yet cottage aesthetics emphasize continuity and stability. The same old silly souvenirs or dried flowers are still here, not to be moved around. Piles of old magazines and mystery stories must line the bookshelves. It is great to walk about in that old straw hat, the one that was once Grandpa's, or to find that worn sweater. (. . . children in particular become the guardians of unchanging summer life.) In town you can redecorate or switch houses, but to rebuild or sell the cottage, that is something different. The past is thus constantly present in the materials and routines of summer . . . Emotionally, second homes often come first."

Returning to a favoured place, owned or not, is a key and appealing aspect of the cottage ritual, and therefore becomes a central part of our memory-making. This is the case for us with the two weeks or so we spend in the BC interior every year; we stay at the same place, jump off the same bridge into Skaha Lake, eat ice cream at Tickleberries, rent a boat for an afternoon, play soccer on the same lawn, visit the same fruit stand. The ritualized and repetitive nature of such holidays becomes a measuring tool, the family vacation equivalent of ticking off your height every year on the back of the basement door, measuring how much the children have grown from marking point to marking point. The relaxed and repetitive summer vacation always has that feel to it. "Hey, last year I was scared to jump from here, now it's easy!" "Two years ago, the cherries weren't ripe this early." "Last year, I had a triple butterscotch waffle cone at Tickleberries, but if I eat one again this year, I think I might have a stroke right here in the parking lot."

On these summery outdoors vacations we tease and stretch time back and forth like a huge strand of warm toffee. Last year meshes with this year. Events from a decade ago are suddenly fresh and relevant the minute you arrive at the same beach. What is it that makes the cottage, or whatever spot you regularly return to, so appealing to so many, that makes it something that so many parents think their families will want and use and benefit from for decades to come? Certainly, there is a romance attached to outdoor life, to summer, to being closer to nature, to being a do-it-yourselfer who either builds or works on the structure themselves. But I think it goes deeper still than that.

Nostalgia is involved, a longing for simpler days, days by the fire, days without the incessant flow of electronic information that now ceaselessly washes over us every minute of every day. It's a nostalgia for what we once had, or, more likely, for that thing we wish we had more fully and completely. It's about longing, and in much the same way that we long for the simplicity of the cottage as it presents itself in our dreams and visions—the log fire, the crickets chirping at night, glass of wine in hand, book by our side—we make our family part of it because of a similar nostalgia, a similar longing. Doesn't every kid deserve a "summer at the lake"? Many of us have a vision in our heads of what a family does over the summer: hang around a lake, go swimming, pick fruit, have barbecues, play baseball, and then do it all again next summer. Isn't that what we're supposed to provide our children? Harmony. Simplicity. Togetherness.

The fact that it never quite works out like that isn't relevant. The fridge breaks down and the place smells like an abattoir. It rains for a month. The guy at the cottage next to you has decided that the best time to chainsaw his firewood is at three in the morning . . . every night.

Still, we hold on to the fantasy. Why? Partly because it's what we want, but partly because it's the fantasy, not the reality, that we want to pass on to our kids. It's part of their inheritance, what one writer called "the nostalgia of return."

It was also on our family vacation this past summer—our carefree sun and water lakeside holiday—that I was given reason to think about the nature of the safety versus experience matrix, about how much risk we want to expose our children to, and about the decisions we make while on family vacation, since such moments inevitably seem amplified on vacation. One day, Grace, Cathy and I went for a walk on the Kettle Valley Trail, a former railbed converted into a six-hundred-kilometre-long trail used mostly for cycling, walking, and jogging. Not too far from our place, over the rail bridge (from which we dive and jump into the lake below), there are rock outcroppings that Cathy suggested we climb. About ten feet up, as I was climbing with Grace, some of the rock started to crumble away down to the path below. At that point, it occurred to me that having a foothold give way, sixty feet up a rock wall without ropes on a face with about an eighty-degree gradient, would not be a good thing.

"This is a bad idea," I said, and started backing down, instructing Grace to do the same. Grace was disappointed and disappointed with me, I could tell, and I think Cathy was, too, but when we got to the top—after climbing a shorter, less steep section—and walked over to stand and look at the face we'd originally thought of climbing, I felt better; it *was* a long way down, with nothing to hold on to but stubbly rocks we couldn't trust. My imagination did what it always does, which is simultaneously hold the best and worst outcomes up for consideration. The best outcome was to do some rock climbing and get a bit of a rush, which we got anyway. The worst outcome was Grace losing her footing eighty feet up and cracking her head open at the bottom. It wasn't likely to happen, but it *could* have happened.

The next day we rented a boat and went water skiing and tubing out on Skaha Lake. I'm no expert boat driver (as evidenced by my crashing into a docked boat at the pier the year before), and the girls are not experienced skiers, though they love the water and are both good swimmers. We were pulling Jess and Grace around the lake in our small seventeen-foot boat with its zippy engine, and every time I looked back and saw them give the thumbs-up to gun the engine, I did, gleefully punching it, sometimes digging into a tight turn at the same time. But now Cathy and I reversed roles. She told me to slow down. She'd become the cautionary parent, justifiably so, of course, given that there was, in fact, a much greater statistical likelihood of Grace or Jess suffering an injury water-skiing—a broken arm or a concussion, for instance—than there was of suffering an injury while climbing a rock face near our condo. Especially given the external factors involved—Grace's high level of dexterity as a rock climber, my own limited boat-driving skills, the crowded lake, the girls' lack of water-skiing experience. And yet I was not at all uncomfortable totally gunning that engine, doing loops in the water, sending them out over the boat's wake thumping up and down. I was willing—no, I was delighted—to scare the wits out of them on the water. Yet on the rock face, I was not willing to have any of us take the risk.

Later on, I wondered why that was.

I realized that I was categorizing risk according to a simple metric: death or not-death. Yes, my overactive imagination could easily envision Grace or Jess falling while behind the boat and suffering an injury that would require, say, a hospital visit and a cast—"Hey, you asked for it by putting your thumb up"—but *they would still be alive.* Whereas the worst-case scenario on the rock face brought death into the equation. As a parent on vacation with one's children, the notion of helplessness certainly comes into play when assessing risk (which seems to arise more often on vacation when we take on activities that are perhaps outside the norm of our everyday experience). I felt more able to take positive action out on the boat, whereas the likelihood of being able to do anything on the rock face, once things went sideways, or rather downwards, would have been almost zero.

The over/under line, I realized, was the finality. For me, anyway. The fact that Cathy operated in the reverse doesn't mean she's at ease putting the lives of her children callously on the line (or perhaps it does; maybe I should ask her directly). It simply means she has a different, and certainly more balanced, imagination. Such a parent operates, wisely, according to likelihood; she lets her children cross the street so long as they demonstrate basic common sense and an understanding of the rules of the road. Whereas I always see the car speeding around the corner with a drunk behind the wheel. The odds of anything happening on a short scramble up a rock face were, realistically, minimal, so Cathy was comfortable with it, whereas boating accidents happen all the time, so she felt that situation called for somewhat more care ("Curtis, slow down!! They're going too fast. It's TOO FAST!! AIIEEEE!!!!").

Having said all that, we haven't really undertaken too many activities with the girls that I would actually characterize as dangerous or overly risky; we've never sea-kayaked, mountain-climbed, sailed the

Inside Passage. The most dangerous thing that happened to any of us in recent family vacation memory occurred when I shanked a golf shot at Panorama, in the British Columbia interior, last year and hit Grace on the ankle—who, it has to be said, was standing ahead of me playing out of turn—causing her to collapse in a heap, shrieking in pain. It was not my finest moment as a golfer, but it did have a few unforeseen advantages: it was a vivid, if perhaps unnecessarily harsh, lesson in golf course etiquette (*The person farthest from the hole has the honour*); it made golf, counterintuitively, slightly more appealing to Grace (If you can get injured playing it, then it must be at least somewhat athletic; she was heard to say later in the round, "Actually, golf is sort of fun"); and it provided the entry point into a great story—not only the getting-hit-by-Dad-on-the-golf-course part of the story, but the follow-up. Because we took a few moments to ensure Grace was not seriously injured, I think we fell a bit behind the pace of play. A few holes farther on, the group behind us—three hipster dudes sipping brews the whole way around—hit into us. It was not entirely their fault, because it was a blind tee shot over a huge hill into a small gully in front of the green on a short par 4. Their three shots from the tee landed within ten yards of one another, and within five feet of us. I ignored my first instinct, which was to chip their balls into the trees, but gave in to my second.

"Look," I said. I reached down and took a couple of the balls and placed them one in front of the other, touching.

"No, no," said Grace. "This is better." She moved them so that they were side by side, still touching. She moved the third ball to within a foot of the other two.

We made our way to the next tee, from where we could still see the previous fairway. The dudes made their way over the hill and arrived at their tee shots. There was disbelief and incredulity, and when they stopped and took out their cameras, high-fiving while they took photos of the incredible moment, it was all we could do not to laugh, hit our tee shots, and move on. Who says golf can't be adventurous?

*

It was a rookie mistake, putting my trust in a single hold. We were half an hour outside of Whitehorse, climbing a sheer wall. I was stuck on the face, and needed a place to put my weight; to my left a small knob the size of half a grapefruit seemed to offer safe purchase. I was wrong. Crack. Gone. It felt as if the Yukon itself was crumbling under my grip. I dropped. My fingers, still curled in a hold, scraped along the craggy surface, shredding off a layer or two of skin, and as I fell I caught the faint voice of Grace, shouting from high above, *"Daaaad! Noohh!"* But there was only emptiness—nothing left to grab, nothing to interrupt my fall. The next thing I touched was the valley floor.

Luckily, it was a drop of only four feet. I also happened to be in a harness, belayed by a slacker kid saying, "Whoa, hang on, dude." On the ground at my feet sat the plastic climbing toggle that had come loose under my weight. The kid looked at the bloody scrapes on my fingers. "Bummer."

We'd come north to ride the White Pass and Yukon Railway, the famous rail line built to transport thousands of stampeders seeking their fortunes on the way from Skagway, Alaska, to Dawson City, Yukon, but as much as we wanted Jess and Grace (who were in grade three and grade seven at the time) to be fascinated by the North's irresistible history and beauty, sometimes a parent needs a little jam to hide the pill. Enter the climbing wall and zip line.

"Dad," Jessica shouted from up high, so that everyone down below could hear. "What are you doing? You fell four feet. Why didn't you just keep going?" When I finally got to the top, I heaved myself up and over the edge, prompting the slacker at the top to say, "Hey, nice walrus move there, buddy."

Above the treeline, the view was staggering and immense. The Alaska Highway snaked away to the north. Whitehorse lay twenty kilometres to the southeast, and beyond that we could see a forbidding ridge of sawtooth mountains, beyond which lay Alaska. It looked an impossible passage.

Early the next morning, we left Whitehorse for Skagway to catch the White Pass train, a drive that would take us through the Yukon, British Columbia, and Alaska. As we drove the empty highway, it seemed the perfect time for a little northern mythology. When I was growing up, my dad frequently played the recorded poems of Robert Service, read out in the stentorian tones of J. Frank Willis, a voice that will forever occupy a basement corner of my memory. And so it seemed only fitting that we listen to "The Shooting of Dan McGrew" and "The Cremation of Sam McGee." The only recording I could find was in the rather histrionic Scottish brogue of Service himself, his voice wheezing out, "The northern lights / have seen queer sights / but the queerest they ever did see / was that night on the marge / of Lake Labarge / I cremated Sam McGee."

I asked Jessica and Grace what they thought of Service's idiosyncratic reading.

"Weird," said Jessica.

"Creepy," said Grace.

There are, of course, things you expect to see in the North—bush and bears and wild rivers and pristine lakes and vast human-free zones—and then there are things that surprise you. Like a desert. Not far from the point where the Yukon, Alaska, and British Columbia borders touch, a fascinating little geographical idiosyncrasy, we came upon the Carcross Desert. A sign on the side of the road declared it "Canada's smallest desert." We stepped out of the car and onto the set of *The English Patient*. An ancient lake bed, part of which still snakes out onto the shore of Lake Bennett, the Carcross Desert is a series of a dozen or so sparsely treed hills that flash up the side of a mountain bowl, all covered in a perfect, fine-grain sand. We doffed our shoes and the girls scampered up to the top of the farthest hill, jumping and gambolling about as if we'd taken them to Arabia not Alaska. It wasn't Lake Labarge, but it seemed considerably more alien. It felt empty, untouched, and for a moment we imagined that we'd discovered it for ourselves.

The history of travel in the great outdoors is long, whether of the adventurous or pastoral variety, but this history was until quite recently almost exclusively individual and largely male; such travel was not a family pursuit. Of course, the world was a vastly different place for the traveller until very recently; the undiscovered actually existed, original exploration was possible, and Google was something only babies said. The hiking and backcountry camping of today evolved out of mountaineering (and overcrowding in the national parks), and although the vacation, and particularly the family vacation, may have been the purview of the upper class prior to the early twentieth century, there were nevertheless genuine travellers, adventurers, and explorers from all walks of life, most of whom looked down their noses at what they saw as poseurs and dilettantes. In the 1870s the naturalist John Muir, writing to a friend from Yosemite, noted that there were too many fancy Easterners around, but not to worry, he said, since most of them did not pollute the backcountry, but instead drifted "slowly about the bottom of the valley as harmless scum collecting in hotel and saloon eddies."

I felt a modern-day equivalent upon arriving in Skagway, from where we were scheduled to depart on the White Pass and Yukon Railway. I had no words to describe the hair-raising descent from the summit of White Pass, snaking down along roads dangling from cliff edges, viewing epic waterfalls and distant gorges, seeing a sliver of town in the distance between slashing peaks, only to get closer and closer and see strange giant white beasts at the far end of the town.

"What are those?" I said, peering out the front window.

Cathy looked out, her eyesight being quite a bit better than mine. "I think . . ." she said. "I think they're cruise ships."

It was true. I hadn't known this beforehand, but Skagway is a deep-sea port, and it's where many, if not most, Alaskan cruise ships dock along the way up or down the west coast. The sight of those cruise ships in that remote little northern town drained much of the sense of adventure I'd anticipated finding in Skagway. It was one of those moments when you realize how difficult it truly is in our modern age to find something you can reasonably call "adventure." Here's my new travel dictum: If you find yourself in view of a cruise ship, you are in a place which cannot, *ipso facto*, be considered adventurous or off the grid.

We awoke in Skagway the next morning and headed down to the White Pass and Yukon Railway station, boarded, and were promptly informed that we were travelling the railway on the exact day it had opened 108 years earlier. Not ten minutes out of Skagway, we were already chugging slowly up some of the steeper inclines, hugging the rock face with thousands of feet of free fall mere inches to our left. How it even occurred to the planners and builders that such a railway would work is a mystery; how they achieved it is a miracle. In the twenty-six months it took to complete the line, thirty-five thousand men worked on it and thirty-five died.

At the peak of the pass, the sky was white and diffuse with mist and the odd snowflake. We'd gained thousands of feet in altitude, and it was hard to even imagine returning to the days of the gold rush, when every gold-thirsty stampeder wanting to pass through that checkpoint had to prove to the RCMP that he had a minimum of one thousand pounds of supplies with him. If he was short, he had to return to Skagway. This was a survival requirement, but also a way to mitigate thievery. We chugged by this point on the train, all silently staring out at the barren hostile rocky summit.

"Isn't that wild?" I said to Jess and Grace. "Wouldn't that be awful to carry all that by yourself, just you and a mule, all the way up *that* trail, and then get turned around by the RCMP because you didn't have enough supplies?"

Unusually for them, both Jess and Grace were wordless, and stared out the window, taking it all in, the stories and the scenery.

And then we were off the summit, on the way back down. Jess was regularly at the back of the caboose, standing on the platform, taking photos, pointing out waterfalls and trestle bridges, enjoying the trip as its operators no doubt imagined enthusiasts might. Grace, on the other hand, had discovered a one-year-old baby at the rear of our coach, effectively terminating her already-tenuous interest in history, trains, or the Yukon.

Our only stop along the way was Bennett, which had been the transition point from trail to river for the stampeders. When we pulled in and walked around, the town's single permanent resident opened up a tiny little hut to sell some of her homemade necklaces and earrings. As Jessica was purchasing a pair of beaded eagle-wing earrings, I asked our host how long she'd lived in Bennett.

"Born here," she said. "Raised here. Still here."

"Oh, right," I said. "And what's the total population of Bennett now?"

She kept her eyes on the wares she was arranging on the small table in front of her. "You're looking at it."

After we left Bennett, the one-year-old baby drifted off to sleep, which caused Grace to turn her attention to one of the young railway coach attendants.

"I'm in grade three," said Grace. "What grade are you in?"

"Uh . . . I'm in second-year university," said the young lady.

"Oh, okay. So how old are you?"

"I'm twenty."

"Twenty!" said Grace. "That's way younger than my dad. He's sixty-four and weighs ninety-one pounds. So where do you live?"

"Skagway in the summer. At university the rest of the time."

"We lived in Paris once. Well, not me, because I wasn't born yet. And I play the piano and the violin, too. Well, not the violin, but we have a violin. My mom plays it, but she doesn't play it anymore."

The conversation, if you could call it that, continued in this vein until the baby came back to life, at which point Grace dropped the young attendant like a slimy bug.

The White Pass and Yukon Railway, once the ligature of an entire historical chapter, is now almost exclusively a tourist attraction. This in some ways mirrors the entire history of rail travel in the tourism industry; for the family vacation the railway has almost always been promotional and transportational, as opposed to being the object of the trip. In other words, train travel has rarely been the point of a family vacation, despite the fact that, for many, travelling across Canada by train with their families was a rite of passage, a way to experience the scope and magnitude of the land. (One writer I read wrote that he wanted to drive across America with his family so that his children would understand "distance," which he felt was a concept lacking in most modern travel.)

In the early days of North American tourism and family travel, the rail network was used almost exclusively to promote western travel, to get families back to the pioneering ways of our forefathers. At the turn of the twentieth century, it was the railway companies themselves who did the marketing, selling trips in 1920s to dude ranches in Wyoming, Montana, and Colorado, close to the national parks, so that families could double up. Susan Sessions Rugh, in *Are We There Yet?*, noted that the rail companies were instrumental in starting dude ranch associations that encouraged owners to upgrade and advertise on the eastern seaboard. Travelling by rail between the world wars was very much tied to the package experience; you went straight there, did your dude ranch fortnight, maybe spent a few nights at the national park next door, and then you went home.

The railroad was central to Canada's creation, of course, and played a huge role in the settlement of the American West, but it has not played as great a role in the tourism industry in either country, partly due to its relative inflexibility (you can't stop and go like you can in a car; you can only proceed along the rail track—your destination is predetermined; you can't pack as much). That doesn't mean it didn't have an impact on tourists and how they came to understand their travels. The elite used the train to a great degree for individual and family travel, primarily between the Civil War and the First World War.

For a brief period of time, rail travel was glamorous and popular and adventurous. It was a new way to see your country, and railways such as the California Zephyr promoted their "Vista-Dome." Every train had five Vista-Domes. "Scenery Unlimited!" they promised. As travellers grew used to the novelty and sensation however, the sense of excitement wore off. Families on vacation did use and continue to use rail. The rail trip from Edmonton to Vancouver through the Rockies, for instance, is still popular today, though you really have to want to travel that way; it takes about twenty-four hours by train and it's less than an hour by air.

Rail travel began to slowly fall off prior to the Second World War due to the increase in auto travel, and by the late 1950s rail passenger travel in general was in serious decline. Not that the mythology of the Old West died out in America. It just became an attraction people accessed in other ways. In Canada, the mythology of rail travel has been linked to the West and the North; that was partly why we'd come to the Yukon, to touch the mythology of our country. We found that mythology everywhere, not just on the rails.

The day before we left Whitehorse, we made a short drive up-river to the Robert Lowe suspension bridge over Miles Canyon, which the Yukon River thunders through. You can visit all the museums and see all the interactive displays you like, but it's not until you step out of the parking lot, pass through the trees, and find yourself on the unfenced cliff edge of the canyon to see, fifty feet below your toes, the boiling, angry rapids spilling through a serpentine basalt chute on their way to Whitehorse ten kilometres downstream that you sense, with adrenalizing immediacy, what it must have been like to try to run a scow on these waters, or, God forbid, a massive steamboat. It wasn't just romantic and adventurous, though it surely was also those things, but truly life-threatening. I find it hard to believe, even today, that such a site wasn't fenced off. This was not rock climbing tied into a harness. Or boating on a lake. One untied shoelace and a bit of bad luck, and it would be the end. Our hike along the river's far edge was not without its nervous moments, and again the safety versus experience debate played out in my mind as we hiked; Cathy and the girls were obliviously traipsing along a couple of feet, sometimes less, from the edge, whereas I spent the whole time preparing myself to have to jump in to save someone who'd tripped and fallen in (ignoring the fact that if Cathy, Jess or Grace fell in and I jumped after them, they'd probably have to rescue me, given that they're all better swimmers than me).

On our way back across the bridge, we stopped in the middle. It was then I knew the pill had gone down with the jam.

"Can you imagine?" I asked Jessica. "Can you just imagine what it must have been like to go through these rapids on a tiny little boat full of supplies, full of every single thing you owned? It would be terrifying, don't you think?"

She peered over the wire railing, down to the churning waters. "Yeah," she said quietly, before grinning. "But so cool."

3

Cruising for Trouble

WHEN IT COMES to family vacations, or life, you can divide people into two categories: amphibious and non-amphibious. There are people who like the water, who play in the water, who swim like dolphins, who like boats, who have sea legs and who, upon encountering a large body of water, will happily envision recreational opportunities, instead of sharks, rogue waves, slimy sub-surface creatures, riptides, and those giant creepy forests of kelp sporting eerily brainlike pods at the end of the stalk which always wash up on beaches. For amphibious people, water (as contained in lakes and oceans) is not simply one of life's necessities, but a glorious thing to gravitate towards, to live beside, or on, and, of course, to vacation around. There are, my research has revealed, many such people.

Then there are the others, people who feel that water is for taking showers, for drinking, who don't particularly like boats, who don't have sea legs, who don't swim, and who are frightened of those giant creepy forests of kelp sporting eerily brainlike pods at the end of the stalk which always wash up on beaches. These are people whose rationale is, *If you can't walk on it, stay away from it.*

People, in other words, like me.

I think it's all about where you grew up. The prairies do something to a person, especially if you spend your formative years wandering around them as I did. Living day after day, year after year, in a landscape where roads end only because the horizon intervenes, where the sky doesn't so much sit above you as surround you, where the fencepost and barbed wire are visible grace notes. The prairies are a place where lightning splits the night sky so fiercely and so vividly that you are sure the world is going to break into halves. It's a place of immense beauty and wonder, most of which is visible and accessible.

Yet it wasn't simply the flat expanse of the prairies that informed my landlubberliness. The spare loveliness of the prairie landscape that stretched out for a thousand miles to the east didn't stretch out at all to our west, since the Rocky Mountains essentially formed Alberta's western border (. . . and still do, I find). Growing up in Calgary, the Rockies were always a backstop, a ten-thousand-foot-high granite fence. The Rockies were a dramatic and always somewhat ominous presence, a reminder that there was no easy passage heading west (towards the ocean, not coincidentally). They were compelling to look at, great for skiing and hiking, but also, to my childhood mind, a constant reminder that natural beauty and danger were always somehow linked. I've never lost that sense, that feeling in the natural world that the more enchanting a spot, the more likely it is to be unsafe. I don't mean this in a negative way; risk and danger can supercharge a situation, make it worthwhile, make something worth doing, whether alone or with your family. When you've scaled a distant peak, or traversed a dangerous hiking path (or, I suppose, sailed a savage passage, which I have never done), part of the beauty of the view is surely that there was risk involved.

Think about it: the view from the mountaintop—yes, it's stunning, but it's a long and deadly drop if you put a foot wrong. The view from the shore of a lake you've canoed in to—stunning, but you're isolated, and bad weather or a broken oar means trouble. The sun bleeding into the ocean as you sit drink in hand on the beach of a tropical resort—an oil painting, but arterial disease from the excess food and drink are surely a hazard.

All of which contributed to my becoming a dedicated prairie dweller, even though as I grew up, went to university, and started working, there were inevitably friends and colleagues drawn to the west coast. "It's gorgeous," they'd always say. "Right on the water. You can swim in the ocean. You can kayak. You can watch the whales."

"And you can drown in it," I'd add. "Or be swept off a jetty by it. Or be eaten by something underneath its surface."

I never really "got" Vancouver, though it is admittedly a beautiful city, and, admittedly, I have a great time whenever I'm there. But there is something oppressive about the place; the giant mountains seem to push you to the sea, even as the sea repels you back to the land, the land where the tall buildings and the low, rainy sky induce a kind of stooped crouch as the default position. I always leave Vancouver feeling a few inches shorter. *Where's the sky?* I want to shout. *Where's the space?*

Don't worry, I use my inside voice.

In my landlocked childhood, we did occasionally camp at lakes here and there in Alberta, but "lakes" in southern Alberta are big sloughs: shallow, weedy, not very impressive, and not very scary. We visited my grandparents once or twice, over the summer holidays, at Ladysmith, on Vancouver Island; their trailer court hamlet was on the milder eastern shore of the island and, strangely, I only seem to recall the lush forest and humid, salty air. I can't even seem to call up an ocean view. Memory is so often tied to incident, of course, which would be why I recall the summer at Ladysmith when my brother

Keith fell off a giant tree swing hanging over a valley and disappeared into a nest of bushes and craggy rocks about ten metres below. We feared for his life, but found him miraculously unharmed at the bottom of it all, save a few scrapes and gashes and a broken arm (the threshold for what constituted genuine injury in our house was very high).

And so water, you will have intuited, is not my natural habitat. As a prairie boy, I am still happiest with my feet on solid earth, and I tend to access large bodies of water only under optimal circumstances or when an even greater threat on shore pushes me there.

Which was why I was so dismissive when the opportunity to go on a cruise came up. The first mistake was mentioning it to my family. All three ladies are such natural swimmers they might as well have fins for arms, but still, I thought: a cruise? We're prairie folk. We camp. We hike. We cycle. We visit great foreign cities. We don't sit on a boat for a week with people in white shoes, where the only adventure to be had would be jostling in the buffet line and wrestling super seniors over the last of the shuffleboard sticks.

"Can you believe it?" I said at the family dinner table one night. "A cruise. A magazine wants me to write about being on a cruise. Ha! Who would ever want to go on something like that? It's absurd. They're just giant floating condos. Why you'd ever want to be stuck in the middle of the ocean on one of those giant tubs is beyond me." I looked in turn to what I assumed would be my like-minded wife and daughters, who were then fourteen and ten.

Six weeks later we left for the cruise.

We flew into Miami the night prior to embarking on the cruise that everyone was now "pumped" and "excited" about, that they'd been "waiting all their lives to do" and that if I'd ever "bothered to ask" I'd "have known" that it was the kind of thing "everyone in the family would love to do . . . except for you."

Our night in Miami was spent at a place near South Beach that, their website said, was "a character motel with vintage furniture and historic value." A dump, in other words. Never mind, we told ourselves, we're not here for the Miami Beach experience, we're here to get on a giant boat, gorge ourselves on food, take part in crass and lowbrow tourism options, get seasick, and then return home ten pounds heavier and unenlightened about the places we would visit. Not that I'd prejudged it.

The next morning, we caught a cab to the pier and were deposited beside a skyscraper that had somehow been laid on its side and placed in the water. It was called the *Liberty of the Seas*, part of the Royal Caribbean line, and it was, at that time, the largest passenger boat ever to have taken to the seas. The cab sped away, leaving our luggage on the side of the road, and we were immediately confronted with a dozen different lineups, organized under various banners and overpass archways, with tour buses pulling in and out, people spilling out of cabs and vans at every turn, anxious seniors hailing harried porters, small children weeping and shouting for Mommy, middle-aged white guys wondering where they'd put those minibar vodkas that were clearly going to be required very soon. There seemed to be no system at all in the sheer chaos. The whole thing put me in mind of the evacuation of Saigon . . . except for the guns, bombs, and choppers, that is, although that wouldn't have surprised me much, either.

We finally found someone who looked like a porter.

"Excuse me," I said above the din. "What are we supposed to do with our bags?" I pointed to our eight bags, slumped against the curb. "And where do we check in? I don't see any signs."

He looked at us as if we were an irritation he couldn't ignore, despite deeply wanting to. Like he'd never seen four pasty clueless Canadians before.

"What class?"

"Excuse me?"

"What class of cabin. What's your cabin class?"

I told him.

"Name?"

I told him.

"Okay," he said, writing it all down on a shredded scrap of paper that he jammed into his shirt pocket. "Just take your personal documents and ship tickets, and go through the far door down there at the end of the pier."

"Okay . . . ," I said. "But what about our luggage?"

He waved me away. "Just leave it," he said. "Don't worry. It'll get taken to your rooms. I wrote it down."

I glanced at his shirt pocket and could see that the little slip of paper was already sticking out, as if scoping things out in advance of making a dash for the gutter.

"Are you sure?"

He gave me a steady gaze suggesting deep tiredness combined with the impatience of one who has seen a few hundred thousand too many tourists in his day.

"Yes," he said. "I'm sure."

"What's going on?" asked Cathy, when I came back to the gang.

"That guy said to just leave our luggage here, and to head over to the end of the pier."

She eyed our luggage skeptically and glanced back down to the porter, who was now frantically unloading bags from a tour bus that had just pulled up to a stop at the curb. We gathered up our passports, tickets, and backpacks, and headed to the gate he'd indicated. Before stepping through, I looked back. The porter had disappeared. Our bags were sitting where we'd left them. I knew in the pit of my stomach that that was the last we were ever going to see of them, and began mentally calculating the cost of new wardrobes and toiletries for four people. I hoped the vodka was in my shoulder bag.

Once inside, it turned out that we were indeed in the right place. There was a line to register, and then a line to get on the boat, and then a line to get our pictures taken, and then another line if we wanted a more formal family picture taken, which we declined. It took the better part of a couple of hours before we were finally on board, checked in, photo ID'd, and oriented. We made our way to Deck 7 and found our cabin. I swung the door open and there, against all logic and expectation, were all eight of our bags. Intact. Lined up. And was I dreaming, or had all our bags in fact been given a little bit of a spit and polish?

"Holy . . . ," I said softly under my breath, not finishing the phrase, given that my children were right beside me. There was no way, I had reasoned earlier, no freakin' way that we were going to see our luggage by midnight. Or ever. Yet there it was. It was all bad . . . and then it was all good. The paradox that is the cruise experience had begun.

*

I woke early the next morning, and quietly slid open our balcony door. The air was warm, the breeze fresh. We were moving. This horizontal skyscraper was actually moving. The sun had just come up, and some eighty feet below our cabin balcony the ocean water was a rich, crystalline blue, the colour of a sapphire, a marked contrast to the brackish khaki of the Miami harbour. I went back inside. Cathy, Jess and Grace were still asleep. I slipped out of our Deck 7 cabin and softly clicked the door shut. It was 6:30. The passageway was silent, the stairs to Deck 11 empty. When the *Liberty of the Seas* had left Miami the previous night it held 3,634 guests and nearly as many staff, but none of them, it seemed, were early risers. I was glad of this, since I'd hoped to squeeze in an hour's exercise as a preventive strike against the food, drink, and sloth the week ahead was sure to hold. Furthermore, the girls had already mapped out the entire day, a planning exercise held the night before which I was helpless to influence. Micro-organized nearly to the minute, unnecessarily, the day's plan seemed to my exasperatingly untrained, unfun, and uncool eye to consist primarily of moving from pool to pool and familiarizing ourselves with the ship's various activity options, which included things called the FlowRider, the H2O Zone, the Adventure Ocean, and something known as a *cantilevered whirlpool*, which sounded both unappealing and structurally dubious.

At the door to the ShipeShape Fitness Centre, I paused briefly to secure a lungful of the morning's temperate saline breeze. Yes, I'd had serious doubts about going on a cruise, but had caved in to family pressure when the opportunity came up. I was worried that it would be too orchestrated, too middlebrow, that it would offer neither rest nor adventure. But as I stood there that morning, at twenty minutes to seven, with the breeze fresh, the air pure, the sea vast and calm, the sun making itself new against the Caribbean's eastern horizon, I wondered what I'd been so concerned about. It was the middle of February back in Edmonton, and I realized at that moment that I was having trouble remembering what it felt like to trip headfirst into a snowbank after slipping on the driveway while shovelling snow in the -20 dark at 5 p.m. This moment was peaceful, serene, and warm. I took one more breath, my doubts all but erased, and pulled on the door of the ShipeShape, ready to get my day rolling with a few endorphins.

"STOP! NOW!!"

I froze, the word *hostage* jangling like a tire iron in my head. *Of course,* I thought, *giant boat, people with money from western democ-*

racies. Of course it's going to be hijacked. But the order to freeze wasn't directed at me. In a faux boxing ring twenty feet away, a female drill sergeant was barking at a ragtag gang of obvious non-boxers. "PUNCH IT! I SAID 'PUNCH IT'!" A matronly retiree gave the swaying heavy bag a limp fist bump.

"NO! NAIL THAT BAG. LIKE THIS . . ."

The sergeant coiled up a biceps the size of an avocado and delivered maximal violence to the bag, which shuddered and swayed from its ceiling chain. Her troop cowered, as did I. Moving gingerly, so as to not attract her attention, I made my way past the ring over to the check-in counter. Just past the ring, ear-splitting techno-pop cascaded in undulating waves from an aerobics studio. Inside, a dozen or so spandexed women were trying to follow an aggressively buoyant instructor shouting above the din. After checking in, I finally located the bicycles near the front windows facing out to sea and began pedalling, but I was soon put off by the fact that I could feel my inner organs vibrating, a state not eased by the odd angle at which the bikes were set, facing out the window at three-quarters ahead, which, combined with the ship's straight-ahead forward movement, gave me the impression that I was pedalling furiously sideways. If there is a horizontal equivalent to the sensation of falling, this was it. I tried to focus and go inward, but I couldn't hear the music coming from my headphones due to the piercing death metal screeching out of the gym's overhead speakers. I left the gym twenty minutes later, appreciating for perhaps the first time why the FBI uses deafening music to drive out bunkered cults. As I passed the exit, the drill sergeant was wiping her face and chew-sipping some kind of lumpy green liquid. I took a mental picture of her face; it seemed important somehow that she be avoided at every turn for the next six and a half days. As I was taking my mental picture she sharply turned her face towards mine. I looked away hurriedly. *Damn,* I thought. *She's ID'd me.*

I returned to the cabin. Grace was laying in bed, stretching out her ten-year-old frame. "Hey, Dad," she said. "How was your workout?"

"SAY WHAT?"

*

I never imagined I'd be the patriarch of a family excited to be on a cruise, probably because one of my lodestars in the world of non-fiction magazine writing had for years been the epic David Foster Wallace piece "A Supposedly Fun Thing I'll Never Do Again," which he originally published as a shorter article in *Harper's Magazine*, entitled "Cruising." It's hard to fully capture the caustic brilliance of his dissection of the cruise industry, and I refuse to quote from it for fear of embarrassing my own prose, but, trust me, find it and read it. (His 2008 suicide, brought on by severe depression, is a blow the literary world has yet to recover from.) To me, the consideration of the realities of a cruise—getting on a big boat, eating from groaning buffets, boozing it up, dipping your toe for a few hours at a time into whatever iota of foreign culture you can find at every port—was bad enough, but this was always eclipsed in its crass negativity by the *symbolism* of going on a cruise. A cruise had always represented to me just about the worst aspects of travel I could imagine: the excess, the vulgarity, the diluted adventure, the conformity of experience, having everything handed to you on a platter, the lack of real interest in the cultures visited. Doing all *that* with my family, exposing my children to it, signalling that this style of travel was acceptable, that this was *us*, was very low on the list of lessons I wanted to pass on to my children through our time together as a family, whether on holiday or not.

But sometimes you're forced to take one for the team, to join the herd.

And it's a growing herd. The history of the cruise industry is not that long, but it has a powerfully accelerated arc; from a decidedly narrow beginning (upper-class liners crossing the Atlantic), it has metastasized into one of the globe's fastest-growing and most popular tourism and vacation options. And in the context of the family vacation, it has transformed itself from a couples holiday into something entire families, and extended families, now view as a standard vacation option. On our cruise, we saw many couples of two principal types: young newlyweds and older forty-something couples (who might have been newlyweds on marriage #2, I suppose). But the biggest demographic were people like us: families. And these families comprised two types: the basic nuclear family, and the intergenerational family, typically a nuclear family accompanied by grandparents. This is why the numbers involved have grown so enormously in the last two decades. The tourism studies academic Ross Klein has noted the cruise industry had roughly half a million passengers in 1970, 3.6 million in 1990, and by 2000 had almost 7 million passengers. That number nearly doubled again by 2010.

The cruise industry, says Klein, could be said to have begun the day in 1958 that Pan American airlines began to offer commercial non-stop flights between London and New York. Up to that point, the only way to cross the Atlantic was by ocean liner. Certainly, the roots of the cruise industry lay in the transoceanic crossings of yesteryear, but those trips, aboard the *Queen Mary* and, yes, the *Titanic*, amongst so many others, were not principally about leisure but transportation. True, for those on the upper decks the *Queen Mary* was an opulent experience, as opposed to the miserable conditions of the third-class travellers below decks. But they all had one thing in common: they were going from departure point to destination point. Upon the advent of mass air transportation, people suddenly had a better, cheaper, quicker way to get where they were going. They didn't need a boat. It was out of this tectonic socio-cultural shift that the cruise industry was created.

The cruise today occupies a well-defined corner of the vacation mentality: giant ships, voluminous food, packaged experience. And they are gaining traction with families so quickly that it suggests something important about the changing nature of the family vacation. Everything about our existence is rapidly changing, of course, and this is illustrated in travel by the intersection between an ease of movement incomprehensible to past generations and a fear of the "other" that might have been equally incomprehensible to a more innocent past. The cruise seems to perfectly fill the desire for travel while satisfying the need for security. A husband and wife can take their three children and maybe a couple of grandparents around the world to see Alaskan inlets, or Jamaican bays, or the canals of Florence, knowing all the while that comfort and security and knowability and risk mitigation are close at hand. In a way, it's the security blanket they find in their cabin. Cruising is not adventurous in any real way, but again, real adventure seems hard to come by these days unless you're a war correspondent, a mercenary, or raising teenagers. In any case, to assume adventure, new experience or authenticity are indeed even potential goals aboard a cruise ship is perhaps to miss the point (which I am admittedly adept at). Much of the research around the cruise industry is starting to show that for many cruisers the ship itself is the chief attraction; the destinations are just add-ons. The writer Polly Patullo quoted Carnival Cruise Lines' CEO Bob Dickinson on the subject: "The limited number of countries and ports offered is not a deterrent to Carnival customers; after all the ship is the attraction, not the port of call." In other words, the Caribbean, or Alaska, or Venice are just backdrops, the set, if you will, against which the real vacation is meant to take place, namely, the experience of being on a giant boat.

Does that make such a trip any more or less meaningful or valuable? To me, going on a cruise puts into stark relief one of the fundamental questions of the family vacation: What is the line between authentic and inauthentic experience, and what is it precisely that you are teaching your children about those things? (Though "teaching" is too didactic a word, when what I really mean is, What are you showing them, telling them, signalling to them, about the world we live in, and how you, as a parent, interpret that world?) Kids remember this stuff. Family vacations form much of the grist for the mill of childhood, and what comes out the other side is an adult. But then, is "relaxation" not an authentic experience? What qualifies as authentic? What are you supposed to do (and how do you define it) if everybody just wants to sit by the pool for three weeks? Or if half the family wants to hike Kilimanjaro and the other half wants to kayak off the coast of Vancouver Island? What, finally, *is* experience, and what does it mean in a family context?

The manufactured, the controlled, the prepackaged, the bland—none of these things are going to harm your kids on vacation, so long as that's not the only experience they ever have. And it's true that there is no such thing as a non-experience, since even sitting by the pool for three weeks will yield something. Yet although everything is an experience at some level, we make judgments as to the quality and authenticity of our activities all the time, and must do the same on family vacations. The answer, like most everything, probably lies somewhere in the middle. Doing nothing can sometimes be attractive, but we also want to expose our family to the new, the different, not just because it hopefully broadens them, and us, but because it also acts as a kind of bonding agent that unites us as a family. "Remember that car trip!" "Remember the time Dad's shorts came off in that tidal pool in Mexico!" It's always going to be tricky to get it right for everyone every time. Democracy is a messy business, after all. Especially when you give the vote to nine-year-olds.

*

Families dove for tables near the windows. Howling children sprinted back and forth down the aisles. Staff hustled about breath-lessly. The breakfast-buffet atmosphere was like a UN food hand-out in a war-torn African dictatorship, so palpable was the frenzy to get one's share. What, I wondered, was everyone so worried about? There was a panic to it all that was as unnecessary as it was unseemly. The food was so endless in its diversity and volume it appeared computer generated.

This turned out to be the case throughout the entire cruise. Food was available everywhere and all the time. You couldn't batten down a hatch without bumping into a buffet. Very early on in the cruise, at that first breakfast, in fact, as I stared at the napkins and various pam-phlets on the table, I realized that the acronym for our ship, *the Liberty Of The Seas*, was LOTS.

Indeed.

Standing in the buffet line, looking at the sheer volume of food (and contemplating what also has to be the massive waste involved)—the eggs, bacon, ham, fruit, breads, cheeses, waffles, pancakes, syrup, all held in tubs the size of the average laundry sink—was a not partic-ularly appetizing experience, simply because there is something unpleasant about the gluttony of it all. Jessica and Grace hit the buf-fet line first and returned with teetering columns of cinnamon buns and watermelon. Cathy and I got eggs, toast, bacon, fruit. To my surprise, the food turned out to be nearly as good as it was plentiful, although that would have been a physical impossibility.

In fact, the general savouriness and tastiness of the food pre-sented something of a problem: it was hard not to eat too much. *Dis-*

cipline is a word I associate with monks, dogs and children, not my diet, but given the savage aural attack in the gym earlier that morning, it was clear there was no way I was going to be able to spend more than about twenty minutes a day there.

Over breakfast, the day's plan was delivered to me. The girls were set to begin explorations. FUN was about to begin.

On the aft outer platform of Deck 13 the lineups for the Flow-Rider wave simulator were already long, and it was only ten in the morning. If there was ever any evidence needed that the cruise has passed from a largely adult and affluent mode of vacation into a mainstream family holiday option, the FlowRider lineup was it. Hordes of kids of all ages waited in line with mothers and fathers, while grandparents holding babies and small children watched from nearby bleachers. The whole set-up looked like a plenary session at a UN conference on intergenerational family unity.

What I didn't realize until I'd been musing on this topic for about fifteen minutes was that we weren't actually waiting in the FlowRider lineup. We were in the lineup to get the registration wrist bracelets that gave us passage to *enter* the FlowRider lineup. After passing through the bracelet lineup, we entered the real lineup, which was long and slow, but saved by the sight of middle-aged dudes showing off for their kids and wiping out spectacularly in the process. I laughed at these amateurs. Even I knew how to ride one of these boards, since it was clear that it was exactly the same principle as riding a toboggan down a snowy hill, an activity woven into my DNA. The water was the snow. It was obvious. You just needed to stay centred and use your knees to steer. Simple.

I got plenty of time to plan my FlowRider attack, given the amount of time we waited in line. This was our first major lineup of the week, and far from our last. In fact, standing in so many lineups allowed me time and reason to ponder the strategy and philosophy of the "lineup" on a cruise. The lineup is the norm. There are lineups for everything. There are lineups at breakfast. There are lineups for towels. You line up to get on the boat and to get off the boat. When tendering (tendering being the ship-to-shore transfer process when LOTS couldn't actually dock at a pier, usually due to rough seas), you line up to get on smaller boats that take you back to the big boat. Then you line up to get off the small boat before boarding the big boat. You line up to get into shows on the boat. You line up to get a coffee on the boat. When ashore with cruise-related activities, you line up to board buses to go to the activity. Then you line up to return to the dock. Then you line up to get back on the boat. After that, you line up . . . well, you line up just because it's muscle memory by then. There were not only lineups for everything, sometimes it even seemed there were lineups for nothing. On two separate occasions I noticed a lineup that seemed to lack a clear terminus.

About halfway through the week it occurred to me that lining up was not simply an unavoidable cruising nuisance, but rather one of its foundational activities. You spend so much time lining up that once you are doing something else the sheer relief of not being in a lineup means you'll be happy to be doing anything other than standing in a queue. The lineup, I decided, is a key, if unadvertised, tool in the managing of expectation. Analyzing the cunning of it helped me pass the time in lineups throughout the week. I don't know if the cruise industry has researched the organization of human movement to the same degree that the Disney people have (books have been written on it), but it's hard to imagine they haven't. The strategy on the face of it seems clear. Because the guests are subjected to lineups of all sizes at all times throughout the day, when genuinely crushing lineups occur people do not panic and push and flee and jostle to the same extent that they would if they were at a sports game or rock concert (all of which is vital when half your passengers are seniors and children). If that were to happen on a cruise ship, with its tight quarters and literally nowhere to go, it would be a tragedy in the making. John Seabrook, writing in the February 7, 2011, issue of *The New Yorker*, on the subject of crowd control, pointed out that "a crowd is at its most dangerous when density is greatest." That danger, of course, would be amplified in small spaces with few exits . . . such as in the middle of a cruise ship. One day, when tendering off the boat over to the Grand Cayman Islands (because the seas were too rough to dock at the pier), the lineup to get off the boat was certainly a thousand people long, moving up and down staircases, through hallways deep in the bowels of the ship. It was a massive, dense, slow-moving serpentining lineup that had the potential to get ugly.

But it didn't.

Why? I wondered. I could only presume that because you line up all the time, everywhere, for everything, including before you even board the boat, you are, in fact, inured to it. You adopt a more laissez-faire attitude. *I've waited for everything else. Another twenty minutes isn't going to kill me. And where am I going anyway?* Sure, there were a few people grousing here and there about the perception that this person or that person had skipped part of the line, or a complaint to a cruise staffing member that grandma or grandpa was getting tired on their feet. But by and large, it was a compliant crowd, so pacified by days of lining up for things of consequence and no consequence that a huge lineup to get off the boat seemed but a minor inconvenience.

Genius.

We did eventually make it to the front of the FlowRider lineup. It was hard to believe; waiting that long and then finally being there. I didn't know quite how to react once we were standing at the top of the FlowRider. It was like waiting for a UFO to land every day for a decade and then one day you walk out to the landing pad, and there it is, without fanfare or warning. A UFO. How do you react to that?

The FlowRider captivated Jessica and Grace, as it would any fourteen-year-old and ten-year-old. It presented itself as a thirty-foot ski hill with water replacing the snow—water pressure-hosed, that is, uphill at a serious clip, allowing the rider to get on a small board and surf while effectively standing still. Jess and Grace were instant experts. In fact, they made it look so natural that the middle-aged guy who followed them decided to showboat a bit. He scooted onto the wave, got riding, got off his stomach and up on his knees. He waved his arms, gave a double thumbs-up, and generally looked like he knew what he was doing . . . until he lost his balance, separated spastically from his board, and was shot back up the slope as if released by catapult. Legs akimbo, he caught his kneecap on the lip of the deck. He limped away, cursing, looking defeated. His kids put their arms around him.

"I hate to say it, Dad," Jessica said to me later. "But you got cocky."

Sitting on the sofa in our cabin, I elevated my leg and gulped down two ibuprofen. Cathy and the girls had gone back up to Deck 13 for more of the FlowRider and a go at the climbing wall. The pain in my knee was severe, a cross between a charley horse and a torn ligament. My ears were still ringing from that morning's ShipeShape aural mugging. My calf muscles were spasming due to excessive queueing. As I lay there, less than a day in, it was already clear to me that a week aboard LOTS was going to require considerable stamina, even a certain inner fortitude. There was no choice and no escape. There was only LOTS.

I checked out our stateroom again. It was nicely appointed, if small. It had a shower, beds for four, a comfy couch, and the thing you need most when on a cruise—a little plasma TV with satellite. I turned it on. The reception was crystal clear and there were many channels. It occurred to me as I worked the remote that a bum knee would allow me to beg out of the ballroom dancing lessons Cathy had spied in the Activities Calendar. Things were looking up.

*

Royal Caribbean says it travels to "The Nation of Why Not", which I take to imply a traveller can find the experience they desire, whatever it might be. Ultimately, they proclaim, "if you want it, we got it." Of course, both are patently untrue. If you want peace and solitude, you won't find it. If you want adventure or even basic mingling with locals, you won't find it. The job of a cruise, however, is not to provide rest or adventure, only the illusion of such. As opposed to the fictions it sells, what a cruise sets out to do in reality (namely, provide bacchanalian amounts of food and drink, decent service, a clean and safe environment, and a narrow sampling of highly sanitized tourism and entertainment options) is precisely what will appeal to a huge cross-section of the population. And there's nothing wrong with that. Not everyone wants to climb Kilimanjaro without a guide or trek through the Australian outback with nothing but a penknife and a water bottle. If you are that type of person, however, consider this fair warning. Do not cruise. You will not win. LOTS will win.

But if it's not exactly restful and not particularly adventurous and not especially broadening, then what, precisely, *is* the point of taking a cruise as a family? It can't really be said that it has always brought families together, given that the industry is barely more than a generation old, and that until a short time ago didn't even cater to families or children at all. It was only when Carnival Cruise Lines began offering cheaper fares in the mid-seventies—explicitly marketing the cruise as formerly for the rich, but now available to the "average" person—that middle-class families began considering the cruise;

prior to that it was simply too expensive for the whole family to go. So much has changed in such a short time; now, according to Ross Klein, half of all Americans report that they are interested in taking a cruise (most of whom were, I believe, aboard LOTS). The cruise is also experiencing exponential growth as a choice for intergenerational family travel, since it offers safe and ostensibly luxurious surroundings for the children, the parents, and the grandparents to travel together. Of course, this has and always will be one of the motivations for parents seeking to create a family vacation—the chance to link generations, to have one's children get to know one's own parents, to signal to both the children and the seniors that family does matter, that familial continuity counts for something (a trend I'll discuss in more detail further on). Also, one should never discount the allure for parents of bringing grandparents along on family vacations to babysit whilst said parents get a night out on their own to finally spend a minute alone with one another without kids pulling at pant legs and skirt hems demanding another juice box and a fresh episode of *Dora the Explorer.*

And so what does the cruise industry do for families? Does it bring them closer together? Is it a good thing for families? It's fair to say that the memory well must be stocked, over and over and over again, with a wide variety of experiences. It's not about good or bad, though on balance, as a parent, you do hope to send your child into adulthood with a hard drive that isn't too corrupted. The cruise may not be my idea of a perfect family vacation, but it was clearly someone's idea, somewhere, of an experience that would generate strong and/or positive memories across generations—LOTS was heaving with newborns, grade schoolers, teenagers, adults, seniors, super seniors, and middle-aged men wearing knee braces.

There is certainly no direct correlation between going on a cruise as a family and hoping to broaden your children in any particular way. Yes, it can be fun (depending on who is handling the definitions) and if the goal of a family vacation is for the family to spend time together, bond, generate some memories, and continue to know and see one another in new ways, particularly at the intergenerational level, then a cruise can (somewhat weakly) meet those goals. But if a family wishes to spend time together while also learning something genuinely new about the world, while seeking a touch of adventure and striving for some form of authentic experience, then a cruise is probably just going to put you in a bad mood. An inherent and intractable problem with the cruise (though not from management's point of view) is that virtually every activity has already been pre-experienced. You are directed, often quite literally shepherded, into experiencing the sight or activity according to how the cruise line wishes you to experience it. You either accept this or you don't. If you accept and understand that what you are really participating in is not so much your own authentic experience as a mass-produced and generic vacation, then you might have a good time. After all, sometimes we do simply crave a Big Mac.

Otherwise, get ready for the lineups, the rip-offs, and the relentless dilution of whatever culture you happen to be visiting. You'll also need to get ready for the fact, if you are a cruise skeptic like me, that you will be mystified to observe, plainly and clearly, that, against all reason, people appear to be having fun.

Including one's own family . . .

*

The ocean was warm, the bright coral close enough to touch, the water brimming with exotic creatures. We were snorkelling just off Haiti. Before we jumped in, our guide told us to watch out for fire coral, the poisonous lime fish, and the spiny sea urchins. This did not motivate Grace, who burst into tears the moment she got salt water in her eyes. About ten metres from the boat, I floated with her for a few minutes trying to get her to calm down, to adjust her snorkel, to assure her that it was unlikely she'd run into lime fish, fire coral, sea urchins, fish, sharks, whales, seaweed, fish, other snorkellers, or anything slimy, spiky, or scaly. Or fishy.

"That was the scariest thing I've ever done," she told us later, proud of herself (once out of the water). This reaction caught us off guard a bit, since Grace has always been a little water sprite, more at home in water than on land. Our guess was that the guide's highly unmotivating motivational speech about the various things ready to kill you or cause you pain didn't have the desired impact on Grace. (It didn't go over too well with me, either.)

Jess, on the other hand, easily adjusted to the snorkel, managed to find and hold a tiny octopus, and was so smitten with the water and the sea creatures, she surfaced halfway through, stripped off her mask and snorkel, and declared, "I'm going to be a marine biologist!" This is the kind of enthusiasm you love to see in a kid, and has resulted in Jess declaring she's going to be an architect (after helping build a tree house), a cardiologist (because she read the word and liked the way it sounded), and an archaeologist (for reasons that remain unknown).

Haiti seemed an odd port of call, given the harrowing poverty and natural disasters the country has experienced, but Royal Caribbean has leased a thumb of land from the Haitian government on the north shore, just over the mountains from Cap-Haïtien, Haiti's second largest city and the root of most of its rebel independence movements. Royal Caribbean has renamed this spit of land Labadee. It felt decidedly odd, and possibly immoral, to be gambolling about the beach in one of the poorest countries on earth. There are undoubtedly rationalizations to be made (it benefits Haitians, it creates work, tourism is good for the economy), but nevertheless it was hard to guiltlessly enjoy one's icy-cold Corona on a beach chair when you know just ten miles over a hillside hundreds of thousands are living in abject poverty. This was precisely the sort of situation that a family vacation, in my world view, was meant to avoid; the blind spot, that is. It raised, again, the question of what it means to travel as a family, or to travel, period. Are we hedonists? Are we curious? Do we want our children to experience the other cultures of the world? Or do we just pretend we do? Perhaps it's more honest—harsh, but honest—to simply admit that we don't much want to investigate the harsher realities of the places we visit, that in fact we prefer to vacation as a family or otherwise not so much to increase what we know, but to *forget* what we know. We did have a couple of conversations with Jess and Grace, pointing over the mountain to the southeast, about how poor a country Haiti was, about how difficult the people's lives were, about how fortunate we were to be living the lives we do. To their credit, they listened, asked questions, were not impatient.

Apparently, we had not had enough water-based activities for one day, because immediately upon leaving Labadee and gaining the boat we hit the main LOTS pool. This gave me the chance to ponder poolside activity in a rather more anthropological way: Why, I wondered, does a man with a large tanned belly, sunglasses, a stud in his right earlobe, a thick gold chain around his neck, and a back tattoo of what looks like Jesus as a floating angel, why does this man require an ice bucket with six Coronas beside his chair? A waiter or waitress passed my own deck chair once every eight seconds, on average, though it did sometimes take as long as fifteen seconds. The bucket of beer seemed over the top to me, a peacock strutting his drinking feathers.

It followed natural law that this would be the same man who joined us on the pool deck when I allowed Cathy to talk me into participating with her and Grace in a team poolside challenge involving water balloons and hula hoops. I don't quite recall the mechanics of the contest, other than it involved passing water balloons back and forth, then throwing them from the last team member to the first. The beer bucket man kept shouting at the rest of us, since of course we ended up on his team, to lick our fingers during the balloon passing; this seemed to me not just strategically flawed, but spectacularly unsanitary. I did not follow his advice and later could only wonder, What sort of existence allows a grown man to cultivate expertise about water balloon finger-licking? We still managed to win, but the crowd, it has to be said, did not reward us with the kind of energetic applause we deserved, even when I raised our winning water balloons aloft like the bloody heads of vanquished gladiators.

"Boy, you really got into that in the end," Cathy remarked later, laughing with Grace and Jess.

The poolside activity wasn't the only place aboard LOTS where I was able to indulge in thinking about what it meant to be on a cruise and what it meant to be a family on a cruise. In fact, although at one level we were travelling as a family of four, on another level we were travelling as a family, a giant family, of 3,634. We were part of a floating community, trapped as we were with one another, which was sometimes problematic—such as when a strange, drunk, heavily tattooed man wants you to lick a balloon that he himself has just licked—but that did, on the other hand, provide for some lovely moments. Such as when our girls made friends with a group of sisters from South Carolina. One night, around 10 p.m., Jess came back to our cabin after being out who knows where on the boat with the posse.

"Hey," she said, flopping onto a deck chair beside Cathy and myself; we were on the balcony, sipping a glass of white wine.

"Hi," said Cathy, peering back into the cabin. "Umm . . . where's your sister."

"Grace?"

"She's your only sister to the best of our knowledge."

Jess shrugged in the way that only teenagers know how to shrug. "She's out running around somewhere with Katie and Andrea." The two younger South Carolinians, that is, one of whom was nine, the other seven.

"Running around? Define 'running around.'"

"I don't know," said Jess. "Running around. I think they were going up and down the elevators, yelling and screaming, sort of playing hide-and-seek on the elevators. You know."

Cathy turned to me, grimaced. "What could happen to them? Nothing, right? There isn't really anywhere they can go."

I held up my white wine, toasting her ability to read my mind. "I'm sure you're right. What could possibly happen?"

Grace showed up about an hour later, exhausted. "Oooh, that was so much fun," she said, collapsing on her bed. "Except for that one guy."

"Which guy was that?" I asked, certain I didn't want to know, but compelled to ask out of parental guilt. "Who was he?"

Grace thought about it for a minute. "I don't know what his name was."

"That's not quite what I meant," I said. "I mean, who was he, as in, What happened?"

She started giggling again. "Well," she said, now laughing. "We were going up and down the elevators. That was so cool. And then we decided to play hide-and-seek, kind of, on the elevators and the stairs."

"On the elevators?"

"Oh, yeah," she sighed, laughing again at the memory. "But then one time, and I swear I had no idea, this one time, I was 'it,' and I was so sure Katie was in the elevator. I was hiding sort of right beside the elevator, you know. I pressed the button, so I was waiting. And I saw her get on a couple floors up. I know I did. I could see her through the glass. Anyway, the door opened, and I jumped in and screamed at the top of my lungs, like I was going to tag her, right?"

I put my hand on my forehead. Cathy took a nervous sip of wine.

"And it was some guy. Some ancient guy. Like you, Dad. Like, that old. I just jumped and yelled when the door opened. But then I saw it wasn't him, so I stopped. Well, I sort of stopped. I didn't hit him that hard."

"You hit him?"

"No, no, no. Well, kind of. Not, like, 'hit' him. Just ran into him. Kind of hard. But I said sorry. Twice. I think he's okay."

"You think?"

"Well," she said, thinking about it. "I'm totally sure he is. When the elevator doors closed, he was still standing there, well, sort of standing. I guess he was more leaning against the railing. Maybe that's because he was so old. He was standing there like this."

She put her hand over her heart.

*

The cruise industry has transformed itself into a massively profitable enterprise, built not least on the tax-evasion foundation of operating in climes such as the Caribbean while being registered in Liberia. But we're not here to be spoilsports. Another way the cruise industry has learned to maximize profit is through realizing that while a boatload of families may not drink as much as a boatload of adults, they spend at least as much on onshore activities. The shore excursion is a key feature of every cruise, whether visiting the Greek Islands, touring the Caribbean, or passing through the Panama Canal. Excursions are, ostensibly, the chief attraction of every cruise; why would you go on a Caribbean cruise, for instance, if you had no interest in seeing the Caribbean? But I use the word *ostensible* because we know that for many, if not most, the boat is the real attraction. What this has meant is that if you are one of those rare people who goes on a cruise wishing to actually experience the countries you're visiting, you may end up being frustrated. Why? Because the excursions are not designed to have you experience the countries you're visiting. They're designed to get you off the boat long enough for the staff to do some housework.

There were two separate "excursions" we took that I would say were indicative of what the cruise industry wants passengers to avoid and what it wants them to do. The first—spent driving the back roads of Jamaica—was an example of what the cruise industry wants to discourage, namely allowing people to operate independently and create their own experiences (although, as parents, we happen to think that's a good thing). The second—swimming with the dolphins on Grand Cayman Island—said everything about how the tourism industry nakedly manipulates situations, in this case, with families, in order to maximize profit while none too subtly containing the potential for new experience.

The night before we docked at Montego Bay, Jamaica, I mentioned to Pretty Shamu (the South African concierge of LOTS, who was, luckily, quite pretty) that we were planning to avoid the sanctioned shore excursions in Jamaica and independently rent a car, so as to explore the countryside on our own. She furrowed her brow both prettily and professionally.

"Oh."

"Is that not a good idea?"

"I don't recommend it . . ."

"Is there a reason we shouldn't?"

"Well . . ." She hesitated, then, "Jamaica is a somewhat wild place. They drive very very fast. You are from Canada, correct? I believe in Canada that they follow the rules of the road. Jamaica is not the same. Also, there is considerable crime. It is a very poor country. However, if you feel you must . . ."

"We just want to go for a drive," I said. "I mean, we're only going to be gone for five or six hours, right?"

The furrows deepened, as if to say, *We'll be happy to notify your next of kin.*

The next morning, we got off the boat and stepped into chaos on shore. The rental car company sent someone to pick us up and take us back to the shop to do the paperwork. We piled in and he sped away, cutting off taxies and buses.

"Ja, good call, mon," he said, often looking over at me, and at Cathy and the girls in the back, at precisely the moment when I, were I the driver, would have been looking at, oh, I don't know, the busy intersection we were barrelling through. "Da tours dey take you on are too busy, too crowded, mon. You don't get fifteen minutes at doze places before you shuttled back on da bus. Better you go somewhere on your own."

I asked about some of the back roads, about taking different routes here and there. We were thinking of going to Negril, I told him. Possibly inland instead of along the coast.

"No, mon!" he said, turning his head rather dramatically to look at me. "Me driving, okay. Yeah. But you, mon? No way. Take da highway. Negril good, though. Go to Rick's."

Once on the road, the reason for Pretty's hesitation made itself known. It's not so much that Jamaicans drive crazy fast—though they do—as much as that based on the evidence at hand there was not a single traffic law in the country. Within five minutes of leaving the rental car shop, we were on the Howard Cooke Highway heading southwest to Negril and already I felt like Charlton Heston in *Ben Hur* racing chariots in the Roman Coliseum, the only differences being that I wasn't wearing a toga and that in the Coliseum chariot drivers had the advantage of not passing into incoming traffic at speeds double the posted limit on two-lane highways. I did my best to keep up with traffic—since it seemed we'd be more at risk going too slow than too fast—but even though I was doing, at times, 50 kmh over the posted limit, vehicle after vehicle full of waving and smiling Jamaicans scorched past us. Jess and Grace seemed oblivious to it all, but I did notice Cathy gripping the dash once or twice. Just as we came into Negril, a truck carrying hundreds of unsecured bags of concrete spilled a few. As we slowly passed, I rolled down my window and asked one of the guys cleaning up the mess if we were on the right road to Rick's Place. He nodded. "Ya mon."

Once we were under way again, Cathy and the girls laughed and asked me if, after two hours in Jamaica, I'd already gone native. Jessica said, "You asked that concrete guy, 'Hey mon, am ah on da rat road to get to Rick's Place?'"

I looked over at them. "What's you point, mon?"

*

After Jamaica, Grand Cayman Island was so clean and orderly—and chockablock with banks—that it felt like Switzerland . . . except for the miles of white-sand beaches, of course. As a playground for rich bankers, it was only fitting that Grand Cayman is where the extortionate practices of the cruise industry began to corrode my spirit. The girls wanted to swim with the dolphins at Sanctuary Bay. This was an activity I'd have felt ambiguity toward even if it were free, but having to pony up $280 US for the two of them introduced a new level of ambivalence, which tipped into outright sticker shock when Cathy and I were forced to pay a $50 "observer" fee.

As Ross Klein noted in his book *Cruise Ship Squeeze: The New Pirates of the Seven Seas*, the gouging of customers isn't just circumstantial, it's a carefully thought-out practice. Get 'em on board, and then soak 'em for all their worth. "Income from sources other than cruise fares," Klein writes, "became serious business in the late 1980s and early 1990s. Carnival Cruise Lines was perhaps the first to realize the potential of onboard revenue but Norwegian Cruise Line reportedly was the first to establish a corporate manager of onboard revenue. The goal was to get passengers on board with low fares and then to generate income by spending once passengers were on the ship. J. Norman Howard, former business director for Cunard Line, succinctly expressed the orientation: 'Attract passengers with good pricing and merchandising. Entertain them at all costs. Fill them up. Strip them clean. Send them home happy.'"

Casinos, bars, onboard shops, spa services, and shipboard photography, Klein writes, augmented the income from shore excursions and shopping programs. By the late 1990s most ships had onboard revenue centres, including art auctions, ship-to-shore communications, in-room minibars, and so on. A huge portion of cruise profits are now derived from sources not related to the fare; the old sources of income have been exploited or turned into loss leaders. For instance, nearly one-third of Royal Caribbean's profit in 2002–2003 was from shore excursions.

Carnival Cruise Lines, in particular, Klein notes, has been a leader in the pack-and-gouge theory of the cruise industry, turning "water into money . . . By equipping cabins with fold-down bunk beds on which parents can stash kids, Carnival can squeeze four guests to a room. Passengers pay less per person, but Carnival gets more bodies that will spend money once on board."

So that's why you're there as a family. Not to lounge by the pool all day, splashing around in all the non-revenue-generating pool water. But to spend on the boat. Or off the boat, on excursions run hand in glove with the cruise lines. Sanctuary Bay, it turned out, was a large open pool, a kind of enclosed bay, where the dolphins were kept, though it would be inaccurate to say they were held there against their will, since they could easily have leapt the two-foot fence any time they chose; being smart creatures, they undoubtedly knew that it would be easier to get fed inside the pen than outside.

Jess and Grace got kitted out with life jackets and, along with the other swimmers, got in the water with the dolphins. Eco-guilt aside, it looked like fun, kissing the dolphins on the nose, catching a ride while holding a dorsal fin. It was spectacularly politically incorrect—I mean, talk about making the earth and its creatures subservient to man's whims—but if you're going to debase yourself, you might as well go all in. Cathy and I watched Jess and Grace frolic with the dolphins, and for a moment I even wished I was in there with them. It was pure rationalization on my part, but to me it even looked like the dolphins were enjoying it. I tried to move onto the pier to take close-up photos of Jess and Grace, but as I stepped forward an employee told me, firmly, that I was not allowed on the pier. It turned out, to my great ire, that our "observer" fee of $50 entitled Cathy and I to stand behind a rope on a walkway much too far away to take a decent picture. The point of this was soon made obvious when a team of staff photographers stood on the pier taking photos; we would have to pay an extra $10 per photo of the girls with the dolphins.

I was a very unhappy dolphin-watcher at that point, and went to stand up closer to the main office—which was in no way differentiated from the "observer" area Cathy and I had just been standing in—hoping to allow my photo-op manipulation steam to bleed off. What is it about human beings? We are offended by tales of Wall Street manipulation in the billions, but when it's twenty bucks of our own money the fury really stokes up. (Mine, anyway, since I have to admit that Cathy has a cooler head under such circumstances; I was standing away from the bay so as to quell the powerful urge to jump in the water, swim with the dolphins, and shout out, "What are you going to do? Charge my Visa for this?! Go ahead. Try it!")

Standing under the alcove of the main building, I struck up a conversation with a local Caymanite. I could feel myself calming down. That lasted for approximately forty seconds. My new friend told me he'd brought some friends from out of country here today because they, too, wanted to swim with the dolphins. It was expensive, I responded, but I had to admit it sure looked like my girls were having fun. "Still," I said, "that's a bit of a rip-off. That $50 'observer' fee, just to stand here and watch them."

He looked at me, perplexed. "There's no 'observer' fee," he said. "We just walked in. Why would you pay $50 to stand here and watch this?"

I had no good answer to that. And neither did the cruise authorities when I asked them the same question back aboard LOTS. They claimed to be unable to control the pricing on shore excursions. I did not share my irritation with Jess and Grace, who labelled the day a highlight, having gotten so close to some of nature's most beautiful and elegant creatures. But the whole experience, it occurred to me later that evening, symbolized cruising in so many ways: the sublime mixed with the vulgar, beauty filtered through naked graft. Vegas is Vegas, and Fiji is Fiji. But a cruise is Vegas pretending to be Fiji. They're going to get their money, somehow, some way.

All aboard.

*

On the morning of our final buffet in the Windjammer, the food was still delicious, the service still friendly, the floors still clean. I couldn't help marvelling at how after seven days at sea we were still being served food we enjoyed, the staff were still able to pretend to be enthralled by our presence, the windows and floors and handrails were still spotlessly clean. Say what you will about the cruise industry, but it has identified what its customer base wants (or thinks it wants) and it delivers. We sat by the window gazing out at the Miami skyline. Grace returned from the buffet with six cinnamon buns on her plate, stacked like decks of playing cards.

"Can I take these with me on to the plane?" she asked.

"No," said Cathy. "We're not even allowed to take food off the boat. The customs people would just throw those out."

Grace, true to her nature, seemed at peace with this obviously draconian law. "I guess I'll just eat them all now then."

The next twenty minutes were spent following the leaps and splashes of a shark-like creature in the harbour. Finally, it was time to go. Our cruise experience was about to come to an end. We walked one last time to our cabin, got our hand luggage. Jess and Grace said goodbye to their South Carolinian friends. We headed down the gangplank to pass through customs—one final lineup to negotiate. As we stood waiting, Jess turned back to face the giant ship. "That was so much fun," she said. "I loved that. But . . ."

This was a moment, I thought to myself, a moment a parent needed to pay attention to. Being a family on vacation was not always about the surface activity, but the overarching meaning. Perhaps Jess was about to give me a glimpse into what she thought of it all, and, by extension, maybe what she thought it meant for us to all experience this together. I hadn't wanted to go on a cruise, but what was true was that none of us would ever forget it, the excitement of being on a large boat, the dolphins, the sense that there were different cultures we'd only dipped a toe into (and which Cathy and I hoped created a desire for more). I also wondered if the less appealing side of the cruise industry had struck the girls, since I'd tried to keep my own skepticism largely under wraps throughout the week. Part of me worried that Jess was even possibly too much in tune with me, wanting to please her father.

"What is it?" I asked, not wanting to push too hard.

"Well, I was just thinking that that was so much fun, it really was. The Caribbean and all. But," she said, putting a forefinger to her chin, "let's go somewhere different on our next cruise."

I nodded and smiled. *It's all experience*, I told myself. *And that can't be all bad.* Whether or not we cruise again as a family, it appears the industry will survive without us; it continues to grow, even after the global economic meltdown of 2008. It has gone from an industry that didn't exist half a century ago to a mainstream tourism option, one that now pays close attention to families. There's no reason for that trend to change, especially given today's climate of growing family economic power tied to concerns around safety and security. As the world becomes a more treacherous place (goes the thinking), the more families will want to travel under benign, or at least knowable, circumstances.

But I believe the equation and the potential implications are considerably more complex than that. As today's parents continue, subtly and perhaps even unconsciously, to place their children under conditions of control and overparenting, the more the cruise is likely to increase in popularity with families. No parent would ever consciously voice it this way, but it seems to me that a cruise represents a default holiday for today's over-controlling parent (and we're all guilty here): a reduction in variables, decreased risk, 24/7 control. I left our cruise unsure if the "packaging" of experience for families (for that is surely what it is) is something parents are unaware of, or if they recognize it but in fact choose to cruise not in spite of the generic prepackaging but expressly *because* of it, in the same way that people cruise for the boat not the destination. Yes, a cruise removes the possibility for a more vibrant experience (as do so many pre-experienced and prepackaged holidays today), but is it possible, I wonder, if because we are instructed on how to ingest our experience, a safe and sanitized experience, that that removes both the headache of planning and the responsibility for the outcome for parents who are already overloaded in today's world. Certainly many of the parents I've talked to who have taken their families on cruises have echoed a consistent sentiment along the lines of "It's just so easy." The pre-experiencing, the regimentation, the control, the lack of variables, may in fact be the attraction rather than the negative we might logically assume it to be. Daily family life is so complicated today, the pressures so numerous, that the added hassle of planning a significant family vacation (*It's got to be new. It's got to be meaningful. It's got to be FUN.*) might just be a bridge too far.

What's the answer? For many, it's a cruise, which perhaps presents the outward signs of adventure to kids who might not know any different (foreign countries, the high seas, giant boats), yet with none of the hassles that so often come with having to plan and carry out something of genuine logistical complexity and/or risk. I'm not opposed to creature comforts. Far from it. But on a cruise, nothing is earned, nothing is new. The "grit" is removed, and, as the cliché goes, no grit, no pearl. But the truth is that the girls enjoyed it. So did Cathy. So, God help me, did I . . . in spots. Yes, I layered myself with heavy sheets of ironic protective coating, but nevertheless, parts of it were, simply, fun. Maybe this is the best you can hope for on a vacation such as this, so long as your children are alive to the complexity of it, which I believe ours were.

I did wonder about the other families aboard LOTS, though I decided not to conduct interviews along this line of thinking. I figured parents probably just wanted to rest and the last thing they needed was some pinheaded (but still sympathetic) journalist asking them if they were taking the easy way out on purpose. But I did wonder. And I still do. Because as the historian John Jakle wrote, diligent and thoughtful tourists "cultivate chance encounters. They flourish on surprises, even subtle surprises, and are open to the paradoxes of life, both big and small. They search for the unexpected by deliberately placing themselves in new situations, shopping for novel experiences. Surprise discoveries and their reactions to those discoveries stand as travel highlights, for chance encounters escape the stigma of contrivance, not only delighting in but appearing patently honest. Unexpected insight seems trustworthy as a candid picture of the world. Chance encounters are also highly personalized because they are the traveller's own experiences, experiences that relatively few others may have had. Chance encounters, better than any other kind, tie tourists to their world while helping them to define a sense of identity."

Which is what you don't get on a cruise. Which means you are not providing it for your family. Which is why I joked with the girls that going on a cruise was "a once-in-a-lifetime experience, literally."

They stopped and thought about that for a second. "Ha ha," Jess said.

"Yeah," said Grace. "Real funny."

I can't see it happening ever again, but then, I never saw it happening the first time. That's part of being in a family, part of the challenge, part of what always makes it new. It's not just about you. And I'm totally okay with that . . . as long as my feet stay on solid ground.

4

A Disney World

*G*UT INSTINCT tells me that going to Disneyland should not scar you for life, at least not in ways that could lead to a lifetime of therapy and an inability to form relationships with people taller than you. I confess I don't know if either of these is true about my youngest brother, Matt, but he has chosen to live in Japan, where he rules as one of the taller members of society. If he's ever had to undergo therapy no one in the family knows about it, though he is such a sensitive and genuinely kind-hearted soul, and so capable of expressing his thoughts and feelings, that it does reek suspiciously of someone who has been in contact with the therapeutic arts.

But if I was Matt I know I'd be scarred for life from what happened at Disneyland in 1974. Not that it was that traumatic on the surface. We had ventured to Disneyland on our way back from Mexico, and perhaps it was due to our general exhaustion that we weren't as pumped as we otherwise might have been. The January weather was not that great. In fact, I remember having to wear a winter jacket whilst traipsing around the grounds. Disneyland was a very different place back then. Yes, there was It's A Small World, which still puts me in mind of what it must be like to go insane, to have that twee music repeating inside your head forever. And there was Space Mountain. But today Disneyland is, to the adult in me, a pure expression of corporate convergence, a cultural product that exists as one pillar in a suite of offerings aligned to the same target (profit, that is). Movies become rides and rides become movies and small versions of both can be sold in a Happy Meal. In 1974, most Disney executives probably thought internal convergence was an intestinal disorder, although the prominence of Mickey Mouse, Donald Duck, and Snow White on site was evidence that if the term *convergence* wasn't on everyone's lips, they were at least evolving the concept. But in 1974, Disneyland was a place that, although obviously run as a business, was still meant to provide dreams of childhood and innocence (not that it did, necessarily, but that was the idea). It was meant to represent innocent fun to kids, and therefore to their parents. Which, for the most part, is still what it represents for kids today. No matter what you think of the Disney brand, it is a remarkable feat of ongoing marketing genius. It has always operated as both a real place (and here I speak of Disneyland, Disney World, and the various Disney parks around the world as one entity) and as a kind of state of mind—in the minds of children *and* adults, it's important to point out. It's both actual (rides, models, theme areas) and virtual (an idealized version of pleasure, free of complication). It's both nostalgic and futuristic.

I don't think we'd actually planned to go to Disneyland on our way back from Mexico. But at some point in our trip, Dad decided it was simply time to get out of Mexico. I don't even quite remember why; possibly because there was the threat of gasoline getting scarce due to world events. Or because Mom was tired of the staring out the window at the desert. Or because of what had happened on our last day in Guadalajara . . .

The Guadalajara that I remember was a city of teeming streets, dust, dirt, smog, but also a place full of the most baroquely stunning buildings, dozens of them on every street, all of them Roman Catholic churches it seemed . . . though I know this cannot possibly be the case. It was the city of the giant market, a structure that if it wasn't formerly a sports arena was certainly big enough to have been. It was, to that point in my life, the most dizzyingly intricate and Byzantine space I'd ever encountered. Floor after floor, aisle after aisle, hundreds upon hundreds of stalls and booths and shops and stands and trolleys, not one of them with any sort of formal signage but every one of them sporting an aggressive huckster willing to give you the deal that would surely break them as businesspeople, but only because you were so clearly a tough negotiator—even as a fourteen-year-old—that he had no choice but to relent and offer you a bargain no one else would ever receive. Such as the onyx chess set and board I paid $12 for, down from $36, but which was still undoubtedly marked up ten times what it cost him.

It wasn't something I was conscious of at the time, but now it strikes me as perhaps the grandest folly of all the follies my parents engaged in during that trip. Letting six kids loose in that ant's colony of a market. It's astonishing they didn't lose one or two of us, though perhaps that was their hope; maybe we were there as barter. This was the mid-seventies, after all, and I'm sure they'd have gotten away with it. I don't recall any feelings of fear or trepidation being in that market, even though I know there were many moments, sometimes stretches as long as ten minutes, when I was not within sight of my parents. What I mostly recall from that day at the Guadalajara market was the simple thrill of being in such a completely chaotic place, a place of thousands of people, none of whom spoke more English than I spoke Spanish, which was four words. The second thing I remember was my parents having one of the few arguments I ever witnessed them having. We'd decided to split up, some of the kids going with Dad to see one part of the city around the market, another convoy of children hanging with Mom to keep walking around the market. There was a miscommunication between the two of them, and since these were the days long before cellphones, there was no real way for them to connect. My mother believed they were to meet us back at where the car was parked, on some side street, at a preordained hour, but my father had heard a different hour. When we arrived back at the car, my mother and the various children with her had been waiting—no keys, no food, no Spanish, no way to contact Dad—for about two hours. My mother was only mildly upset at the inconvenience of having to sit in the hot sun with three screaming, blistering, thirsty, unwashed small children, but she was beside herself at the thought that something bad had happened to one or all of us in Camp Dad. When reunited, they stood on the Guadalajara street exhibiting, in my mother's case, an anger rooted in fear (as in, *I'm angry because I had no idea what happened to you and that scared me*), and, in my father's case, exasperation rooted in his own sense of blasé confidence (as in, *What were you so worried about, we were okay and even if we got separated we'd have eventually found one another*).

The mood in the car was not improved once we got out of Guadalajara and back on the highway, mostly due to the bullwhips. Bruce and I got them at the market in Guadalajara, paying a couple of dollars for them. Why our parents allowed us to purchase them in the first place, I'll never know, but we revelled in flicking and snapping them at each other, and at our siblings. Bruce seemed to single out Matt more than the rest, for what I suppose were obvious reasons.

As we left Guadalajara, through the semimountainous high desert, the plan was to take the inland highway for a stretch and then turn west, back to the coast. It was a scorching-hot day, and though we had no air conditioning we drove with the windows up because the air outside was even hotter and full of sand and dust. The fact that both my parents were chain smoking didn't make the car any more pleasant.

Bruce and I had no trouble occupying ourselves, however. We'd fallen in love with our whips. They were the perfect length; not so short that there was no snap, and not so long that we couldn't control them. Bruce, in particular, was getting adept very quickly at picking out targets and snapping them off. We were envied and feared by the rest of the horde. Somewhere outside of Guadalajara, Bruce and I got into a bit of a scrap. He was sitting in one of the rear jump seats, and I was seated in the middle row of seats, on the right-hand side behind my mother. I can't recall what started the dispute. Not that it mattered; we never really needed a reason to fight beyond a sibling drawing breath the wrong way . . . or at all. In any case, it quickly escalated into a whip fight. We flicked the knouts at each other's faces, aiming for the eyes, the nose. The other kids ducked away a bit, not interested in the fight so much as simply knowing how best to avoid becoming collateral damage. My parents weren't paying much attention to such a garden-variety scrap; nobody had been injured yet. My mother was gazing out her window, staring into the Mexican desert, dreaming about something—who knows what; a spa, a quiet bath, multiple homicide. She was quietly smoking a freshly lit cigarette as she watched the desert whiz by. Bruce still will not say whether he was aiming for me and I ducked, or whether he simply saw an inviting target and reacted, but he cracked his whip and perfectly caught my mother's burning cigarette, snapping it out of her lips like a circus pro. The cigarette dropped onto her lap, and she jumped like she'd been stung by a scorpion. "Ahh! Gerry. Stop the car! My cigarette. Where is it? Ah, ah, ah." She found it and picked it up. "That's it!! Gerry, stop the car! Now. That's it. I've had it. Stop the car. NOW."

My dad pulled over. Silence ruled in the back seats.

"You are so dead," Keith whispered to us, grinning widely.

Mom opened her door and burst out, stepped back, and yanked our door wide open, flinging it so hard it recoiled into her hip. She thrust her head into the car, so that her face was about two inches from mine.

"It was Bruce," I said.

Bruce was hidden from view, having worked himself practically under the jump seat, down near the wheel well.

"I don't care who it was!" she shouted. "That's it. Give me those whips. Give me those whips, NOW!"

A disembodied arm rose from behind the jump seat, like some undead creature emerging from a grave. The arm was holding a whip. My mother snatched both of the whips from us, muttering the whole while. She stepped backwards out of the car, and then in one smooth motion pirouetted and flung the whips into the desert with all her might. They spiralled through the air like snakes and hit the cactus and brush, disappearing into the khaki landscape.

Every occupant in the car was deathly silent, my father included. My mother, who was and still is an unfailingly supportive and loving person, stepped back in, sat down, shut her door. I can still recall the solid physical weight of the tension. She picked up the cigarette in question from where she'd placed it in the ashtray. She relit the smoke, stared straight out the front window, waited a beat, and said one word that seemed to sum up so much of what our trip, and our society at the time, was about.

"Drive."

*

After Guadalajara, the beaches beckoned, and we all needed it, although by that time, I think we were all probably anxious to make our way out of Mexico and back to a land where our speech was understood, the money was more or less the same, and the food was something we recognized. It seemed as if the cathartic act of hurling the whips into the Mexican desert was a signal. I know my parents felt it, too, and not just because of the passion and fury my mother—who as I have noted was normally a woman of great patience—invested in flinging those whips as far away as she could. The shark episodes at Mazatlán I mentioned earlier probably hadn't helped: first, my mother's panic attack over what turned out to be dolphins; second, Keith insisting, and my parents' agreeing (an agreement they regretted, surely, once it started to smell), that carrying a shark head four thousand miles across two national borders for a grade-seven show-and-tell session was actually a good idea.

And then, as if stepping through a magical passageway, we were suddenly back in America, in California, passing through San Diego and ending up in Anaheim. The day after arriving in Anaheim we headed for Disneyland, where we strolled around for a while, getting familiar with the size of the park, the placement of the rides, mapping out a strategy to do everything we wanted to do and see. Disneyland that day was mostly empty and the weather was blustery; it was early January, after all. I have a photo of Matt, who was four years old at the time, standing wearing a red winter jacket with a fluffy hood encircling his head like a halo.

After setting out a plan to make the most of our day there, we hit the rides. Space Mountain was thrilling (and still is, actually). Big Thunder Mountain was jarring and fun. Soon enough, it was time for lunch and so we went strolling down Main Street. A huge cast iron statue of Frankenstein's monster happened to be plunked right down in the middle of Main Street—which perhaps says something about what Walt Disney thought went on in small-town USA—and we all ambled by it. Except for Matt. He was riveted. The monster was at least double his height, maybe even triple, even though it was already slightly bent over at the waist, as if frozen in the act of stooping down to pick up a small child to tear apart limb by limb. We stopped when Matt did. The monster was stunningly realistic. The blood leaking from the side of its mouth seemed wet. Its eyes were open and staring right at Matt. After a second or two, it began to creep me out and so I stopped looking and started to move away.

But Matt stayed. He stood looking up at the monster, at its pale face, the stitches, the metal battery posts jutting out from either side of its neck. I remember not wanting or needing to study it the same way Matt was, probably because, at fourteen, I'd already seen my share of Frankenstein movies and cartoons, often in parody form. And so the monster, while interesting enough—and, as I say, impressively realistic—didn't really draw me in. I was more fascinated by how fascinated Matt was, and it only occurred to me later that he'd probably never encountered the figure before, being only four and likely not having seen any movies featuring Frankenstein's creation. All six of us kids were devotees of the campy cartoon *Scooby-Doo*, which featured a variety of monsters in the opening credits, but that was funny, not scary, and, in any case, was always watched on a dinky little black-and-white TV at home. There was, therefore, no Frankensteinian precedent for Matt, and so it was only natural that he was captivated and kind of grossed out by this creature. I think my mother was about to say something to him to get him to move along, but he was concentrating, as if trying to stare into the soul of the monster.

He'd been standing there for a good thirty seconds when, with no kind of warning—no movement, no breath, no eye blinking—the monster came suddenly, horribly, to life. It half-gargled, half-growled in a loud and horrible way while simultaneously making a desperate jerky lunge at Matt. The monster's eyes were wide open, his mouth agape and roaring, spittle flying. His hands were the size of Matt's head and they came at his face like a pair of T. Rex claws. I was standing ten feet away and I jumped.

Matt let out a terrible shriek and burst into tears, but didn't seem able to move. He'd grown roots into that tarmac and, though the monster loomed over him, stood where he was. But he could yell, and he did. He shrieked, cried, howled. Other people stopped to look. My mother and father immediately ran towards him and gathered him up, bundling him away. The monster must have had some sort of clause in his contract forbidding him to break out of character, because as soon as my mother stood up and walked away with Matt in her arms, he simply walked another ten feet down the lane, stiff-legged, arms outstretched, and took up another statuesque position, waiting for his next victim.

Matt was a basket case for hours afterwards, unmoved by multiple hot chocolates and cinnamon buns. It wasn't until we left the park later that day that he seemed to have recovered.

I remember thinking then, and thinking even more strongly now, that that wasn't quite the message Disney wanted Matt and my parents to go home with. Matt, to my knowledge, has never returned to Disneyland or gone to Tokyo Disney, close to where he now lives. But as I alluded to earlier, he has lived in Japan for more than a decade now and seems to quite like it. Whenever he sends pictures of him and friends out at a party, playing music, visiting one Japanese shrine or another, he is invariably the tallest person in the photo. He will never again be attacked from above, is my thumbnail psychological analysis of this fact. Come to think of it, I've never seen him watch a horror movie, either.

The rest of that Disneyland trip, and in fact most of the rest of our trip home, is something of a blur, though we did make one more major stop on our way home to Calgary, which was Las Vegas. Fittingly, given our family dynamic, we stayed at Circus Circus. Las Vegas has gone through numerous reinterpretations, of course, including a period in the 1990s when it aggressively, counterintuitively, and, by wide agreement, disastrously, marketed itself as the perfect family destination. Various marketing brains decided that Vegas was ideally situated to serve the family vacation market, and although I don't know how many families actually vacationed there during this particular marketing cycle, it didn't take long for the marketing brains, and every retailer in Las Vegas, to realize that Las Vegas was about the fantasy of *escaping* family, not celebrating it. There are even certain hotels now in Las Vegas that have gone actively anti-family, such as the Bellagio and Wynn Las Vegas, which ban children not staying in the hotel from entering the hotel. Frommers.com reported that these hotels have begun to make it a practice to ask children for room keys to prove they are in fact staying at the hotel. But to me, one of the ironies of the whole *What happens in Vegas, stays in Vegas* marketing campaign and civic websites promoting the adoption of fake identities is that it has taken the air out of the subversiveness balloon such activity might once have had. The minute "the man" is giving you permission to be subversive it immediately ceases to be subversive.

Not that we were thinking of any of this in 1974, although by the time we got there, after five and a half weeks on the road and thousands of miles, hundreds of fights, numerous vomiting episodes, and with Keith's rotting shark head still tied to the roof of the station wagon, I feel confident in saying that my father was probably open to adopting a fake identity and catching the Greyhound to Miami to sell hot dogs on the beach and never again be yelled at to stop the car due to urination, defecation, evacuation, or impending assassination. Impersonation might have appealed to him, however, so I'm glad Las Vegas had not yet popularized the notion.

*

Despite the Frankenstein's monster episode, Disney has survived and done rather well for itself since the early seventies, although it didn't impress immediately upon opening; the first few days of operations, in 1955, went so poorly, in fact, that Disney executives decided to close the park and then reopen some months later, simply to correct the opening-day mistakes and get a fresh start. This was to be but the first of their thousands of adaptations, improvements, ameliorations, and corrections, all geared towards an ever-more-seamless escape from reality.

Theme parks, or amusement parks, as they are sometimes referred to, are actually a deeply historic institution; Disneyland was hardly the start of this history. The first of them, the Bakken, was opened sometime around 1550 in Copenhagen; it's still running today. They weren't known as amusement parks at the time; "Pleasure Garden" was the preferred term (a phrase that seems purpose-built for witty innuendo, though perhaps not in a book oriented towards families). In any case, these Pleasure Gardens, according to the National Historical Amusement Parks Association, were the first such areas designed purely for the purposes of outdoor entertainment, and featured a wide variety of attractions that included fountains, flower gardens, bowling, games, music, dancing, staged spectacles, and a few "primitive" amusement rides. An example of these "primitive" rides would have been the ice chute rides introduced at parks in Moscow and St. Petersburg. For some reason, these parks seemed to drop out of favour in the eighteenth century— the Industrial Revolution and its focus on machine versus manpower perhaps caused a drop in popularity in what would then still have been largely pastoral amusement parks—but they made a comeback in the nineteenth century.

The precursors of what we would recognize as today's amusement park attractions began with the introduction of machine-driven rides such as the Switchback Gravity Pleasure Railway created by La Marcus Thompson at Coney Island at the end of the nineteenth century. It went on to evolve into the roller coaster, although some have said the roller coaster is actually a derivation of the Russian ice chute ride mentioned above. The introduction of large-scale machine-driven rides at these parks continued in 1893, when George Ferris took the ribbon off his new wheel ride at the Chicago Columbian Exposition. At 250 feet high, it astonished all when it opened. It was the very next year that the first fully enclosed amusement park, the Water Chutes park, opened in Chicago (as opposed to the amusement parks of the past, which were largely set in open and unfenced public spaces, hence the name Pleasure Gardens). Sadly, Water Chutes park went down the drain in 1908.

A series of historical circumstances—the First World War, the stock market crash, the Great Depression, and then the Second World War—led to a severe contraction in the amusement park industry; of the nearly 2,000 amusement parks in the United States before the First World War, only five hundred were left by the start of the Second World War. A hangover after the Second World War lasted for a few years, and then in 1955, everything changed. An optimistic illustrator named Walter Disney took his cartoon success and decided to create an amusement park based on two primary factors: the promotion of his cartoon characters tied to a celebration of what he saw, or wanted to promote, as the American way of life. This kind of re-creation of reality, according to Walt and reflected back on to us, was central to what he was up to when he created Disneyland. As the writer Margaret J. King quoted Walt himself saying, "I don't want the public to see the real world they live in while they're at the park . . . I want them to feel they are in another world." His world, that is.

Disneyland cost $17 million to build, the most by far that had ever been spent building an amusement park. There was skepticism, but after the initial setback, the park still drew nearly four million visitors its first season.

One could make the argument that the *amusement* park morphed into the *theme* park the day Walt cut the ribbon on Disneyland.

Keith Hollinshead, writing in *The Sage Handbook of Tourism Studies*, noted that the mid- to late-twentieth century saw parks move from being about rides and shows to being much more all-encompassing, assuming a more mass-market and multi-dimensional "themed" activity. They went, in other words, from being about fun and games to being about fun and games according to a theme. Today, estimates Hollinshead, there are over seven hundred theme parks in the United States alone, although it's also getting to the point where, he says, it is "becoming increasingly hard to distinguish what is a theme park from what is a mammoth-sized hotel or resort complex, from what is a massive regional retail complex, from what is a crossroads leisure and education play park."

His point is significant for vacationing families, because he's asking us to consider that the modern leisure landscape has, in fact, created a daily existence of never-ending tourism. There is no better evidence of this than in my very own neighbourhood, where we happen to live not far from the gigantic West Edmonton Mall, a shopping complex that features roller coasters, submarine rides, seal shows, a large hotel, a skating rink, a casino, a beach, a wave pool, a waterslide park, a bungee jump, a live-music venue, and, almost as an afterthought, a few hundred shops and department stores. We could travel to Disneyland and ride the roller coaster, but we can ride what is more or less the same roller coaster five minutes from our house. West Edmonton Mall statistics regularly indicate that a significant percentage of their patrons are out-of-town parent and children visitors who are shopping *and* staying at the mall. In other words, they are families on vacation.

Still, Disneyland remains categorically different from "everyday" tourism. What Walt Disney did was two very significant things, especially as it relates to the family vacation. First, he created a theme park that, as one writer put it, "expanded the concept of amusement parks from simply rides and carnival barkers to include shows, shops, and restaurants in theme settings with immaculate cleanliness, promising adventure, history, science fiction, and fantasy."

The other pioneering Disney twist was that he created an all-encompassing space purely devoted to entertainment and leisure and travel and vacations *for the family*. It may have been the first purpose-built one-stop family vacation destination. You didn't need to go anywhere else. You could go to Disneyland. That said it all. It became, and has become, shorthand for the family vacation, for better or worse. If you were going to Europe as a family, that entailed all kinds of complications. If you were going to the lake for the summer, that involved logistical details. But if you were going to Disneyland, that said it all. You could do it all, see it all, have it all. There was no need to add anything more. No wonder it was, and remains, popular; because it was easy for the parents and represented something iconic for the kids. It did, and does, represent something that families can trust (or *think* they can trust—an important distinction): the rides are fun; the grounds are clean; it's efficiently run; and, if you plan ahead and organize your day properly, it's good value. In short, it has covered all the bases and allows for a family vacation that forms a kind of insurance policy against the unknown.

There are drawbacks, obviously. The notion of control at Disney parks—of control of the park, the employees, the visitor experience, and the visitor's understanding of society, and of the past, present, and future—has been widely written about, but social scientists have summed it up well by noting that, in fact, the high level of control exerted upon visitors at every level at Disneyland is often seen as a positive. "Many parents," one social theorist wrote, "relish the control exercised over them at the Disney parks because it enhances the predictability of the tourist experience." In other words, from the family vacation point of view, a trip to Disneyland is knowable and reliable. Its predictability has become a virtue. It is a risk-averse trip, not just in terms of what might happen or go wrong or even (in terms of physical or emotional injury) what might be risky, but also in terms of being on-the-ground bulletproof parental Kryptonite. It inoculates parents against complaints from the kids. *It's Disneyland! How can you not like it? If you're not having fun, that's not my problem.*

Of course, there are always things you can't control, things you can't predict. A friend tells the story of another friend whose family drove from Calgary to Disneyland when they were young, some twenty-five years ago, a trip that featured seriously poor behaviour from the children in the back. The father lost it as they entered California. "That's it," he half-shouted to the throng in the back. "If there's one more fight back there, I swear to God, I will turn this car around and drive straight back to Canada. I don't care if we're stopped at the Disneyland gates and you start fighting; I'm turning around." It wouldn't be a story without what happened next, which was that the kids got into a fight about halfway between San Francisco and Los Angeles. The father said not a word. He pulled into a gas station, filled the tank, and turned the car onto the highway heading north. They never did go back to Disneyland, and, sadly, the parents divorced shortly thereafter. Reaching Disneyland probably would not have saved the day, I'm guessing.

The predictable nature of the Disney park experience, then, means that there is no guarantee it will be an especially unique or insightful or memorable family vacation, especially upon repeated visits. There is something highly anodyne about the Disney experience. But then that's part of the plan, part of the appeal. Unsurprisingly, what is a deeply conservative Disney view of the family and history in general (nuclear families, American transcendence, the predominance of positivity, simple mythical tales of frontier and adventure wherein good always vanquishes evil) has been translated into the most conservative of family vacation choices.

But it has, I think, an expiry date in the life of a child. Our inaugural trip to Disneyland with Jess and Grace was in 2006, and the excitement in the household was palpable, although perhaps not so much amongst those—okay, me—who were not looking forward to the crowds, the noise, the lines, all of which would have been bearable except for the thing I was dreading most, which was what I imagined was going to be the relentless push of the Disney mindset, the false cheer, the unshakeable positivity, the ever-smiling cartoon characters. I imagined it was going to be four days of being stuck inside It's a Small World, which, to me, is more or less exactly what Disney represents. But I was pleasantly surprised by Disneyland, even if most of my enjoyment of the park came through witnessing the pleasure Jess and Grace took in it. Still, I appreciated the things I alluded to earlier, that it was clean, efficient, decent value. The fun Jess, Grace, and I got out of teasing Cathy for shrieking in the Tower of Terror was probably worth the entrance fee alone.

When we returned in 2011, for one day, it seemed the magic had in many ways dissipated. The rides were still fun. California Dreaming was still exhilarating. The only live-monster encounter came when Jack Sparrow—the Johnny Depp character from the *Pirates of the Caribbean* franchise—stopped us along Frontierland. Cathy and Grace stood with him while I took their picture, and Captain Jack, instead of looking at the camera, fixed a steady, and I have to say somewhat lascivious, gaze on Cathy. Perhaps he recognized a fellow traveller; Cathy's mother's maiden name is Morgan and family lore has it that they are descended from the infamous pirate Captain John Morgan. Maybe his swashbuckler's radar picked up something in Cathy.

But despite the engaging rides, despite finding the same cleanliness of the park, despite being impressed again by the overall efficiency, there was still something missing, though it was obviously more engaging for Grace, who was eleven at the time, than Jessica, who was fifteen. Perhaps that something was simply that our girls were growing up. It seemed, too, that when it was less magical in their eyes, it became less magical in ours. I asked Jessica afterwards what was different about it the second time around, what made it so clearly a different experience for her, as opposed to when she was younger. Her point was, I thought, dead on. "The thing is," she said, "is that when you're little, when you're a little kid, your whole world is wrapped up in fantasizing about those characters. Little girls are just obsessed with the notion of princesses, and I was when I was little. And then when you're actually there, at Disneyland, and there's a princess right in front of you, you can't believe it, you just can't believe that Cinderella is right in front of you and she looks exactly like she does in the movie. It's like other kids, boys, maybe, are obsessed with the Pirates of the Caribbean, and then they get to go to Disneyland and there's Jack Sparrow." She stopped to think about it a bit more. "It's kind of like Disneyland is their fantasy world come true. But then when you get older, and especially once you've already been there, you go back, and you don't really see the characters the same way. It's sort of fun, still, but it's just not, you know, your whole play world coming to reality. It's not your whole world anymore."

She got her brains from her mother, as must be obvious.

But it does point to one of the fundamental debates of theme parks like Disneyland, and therefore of the family vacation on the whole: Who is it *for*? Much of the current research into the nature of the family vacation—what little there is—has begun to focus on the "agency" of children. As Neil Carr writes, "studying children and their holiday desires and experiences is important from a tourism industry perspective and . . . offers an insight into the social constructions of childhood, contemporary intra-familial relations and the identities of children."

In other words, it's worth trying to understand how family vacations change, or don't, when children's experiences are considered in as unmediated a way as possible. And so, knowing that a trip to

Disneyland, for most relatively well-adjusted adults, is and should be about the kids, our adult—read, parental—interpretation and evaluation of the experience will inevitably be filtered through their eyes, presuming we hear them properly. And there is nothing wrong with this. If they enjoyed it, then Disneyland was great. If they thought it was so-so, then Disneyland was so-so. There are two sides of the debate, of course, the one I've just articulated, wherein the children's interpretation is valued above the adult's, but the other side would hold that children aren't in a position, and can't be expected to be in a position, to make fully informed choices as to what constitutes valuable experience, and therefore their choices must be at the very least guided by adult experience and insight. At the risk of seeming like a fence-sitter, I see both sides. Clearly, much depends on the age of the children. At the age Jess and Grace are as I write this—sixteen and twelve—they are not only capable of understanding the world in sophisticated ways and making decisions consonant with that understanding, they are probably in a better position to make some decisions than Cathy and I, given their lack of jadedness, their openness to experience, their sense of adventure, their trust in others, their sheer enthusiasm. Yes, we'd need to be there to advise obvious safety measures ("No, Grace, that's not a fake crocodile in that river you want to swim in."). But my sense is that a vacation planned exclusively by them, at this age, would be fresh and fun. Having said that, when we went to Australia a few years back, we decided we'd give them some control over daily events, and Grace, who was seven at the time, was somewhat, shall we say, repetitive.

"What do you want to do today, Grace?"

"Swim!!"

"And then what?"

"Go for ice cream!"

"What should we do tomorrow?"

"Swim!!"

"And . . ."

"Go for ice cream!!"

*

The spectrum of what's on offer to vacationing families is, naturally, going to change how families evolve. As we grow up we define what a "family" is by casting back over our childhood, over our evolution as both individuals within a family, and as a family unit, and a significant portion of the raw material we use to form these impressions is gathered on family vacations. They are highlighted in our memories. They are moments in time caught in amber, in ways daily life rarely is. They provide powerful memories, often positive, sometimes negative. And although daily life is, of course, also a significant part of the data we use to form an understanding of what a family is—what it means, what it represents, how it works, how to make it function or not, how to create a sound version of one—daily life nevertheless does not always carry the same emotional weight that family vacations do, although now that I think about it, having access to my mother's daily calendar as we were growing up would perhaps have been revealing. I can imagine it:

  7 a.m. – make six lunches

7:20 a.m. – wake six children

  8 a.m. – quell preschool chaos, separate bickering children in single bathroom, ensure children are clothed leaving house

  9 a.m. – devise new grade-appropriate punishments for insubordination, backtalk, bad manners, fighting, poor

hygiene, forgotten homework, food wastage, deceit, and
potty mouth

10 a.m. – do nine loads of laundry

Noon – shower, get dressed, eat lunch, take time for myself,
meditate

12:05 p.m. – control panic

12:30 p.m. – shop for eight on a budget of four dollars

2:30 p.m. – clean house left in post-hurricane state every
morning

2:35 p.m. – abandon cleaning house as pointless

2:36 p.m. – prepare for return of six children, put out snacks, clean
kitchen table for homework duty, put empty laundry
baskets in bathroom

3:00 p.m. – greet children coming through door

3:05 p.m. – control panic

4:00 p.m. – prepare dinner for eight

4:05 p.m. – introduce and apply new grade-appropriate
punishments for insubordination, backtalk, bad
manners, fighting, poor hygiene, forgotten homework,
food wastage, deceit, and potty mouth

5:15 p.m. – welcome husband home and remind him to never touch
me again

6:00 p.m. – serve dinner, ask children to do dishes, end up doing
them myself

6:15 p.m. – attempt to cajole children to do homework, clean
rooms, brush teeth, prepare for bed, then ask husband
to re-apply, with interest, new grade-appropriate
punishments for insubordination, backtalk, bad
manners, fighting, poor hygiene, forgotten homework,
food wastage, deceit, and potty mouth

8:00 p.m. – have glass of wine

9:00 p.m. – close bedroom door, control panic, remind husband

never to touch me again, have another glass of wine,
drift into sleep

11:00 p.m. – rise to instruct older children to shut TV off and get to
bed, as it's a school night

11:01 p.m. – beg oldest child to apply to younger siblings, with
extreme prejudice, new grade-appropriate punishments
for insubordination, backtalk, bad manners, fighting,
poor hygiene, forgotten homework, food wastage,
deceit, and potty mouth

11:05 p.m. – return to bed, shake awake peacefully sleeping husband
to remind him to never touch me again.

Repeat daily for 20 years.

A visit to Disneyland would certainly have been a nice change
from that routine. Although the industry has contracted somewhat
in the last couple of decades, in terms of new park construction, there
are still thousands of theme parks across North America, which
makes it a fascinating source of study, given that there are still over
thirty amusement parks in operation that started before 1900 (most
of which are in Europe). Of course, it wasn't until the advent of mass
travel by car that families were able to make amusement parks and
theme parks that were some distance away from them part of a larger
holiday option. It's no accident that Disneyland opened in 1955, just
as cars were being purchased en masse by a burgeoning middle
class, and as the Eisenhower grand-highway construction project
was being realized. Disneyland flourished because people could get
there. Prior to the Second World War, amusement parks, though
plentiful, were not necessarily family vacation destinations. What
Disneyland also did, in conjunction with creating the park itself, was
build a contiguous hotel district; they didn't wait for it to evolve.
They knew that to get four million people visiting the first year,

they'd need room for most of those four million people to stay; only a fraction of them were one-day local visits. It was a strategy that you could say met with some success.

Disney parks are now but two of thousands dotting the North American landscape, yet they stand on their own as both place and symbol. As *place* Disneyland is a well-run, clean, convenient holiday option, if still, to an adult, cloying, overly cute, and maddeningly simplistic in the world view it espouses. As *symbol* Disneyland is much more complex, which is ironic given the simplistic world view it lays out. The complexity lies in the gap between what we want our children to experience today and who we hope they become tomorrow. So much of what I have written about in this book can be made to fall into either/or questions: Do we want our family vacations to be about experience or safety? Do we value risk over security? Do we seek authenticity and originality or do we willingly ingest the pre-experienced and predetermined? (And this does not just refer to Disneyland; the cruise, certain camping experiences, and other family vacation options raise similar questions.) To be sure, Disneyland is about as risk free a family vacation as you can find. Not just risk free in terms of physical safety, but risk free with regard to the confidence of the decision-making process. Family vacations are rare commodities. As children reach their teen years, parents begin to realize time is running out, that there won't be that many more chances to be together as a family—only this family—on holiday. You don't want to ruin one of these increasingly rare opportunities by choosing a lousy resort or an overlong drive or a place where someone will get sick or mugged (although, as I alluded to earlier, sometimes it's those very things—all those things that are unforeseeable or at least unprogrammable—that make vacations memorable, that give us things to bond over). The problem is that it's difficult to just flip a switch and make those moments happen, because you can't make them happen—you can only create the conditions and hope for the best. But instead of taking that risk, many parents choose the easy answer, the simple and admittedly tasty fast food over the risk of trying an untested home recipe or stepping into the new ethnic restaurant down the street.

Disneyland, for all the fun and joy it gives children, and some adults, has masterfully turned a conservative and even reactionary choice into a default family vacation option. It does not promote new experience, and in fact in creating and circulating characters and rides throughout the grounds that are already known to us through movies and cartoons, the park takes the already familiar and deepens the relationship. To use the parlance of marketers and political strategists, Disneyland's relationship with its audience is an inch wide but a mile deep. This refers back to Jessica's wise words about how children get excited to an intense degree by the thought of visiting Disneyland precisely because their whole world is wrapped up in one or two characters. The scope is narrow but the focus is total. And its success in entrenching itself in our collective consciousness as a kind of default family vacation option strikes me as limiting. This is true of the theme park experience in general; Disneyland may be at the top of that particular heap, but visiting Universal Studios is an experience not unrelated to visiting Disneyland. The details differ, but only because they're marketing *Finding Nemo* instead of *Jurassic Park*.

All of this is limiting not just in terms of the true choice available to families, but also because it discourages children from using their imaginations; everything they could imagine has already been provided and made "real." Every fantasy and every dream has already been supplied and prepackaged. In a way it disallows, even denies, the existence of one of the key building blocks of any child's creativity, which is boredom. At Disneyland boredom is the archenemy. Disneyland is so hyper, so full, so relentlessly *on*, that boredom and/or reflection, and therefore one's inherent individual creativity,

are strangled. You don't need to imagine anything, because everything has already been imagined for you and is in front of you. Yet, as
every researcher investigating child psychology will tell you, boredom is a key portal children take into their imaginations. Ample
research has shown that so-called "boredom" is, in fact, vital to one's
psychological health, and that it contributes to creativity. Writing in
the *New York Times* in 2008, Benedict Carey noted that researchers
are increasingly finding that boredom "allows the brain to recast the
outside world in ways that can be productive and creative at least
as often as they are disruptive." He went on to refer to a recent
paper in the *Cambridge Journal of Education* by Teresa Belton and
Esther Priyadharshini, of East Anglia University in England, which
reviewed decades of research and theory on boredom, and con-
cluded that it was high time boredom "be recognized as a legitimate
human emotion that can be central to learning and creativity."

A child "needs enough downtime to be bored," wrote Christina
Schwarz in *The Atlantic* in April 2011. "Yes—bored enough to stare
at the sky and study the imperfections in his own eyeball. That's
what makes for a childhood worth remembering for the whole of
one's life." Children, she writes, have always taken risks and are driven to experiment and create, but we seem to have returned to "the
18th-century notion that play for its own sake is a waste of time, that
children can be allowed to pursue their natural inclinations only if
those can be channeled into activities that will prepare them to be
orderly and productive (and now, God help us, creative) adults—
even today's play movement stresses the uplifting educational value
of play."

But she argues that perhaps childhood—"those first, fresh experiences of the world, unclouded by reason and practicality, when
you are the center of existence and anything might happen"—
should be seen less as "a springboard to striving adulthood than as
a well of rich individual perception and experience to which you

can return for sustenance throughout life, whether you rise in the world or not."

In other words, we must supply the memory well. One of the best sources of that supply is the family vacation, where there may very well be adventure and event, but where there may also be room for children to dream and play. Perhaps one of the greatest dangers in our desire to give our children everything is that it interferes with the ability of their imagination to create something out of nothing (the nature of that "something" being largely irrelevant, so long as they're the ones coming up with it). Just a thought. A thought related to what I see as the threat to the lazy-day do-nothing family summer vacation (when all manner of things were given room to happen), which has also been rendered nearly extinct by our desire to inflict upon our children the endless push for excellence, for self-improvement, for the development of the skill set we believe is required for our children to succeed as adults in an ultra-competitive world. Various media outlets have reported that there has been a noted rise in the "learning vacation" amongst families, wherein families travel great distances to faraway lands only to place their children in highly structured and supervised learning environments. I've read of recent family trips, sometimes taken over considerable periods of time, conducted according to rigorous academic, intellectual, or cultural agendas (two months to see every endangered species along the west coast, two weeks to visit every major museum in New York City, and so on). These children will gain knowledge, to be sure, but will we ever know if they saw it as a family vacation or as school in a different classroom? One person I interviewed told me that her parents "had the good sense to steer clear of educational or cultural aspirations" on their family vacations. That sounds about right to me, although there are obviously circumstances where such trips can act as positive life-changing events for children. I read about one couple who took their two teenage daughters

on a three-month trip to South America, but who insisted that along
the way they perform some sort of volunteer service. They asked
their girls what volunteer service they'd like to perform and both
responded, *Work with animals!* They worked at an animal rescue
centre in Quito, Ecuador, for three weeks, after which they visited
the Galápagos. The beauty of this is that they let the girls choose the
form of service, although part of me still hopes that such families
occasionally holiday in a place, a space, where there is room and
time to do something less heroic. This is ignoble of me, I admit; I
admire the impulse to take one's children on a "learning" adventure so as to teach them something about treating their world with
respect and responsibility. I can only imagine my parents trying to
cajole six kids into volunteering at a Mexican zoo. I suspect diplo-
matic intervention would have been required.

*

What Disneyland ultimately asks us to consider is whether we seek
authentic or predigested experience when we vacation with our families, begging the question, again, of what constitutes an "authentic"
family vacation experience. What's not *authentic*, after all, about a
visit to Disneyland? It's there. We're there. It seems real enough. But
even if it is "fake," then what's inherently wrong with consuming
something fake? We do it all the time with other products and experiences. We play video games. We eat cheese spread. We go to Las
Vegas and stay at New York, New York. All true, but that still does
not mean that authentic experience isn't worth striving for. None of
us are perfect, to use ourselves as an analogy, but that doesn't mean
we stop trying to be kinder to those we love, to do our work with
an ever-increasing integrity and application, to find more harmony
with the world around us. That strikes me as a pretty good way to
travel through life, to never accept stasis, to ask more of ourselves. In

some ways, the simple goal is to make the process a better one, and the family vacation is part of that because it's a significant aspect of how we create and define our families and ourselves. I think the fault line lays along the goals and notions you have for the family vacation, and, by extension, for how you interpret the family compact. Disneyland represents the sanitized version of the family, wherein everyone gets along, has fun, never bickers, never suffers hurt feelings, and always shows their shiniest face to the world. Real families are not like that, which is why we grow out of Disneyland, and seek out different and more complicated experiences, experiences that might better reflect who we are, or aspire to be, as a family. Either that or we stay stuck in a kind of eternal childhood of the mind and soul.

I actually first began to think about the authentic as opposed to the manufactured and simulated while on a ride at Disneyland the first time we visited. Grace was, at the time, too short to go on California Dreaming, the wickedly fast giant roller coaster, and so she was relegated to the little kiddie roller coaster, Mulholland Madness, over in the Paradise Pier section of California Park. It is (or was, since it closed in October of 2010) a classic Wild Mouse–style roller coaster, with plenty of sharp turns and tight spaces. I found it utterly terrifying. The big roller coaster, with all its speed and upside-down sections and hyper-G banks, was nothing compared to this rickety old death trap of a ride. And because Grace was only allowed on this roller coaster, and because Cathy doesn't do rides, and because Jess felt it was beneath her, I was forced to endure a good half-dozen spins on Mulholland Madness. Every time we took a hairpin bank swinging out over the park, I was sure we were plunging to our doom.

After getting off the fourth time, I said to Grace, "I just don't think I can do that again, Grace. It's terrifying. Aren't you scared?"

She looked at me as if I was scared of a spider in the bathtub. "It's a ride."

"I know it's a ride. And it's terrifying."

"Dad," she said. "It's for *kids*."

It didn't matter. It was still the scariest thing in the park, and therefore for me it was the most vivid, most real, most authentic. Perhaps they didn't mean it to be that way, but it felt like something that was just slapped together and not tested to within an inch of its life. It may not have been a trip along the real, winding and sick-making Mulholland Drive, but the sensation was close enough. In any case, the irony was there; the lamest ride in the park, the kid's ride, was the one that brought about the strongest physical sensation. That didn't make it authentic, per se, but it gave me reason to think about the question. The first time we were there, seeing Disneyland through our children's eyes, it was clear that it represented something special to them, a kind of rite of passage, though they'd never have used those words. And that made it good to be there. The next time we went, five years on, the girls had grown up. Grace, now eleven, enjoyed it, but didn't argue when we suggested leaving at 4 p.m. Jess had largely outgrown it and while she would go again, I suspect she'd never again suggest it as a first option. We evolve and change as individuals, of course, which means the family we're part of must do the same. The family vacation evolves and changes along with us, and if it doesn't perhaps that means we're stuck in a family dynamic that has failed to develop into something through which we can better communicate with and understand one another.

The afternoon we left Disneyland, I saw many couples strolling around without children in tow. I wondered why they were there. It would be uncharitable to assume they were trapped in their adolescence, though that must surely be the case with some. But perhaps it's simpler than that, less psychologically tormented. Perhaps they weren't trying to rediscover or revisit their childhoods as much as they were simply hoping to participate in something else. I can almost see the appeal of going to a theme park like Disneyland if you were a couple without children. Maybe they were just wanting to be part of what they see as Disney's single greatest asset, its best ride of all, even if it is the one it doesn't own or control. Family, in other words. We were all together, in some strange way, all of us there to express something central about ourselves as families. That's why you go to Disneyland. Because you're a family, hopefully one in evolution. I'm glad we went. But I'll be surprised if we ever go back.

5

Vehicular Recreation

WHEN CATHY AND I sat down to talk about going to Australia with Jess and Grace, it felt very much like we were planning a rather grand adventure. A land so far away. A place so different than our home. At times it reminded me of sitting around the kitchen table in Dalhousie, circa 1973, when Dad had the big maps spread across the table highlighting our route to Mexico City and back. The excitement of Australia was real, the enthusiasm high amongst all four of us. We had total buy-in, which always helps.

The history of middle-class North American family travel to the southern hemisphere is not extensive. My astute investigative journalism practices revealed, further, that this history is even sparser when a recreational vehicle is added to the mix. That's correct. An RV. That may have been the most adventurous decision we could have made, given that I'd never driven such a machine. Naturally, there are always going to be limits to the definition of "adventure" when you've got the family along with you; war zones, Himalayan climbs, and Indonesian jungle treks may prove trickier than would otherwise have been the case if forced to haul along fourteen brands of crackers, two Nintendo Game Boys, two Tamagotchis, and four special blankies, although I'm sure there are people who try. If travelling widely reveals anything, it's that no matter where you go, or what you do, or what you can possibly imagine doing, the likelihood is that someone has already done it. Or at least tried it; someone else's failed attempt usually being enough to warn you off pursuing the family tour of Africa's military dictatorships or the Ten Days Through the Axis of Evil tour you saw advertised in *Ordnance Magazine.*

But until the relatively recent past there simply was no affordable way for middle- or working-class families to get to Australia, or Africa, or Asia. Yes, they emigrated, but that was to live and work, not holiday. They had to go by boat and train, trips that would take weeks. Even if there had been easier and cheaper ways to get to distant lands, it wouldn't have mattered, because, as alluded to earlier, until the period between the wars the middle-class worker didn't even possess legislated time off, let alone enough time to take the entire family to far shores. But following the advent of cheap automobiles and the construction of the highway system, which liberated the North American family from their homes and put them on the road for regular vacations, it was only natural that at some point that great accumulation of people, the millions upon millions of North American families who holidayed all over the continent, would sit down at the kitchen table early in the new year and say, *Do we really want to drive all the way to Yellowstone Park again, for the fifth year in a row?*

For many, the answer was no. But for people like my parents, who, in the early seventies, couldn't afford to take us to Australia, Asia, or Africa (the mind boggles at the calamities that surely would have unfolded), but who thought, *We want something different,* the answer was yes. And so we drove to Mexico City and back. Yet for many other families at that time, with fewer children and more discretionary income, the timing was right to start exploring the wider world. Mass air travel did not change things much for our family when I was growing up. I had never been on a plane with my parents or siblings until very recently, within the last couple of years, in fact. I suppose that's because in our heyday as family travellers—from, say, the late 1960s to about 1980—mass air travel was still relatively new . . . especially for a family of eight. Okay, it wasn't just new for a family of eight; it was unheard of, at least in our circles. The thought of cramming eight of us into one of those airborne cigar tubes is beyond me, unless my dad was piloting it; then I might have gotten on. Not to mention that it would have cost a fortune we didn't have. I didn't make my first airplane trip until I was seventeen and didn't make my second until I went away to grad school eight years after that.

A generation later, when we sat down as a family, Cathy and the girls and myself, to talk about our trip to Australia, it was within the context of having been abroad before as an entire family, to live in Scotland, and to spend a summer in Paris. But those were different; Scotland was a move—we lived and worked there, and Jessica went to school, and so we didn't consider it a vacation—and Paris was an urban sojourn, the vacation as a summer abroad.

But not only was Australia something else altogether, Cathy and I wanted to do things differently with the girls in Australia. There was the opportunity to pursue the standard course: arrive, stay in hotels, take guided tours, visit the sites everyone else saw. A second option was to drive across southeast Australia in a beast of an RV, get lost, take roads that made our brakes smoke, get sick, visit hospital emergency wards, and place our lives in the hands of incompetent strangers. Of course, we didn't quite anticipate the full playing out of these scenarios as we discussed the trip. We just thought, hotels or RV? And the RV it was.

We also decided that this would be a good trip to let the girls have a larger say in the itinerary. In fact, we agreed that beyond securing the continuation of life (yes, Grace, you must eat more than ice cream for two weeks; no, Jessica, you are not allowed to drive the RV), we would let the girls map out the broad strokes of our daily itinerary. Too often we adults impose a holiday routine, a schedule, on our children, as if we know not only what's best for them, but what's fun for them. But is this always true? If, as we so often claim, we take holidays to be with the family, to create a solid family construct, to be good parents, to provide recreation for our children away from the daily demands of all our lives, then why is it that we don't let them make the plans more often? Possibly we're worried— well, I know *I'd* be worried—that if we left it in the hands of our kids, they'd ditch us. A 2006 study of holiday preferences for children aged 8–14 showed that when children were asked "who they would most like to be stranded on a desert island with," friends topped the list at 49 percent with parents second at 25 percent. Not that Cathy and I were particularly worried about such things in Australia. We knew our girls. We trusted them. We told them they got to choose. Whatever they wanted, that's what we were going to do . . . and sometimes it even worked out that way.

Following two days in Sydney spent exploring the wonders of The Rocks, the Opera House, Bondi Beach, the harbour ferries (all of which the girls chose), we were on our way to the coastal highway, on our own, in our RV, ready for anything. (And I will note here that for the purposes of continuity I'll refer to the various incarnations of the vehicle—the RV, the motorhome, the trailer, the camper, and so on—as an RV unless I am discussing the differences between them and their separate paths of development.) As we tried to follow our maps to find the Southern Freeway leading to the Princes Highway, which would lead us finally out of Sydney's vast suburbs, Cathy and I overheard Jess and Grace discussing Sydney.

"That was an awesome city," said Jessica. "I loved those harbour ferries. And those kangaroos at the wildlife centre. It's such a pretty city."

"Oh, those kangaroos were so cute!" said Grace. "Yeah, I loved Sydney . . ." She paused and looked out the window at the last of Sydney's monotonous outer burbs; it had been perhaps forty-five minutes since we'd picked up the RV. "But I don't like Melbourne." This was the same girl who in the taxi halfway to the Edmonton airport for our seventeen-hour flight to Sydney said, "How much longer will it take to get to Australia?"

As we left Sydney, the realities of driving an RV for the first time were hitting home. Frankly, I'm surprised there aren't more RV accidents, period. You rarely read about them or see them. The Recreation Vehicle Industry Association has reported that RVs are statistically amongst the safest vehicles on the road. It sure didn't feel safe on the Australian roads. The fact that my first experience driving an RV was in Australia didn't help—a first-time visitor leaving a city of five million people in a big RV while sitting on the wrong side of the vehicle, driving on the wrong side of the road, shifting six speeds with the wrong hand. Add to that the RV reality of not having a rearview mirror, and it would be fair to say that I was less than comfortable. We'd hoped that coming to Australia would be a bit of an adventure for the girls, but we didn't think the adventure would be surviving the RV.

Two hours later, we were easing the RV inch by inch down the tenth of some thirty steep-descent single-lane-road hairpin turns along the recommended route of Kangaroo Valley Road to the Bendeelah campground in the rainforest-draped escarpment inland from Berry. I could have used crampons to *walk* the road. Soon the acrid, yet oddly thrilling, stink of a burning clutch began to fill the cab of the RV. It was here that a rather fundamental question entered my mind, namely, "What precisely *is* the point of trying to find some adventure on a family vacation, anyway?"

Before I could find a reasonable answer to that question, it occurred to me, not at all happily, that the smell was not the clutch, but the brakes. It was the smell of imminence, a smell you sense will not contribute to your immediate or long-term happiness. Right then, Grace barked out from the bowels of the RV, "Mom, Dad! Jess looks sick. I think she's going to barf."

Our dipping, dropping, swaying, and lurching—all accentuated back in the hold of the supertanker—had gotten to Jess, and the poor thing was both pale and green, pretty much the colour of the eucalyptus leaves that surrounded us. I didn't say as much, but at one level I was pleased that Jess (who has inherited my predisposition to carsickness) was about to be sick; one of my rules about family vacations is that every trip has to involve somebody throwing up somewhere. If somebody doesn't throw up, it doesn't qualify as a family vacation. If you're returning home, in the cab, and it hasn't happened yet, jam a finger down your throat and get it done. On another, more urgent level, Jessica *was* about to be sick, so we pulled over on a hairpin cliff in the middle of the fragrant eucalyptus forest. While Jess got some air, I pondered the nature of the Australian sensibility as we'd found it so far. We'd been led to understand Australians were an easygoing, laid-back species, but that didn't seem to quite capture what the nonchalance of the last couple of hours had led to. First, the amiable fellow who'd handed over the keys to the RV in Sydney had given me an almost comically abrupt tour of the vehicle. It began when he opened the driver's-side door and put a palm on the steering wheel.

"Steering wheel," he said, looking back at me.

I nodded to indicate that that had registered.

"Gearshift." He pointed at the gearshift. "And important," he added. "Turn signals on this side of the wheel and wiper blades on the other."

He shut the door, ushered me around the back, and pointed underneath the rear bumper. "Spare tire under there, mate."

That was the vehicle orientation in its entirety, although it was longer if you included the five-minute lecture about emptying the septic container before returning the vehicle. "We fine you $300 if you don't," he emphasized.

With nothing left to do but drive off in search of the Princes Highway—a greatly underappreciated part of the Australian experience, we would come to learn—we'd hit the road, following some breezy directions to what sounded a charming campground. "Once past Sydney," it read, "proceed to the town of Berry, then turn inland to take the delightful, scenic Kangaroo Valley Road to the Bendeelah campground."

It occurred to me that perhaps, just perhaps, given that it was principally tourists who'd be reading this directional material, it should have read, "Once past Sydney's endless mazelike suburbs, spend another half an hour finding the Princes Highway. Proceed to the town of Berry, then take the delightful, scenic Kangaroo Valley Road to the Bendeelah campground, or as we say here in Australia, take the spiralling, clutch-burning, hairpin-filled Escarpment of Stupid Dead Foreigners Road to a remote campground overrun by brake-line-nibbling wombats. Here you will find no food, water, or services. Have a great day, mate!"

Jess pronounced herself over her nausea, and so we pressed on, eventually making it to the valley floor after another twenty tight hairpin turns, insanely vertical drops, visible smoke in the cabin, and one or two milliseconds of genuine full-cabin terror, causing Cathy to cover her eyes. "OH, NO. NO," was all she said for about half an hour. From the highest point of the descent to the lowest was an elevation change of about four hundred metres. On a two-kilometre stretch of road. It would have made for a thrilling, if hair-raising, ski run. As we passed out the bottom, I looked in the side mirror and saw a large road sign that could be read only by those heading up the road we'd just come down. We stopped and got out.

ROAD AHEAD **UNSUITABLE** FOR CARAVANS, COACHES AND LARGE VEHICLES.

"That might have been good to see at the other end, too," deadpanned Cathy. We reasoned the sign's perplexing location signalled more about Down Under nonchalance than any grand plan to mock our suffering. Or perhaps it was simply natural law, a hemispheric reversal, the Australian roadside equivalent of the toilets flushing in the opposite direction. We waited on the side of the road until I could no longer smell the brakes. When the dominant scent was eucalyptus, we pressed on.

*

It certainly wasn't Australian unfamiliarity with RV culture that created our troubles. There was a sign, after all, even if it was perversely located. There is also a long history of RVing in Australia. "Caravanning" has been around for decades, and Australia even has a significant subculture of older adults—the Grey Nomads—who tour the country in their RVs. My dad's nickname for most of his family life was Ghost, due to his beard and head of white hair. He was a bit of a nomad, himself, and I suspect he'd have fit in as a Grey Nomad. Not only that, our family had a bit of an RV history, if you want to call it that. Following our grand adventure to Mexico and back, my parents somehow got it into their heads that regularly travelling considerable distances with their six children in tow was a good idea. Although they were clearly suffering from some kind of post-traumatic amnesia—given that any sane parent would never forget the vomiting, whips, heat, fighting, and smoke suffocation of eight people in a car for six weeks—they were nevertheless not so foolish as to think piling into the Country Squire with a few sandwiches and a tank of gas was enough preparation to zip down to Rio de Janeiro, though I wouldn't have put anything past them.

Yet far from making what would have been the reasonable decision to never again go anywhere with six children in one car unless it was to Family Services to give one or two of us up for adoption, my parents went the other direction. *Let's go on a lot of vacations!* they said. *Let's do that sort of thing again. In fact, let's buy a full-length partially converted school bus, keep it parked in our tiny backyard, and then travel all over western Canada!!*

Yes, a school bus. As kids we religiously watched *The Partridge Family*, a TV show about a single mom and her musical family, in which Mama Partridge put herself behind the wheel of a giant school bus painted, inexplicably, in the manner of Mondrian's *Composizione 1921*, and travelled around on tour with her five musical and formulaically quirky children. It was a fairly awful show, but we loved it . . . until it became our life. The potential excitement of a school bus RV was tempered by the fact that we were becoming the Partridge family. Even our friends would later on always refer to it as the "Partridge Family bus." The only two differences between us and the TV show were that we had a dad and none of us could sing. Although, if memory serves, neither could anyone in the Partridge family.

It was hard to believe our parents were going to do it, but do it they did. One day, there it was—a school bus parked in our backyard. Or more accurately, our backyard now *was* a school bus. There was hardly room to let our dog, Tommy, out into the yard. It was a gigantic thing, and my father had to create a special gate in the fence for it. I still can't quite recall how he managed to fit it into our backyard when we weren't out on the road with it. We lived in a small bungalow in Calgary's northwest, after all, and our backyard already had a garage.

When my dad bought the bus from a friend in Wetaskiwin it was already partly fitted out. He paid $3000 for it, even though it was missing a couple things, like beds. He didn't paint it like a Mondrian. He didn't need to. It already had its own signature. It was completely white, except for a single bright red stripe that ran straight down the middle of the bus from nose to tail. It seemed to suit us, somehow. Dad left a couple of the bench seats in up near the front for those who wanted to ride with the driver. He also left the original steering wheel in, which was about the size and thickness of a hula hoop. The gearshift was a scary contraption; it rose from the floor like a golf club with a golf ball glued to the top of the shaft. Shifting it from one gear to another often involved a series of semi-articulated jiggling movements interspersed with double-clutching and pauses in neutral. Putting it in reverse was even more compli-cated; he had to lift a safety-catch mechanism attached to the shaft of the gearshift, while simultaneously forcing the stick as far towards the door as he could and then jamming it north. They didn't call it a manual transmission for nothing.

We had the Big Red Stripe for a few years, and mostly drove around western Canada, frequently visiting my grandparents, who'd moved to Vancouver Island. The summer of 1976 we drove to Long Beach on Vancouver Island. I remember it was 1976 because I recall listening to the Summer Olympic Games from Montreal on the radio as we drove through the Rockies, the signal fading in and out, the tension unbearable as we tried to hear whether or not Greg Joy won the high jump. My mother was trying to quit smoking that summer, again, but my dad was still puffing away (he hadn't stopped since picking cigarettes up again when I threw up in the car on our first day's driving to Mexico City). Knowing my mother was serious about quitting, my dad took all his cigarettes and hid them somewhere in the bus. One day, halfway to the west coast, we found Mom cleaning the bus to within an inch of its life, which was unusual for her only because she'd vowed a couple years earlier to stop cleaning up after us. But she wasn't really cleaning. She was looking for my dad's smokes, which she never did find. My dad eventually took pity on her and broke out his stash.

*

When we left Bendeelah (after a sleepless night on my part, due to a chewing sound and gentle rocking motion that I was certain were wombats snacking on the RV's brake lines; an impression I'll admit was perhaps a hallucination influenced by the previous day's drive), we had to force our RV back up a different but nearly as treacherous road in search of the Princes Highway. I was starting to get the hang of driving the RV, and only stalled it out once while shifting as we climbed the steep buttonhook turns going up and out of the valley, a stall that caused the massive unit to briefly achieve weightlessness and then slide noticeably backwards. "AGGGHH!" said Cathy, helpfully. The brakes caught. I fired the unit up again, put it back into gear, revved the engine, and then eased the clutch out slowly before popping it, at which point we jerked forward and kept moving. "We're good," I said, looking over.

Cathy had her hands over her eyes. The girls were shrieking with delight at the sensation now that we were going up instead of down.

If the car road trip was the iconic family vacation of the generation following the Second World War, then the RV trip (including trailers and caravan) wasn't far behind, particularly as the 1960s dawned. The development of the RV as we know it today actually began between the world wars and for most of those years the RV and particularly the travel trailer was popular with a small segment of the vacationing public, even though they were expensive and the road networks were poor (two factors that combined to keep the RV something of a novelty). Not that their potential for mass popularity wasn't recognized: *Popular Mechanics* magazine, Orvar Löfgren noted, predicted in the 1930s that trailering would become so popular, America would eventually be converted into a land of nomads wherein fully half the population would be living in some sort of wheeled home. Even though it was Volkswagen that instituted the mass production of the campervan after the war, it was the Second World War that created much of the technology and mechanical know-how that allowed RVs to take vacationing to new places in the postwar period. During the war, RV-style vehicles were used for transport, housing, and even field hospitals. But the RV, in this case the campervan, had its mass-market fulcrum point in 1947, when German engineers working for VW first put a camper on a Beetle chassis. VW went on to develop dozens of styles of campervans, and by the 1960s, there were close to 150,000 VW campervans in North America. By 1975, VW had produced over four million of these iconic vehicles.

RVing really came into fashion in the 1950s. Near the end of the decade the "slide-in" camper for a pickup truck began to go into production, and in the sixties the trailer industry coined the term recreational vehicle, the RV, primarily to differentiate it from what was then becoming a residential alternative, the "motorhome," never driven anywhere except to a trailer park, after which it was used as a primary residence. RVs became increasingly popular through the sixties. Families and other vacationers were starting to realize that they could take a small house with them. "Tin can tourists," they were labelled. Even John Steinbeck wrote about them in *Travels with Charley*: "They are wonderfully built homes, aluminum skins, double-walled, with insulation, and often paneled with veneer of hardwood. Sometimes as much as forty feet long, with air-conditioners, toilets, baths, and invariably television. . . . A mobile home is drawn to the trailer park and installed on a ramp, a heavy rubber sewer pipe is bolted underneath, water and electrical power connected, the television antenna raised, and the family is in residence."

RVers didn't need a tent, they didn't need to pack up a suitcase every night. There was a fridge to store milk, a stove to boil up some spaghetti. The RV Hotline, in its short history of the RV, reported that the demand for the RV grew so steadily throughout the sixties that it was the trailer manufacturers who forced truck manufacturers to not even install the beds on trucks, but to begin welding the housing unit straight onto the chassis.

From there it was just a short step to open the driver's cab up to the trailer unit. Every development since has just been refinement. RV sales dropped off in the seventies with the oil embargo—since they tend to use only slightly less gas than an aircraft carrier (although a family of five travelling cross-country in an RV will still use less gas than the same family of five travelling round trip by airplane)—but the RV had a firm place in the family vacation rota by then. The North American family was by this time fully into the habit of vacationing as a unit, travelling throughout the continent, taking advantage of state and national parks, enjoying increased motel and gas station facilities, driving on new highway systems. It was only natural that a segment of this demographic would prioritize the comfort of an RV over the "closer to nature" feel of a tent.

Like my parents. I will label it an educated guess, but I am pretty sure that my dad only bought the Big Red Stripe because he never wanted to have to put that damn tent up again. In any case, in 1978 we sold the bus for pretty much what we paid for it. The guy who bought it was planning to live in it, I think. By the summer of 1978, I was closing in on my eighteenth birthday and would only be living at home for two more years. My parents were probably sensing—with what I can only assume was the kind of relief that the construction manager of the Great Pyramid of Giza must have felt when the Pharaoh proclaimed it complete—that our family holiday era was drawing to a close.

The end of the Big Red Stripe wasn't the end of our RV experience, however. In 1979, over Christmas, we borrowed my aunt and uncle's RV, and the eight of us drove down to Arizona for the holidays. That was something of a hybrid vacation, in that we stayed at a motel and left the RV parked outside. Us four older boys slept outside in the RV for the week, while Mom, Dad, Janine and Matt slept in the motel. It seemed to work. And it gave us access to the pool, which we used for many hours a day, surely driving away any other patrons in the process. I do remember being a little curious why the motel seemed so full, yet there never seemed to be anyone else around the pool. Maybe it was because we were in the shallow end the whole time using Matt as a football.

If it was around that era—roughly the 1970s—that the RV went through a slight decline in popularity, they did begin to slowly win that popularity back, and in our post–9/11 world of holidaying closer to home (a bit of a myth, actually), RVs are now a massive business again. The old Big Red Stripe may have been a beast, but it was a cheap beast, nothing like today's RVs, these monsters of the road that criss-cross the landscape towing *behind them* the kind of cars we used to squeeze eight people into. I visited a friend in Key West not too long ago, and he took me to visit mutual friends in an RV camp about fifteen miles up the Overseas Highway. I suppose I still had this idea that RVs were rather utilitarian, just a step up from the Red Stripe. I assumed that if we were going to something called an RV *camp*, surely it was the kind of place where the common folk hung out.

Or not.

At this "camp" we found row after row of gleaming mansions on wheels. I went inside our host's recreational vehicle, something called a Featherlite, to find a space almost as big as my home and with better interior decorating. It had to be fifty feet long. If this was a motorhome, there was a lot more home than motor. A couple of beers into a conversation with our host, down at their private jetty just off their private RV pad, I was able to finally ask, in as subtle and indirect a manner as I could muster, what kinds of sums were now involved in purchasing an RV.

"What'd this sucker set you back?" I said.

He sipped his single malt, puffed on his cigar. "One point five."

I'm not often speechless, but this was one of those rare occasions.

"And that's just for the rig," he added.

"What do you mean?"

"Well, gas ain't cheap on a baby like this. Thing weighs fifty thousand pounds. And then there's the pad and stall." He waved a hand around the cabana and pier that was dedicated solely to the RV he and his wife were occupying. "We're just renting this one, but it ain't cheap. They want people to buy them now. I think they're going for about two hundred K."

I thought back to my dad, driving the big bus, filling it with gas, shifting the big stick. It had never really occurred to me before, but I wondered then if it really was as cheap a way to travel as I remember thinking at the time and since. Three thousand dollars was hardly one and a half million, but in our world it was still a lot of money; I know that now, but at the time I don't really think I ever wondered how my parents could afford it at all. As I wrote earlier, my dad ran his own glass and trim business, and while he made a living, we were not what you'd call well off, graduating from being poor when I was little to somewhat less poor when I was a teenager. We always lived in a small house. We didn't have the toys and gadgets other kids did.

My parents drove old junkers. I suppose it's possible my parents had more money than I thought. Or, more likely, they simply spent what little money they had on their family because they wanted to, because they thought it was the right thing to do, because that was their understanding of what parents did. I guess, in the end, for them it was about the bus. Or us.

*

The history of the RV may be rooted in postwar mass-market utilitarianism transformed into boomer luxury, an evolution that, like so many things about the tourism industry, is a reflection of class distinctions and social status, but the one thing I've still never been able to figure out is that if you're wealthy enough to own a $1.5 million RV, and can afford a two-hundred-thousand-dollar pad to put it on, why wouldn't you just stay at the best hotels? If it was that you liked the camaraderie of it all, why not find a cabin in a community where you could develop a social network to return to every summer? Or if it was to do with the *getting out on the open road* angle, then, well, why weren't they out on the road? So many RV owners drive somewhere and put down roots for weeks at a time. I make no claims to understanding the mindset of the luxury-RV owner, nor do I make claims to sharing equal-sized bank accounts. But it just seems to me that if the point of having a luxury RV is to take your home with you, then why don't you just stay home? I don't mean that in a mocking way, not at all; I'm truly curious.

I certainly can understand the postwar development of the low-budget RV as a vehicle for family travel. It's a tool that, like every vehicle we use for vacations, helps bracket our experience. (One Swedish researcher I read wrote that the car "is a family pack, a preserving jar for people's relations with one another.") After the Second World War, camping and communing with nature in general were seen as not only the newest and best ways to have a family vacation, but the cheapest. It was free of class structure, at least at the start. The flood of tourists and families into the wild meant there was inevitably going to be a segment of that population that did not like putting up tents and cooking over an open fire. Enter the RV. Some writers have pointed out that, in the aftermath of the Second World War, the family vacation was marketed across North America as an irony-free tool to bolster family unity and, in America, manifest destiny. Canadian marketing was focused primarily on the trip and the family, but American marketing for the family vacation, and for tourism generally inside the United States, framed it as a patriotic act. This kind of American patriotism still holds sway today, even in scholarly works such as Susan Session Rugh's, who, writing about the golden age of the family vacation, said in the conclusion of *Are We There Yet?* that no matter what your family makeup, "going on vacation together is a declaration that you are indeed an American family."

But whether it was patriotic or quixotic, the family vacation was gaining in popularity throughout the fifties and sixties, and along with it so, too, was the RV. They were getting better and cheaper all the time, and as the historian Roger White noted, it simply meant family travellers could be "at home on the road." In 1961, 28,000 travel trailers were sold in the U.S., and in 1965 that number had nearly tripled, to 76,600. Travel-trailer companies advertising at the time illustrated how revolutionary they thought their product was, or at least how revolutionary they wanted people to *think* it was. In the late fifties, magazines such as *Life* and *Westways* were running ads for travel trailers with tags like, "This resort home goes with you any time . . . any place you like!" or "It's the ideal summer family home" or "After a day's hiking in the woods or trolling out on the lake, there's nothing like pulling off your boots and sinking into one of those easy chairs in your travel trailer!" *Motorland Magazine* felt that vacationing by travel trailer was a way to hearken back to the frontier spirit still lurking in all of us, by comparing RVs and trailers to the pioneer wagons that were used to settle the West: "Today's nomad sits at the wheel of the station wagon; the prairie schooner spirit sails highways on the wheels of a house trailer."

The appeal was obvious. You could carry everything you needed. It was cheaper than staying in a motel every night. You could park in a camping spot and have an open fire. It was almost too popular; state and national parks were for a time overrun with RVs in the early sixties and new national standards had to be devised. The popularity and pressure on the National Park system also led to the rise of privately owned campground chains, such as the aforementioned KOA, which was founded in 1963 and grew to multinational status.

I don't think I ever recovered from what happened to us in that KOA campground in Mexico City in 1974, and I was somewhat relieved not to have to stay in any KOAs during our Australian RV journey. The caravan parks we stayed at may have been owned by one person or a multinational, I don't know, but they sure didn't turn the water off at 10 p.m. As we crossed from New South Wales into Victoria, and hit the town of Metung, we gave ourselves a night off from the RV to stay at The Moorings, where the balconies opened straight onto the dock. After getting settled and renting a boat, we set out on Lake Victoria to do a little fishing. While baiting the hooks, Grace pointed at the bait and said to Cathy, "What is that you're putting on there?"

"Mussels," said Cathy.

"Whose muscles?" was Grace's alarmed but quite logical reply.

We caught no fish, though Jessica repeatedly had something tugging on her line. Time after time, she pulled her hook up to see her bait gone. She began shrieking at one point, "I've got something! I've got something!" Her rod was bent to a C-shape, but it soon went slack, and the hook, again, was empty.

"That was something big," Cathy said.

"How is it getting the bait off?" asked Jessica.

"It's eating it off," said Grace.

"It's The Nibbler," said Cathy, raising her eyebrows.

Moments later, Grace got a bite, and this time the hook did not come up empty, though we wish it had. Attached to her line was something resembling a lobe of brain. Hauling it aboard caused the girls to recoil. "That is dis*gusting*!"

"It's like a brain," said Grace.

"Exactly," said Jess, with B-movie portentousness. "The Brain of Doom."

I tipped it back into the deep, and Grace watched her catch sink and disappear. She shuddered, trying to match Jessica's theatricality. "Maybe The Nibbler will eat The Brain of Doom."

The next day, swaying down the highway, Cathy and I were horrified to hear Grace shrieking at the top of her lungs. I pulled the beast to the side of the road.

"What?" said Cathy, undoing her seat belt and climbing back. "What? What is it?"

Grace pointed to the small TV mounted on the wall (which we'd never been able to figure out how to work). There was a blue slime running from the cupboard above all the way down behind the TV and into the cabinetry below. After checking various hoses, tubes, and manuals, Cathy was able to deduce, by opening the cupboard door above, that the dishwashing soap hadn't been properly closed and half a bottle of it was now covering the side of the RV. At least the walls were clean.

That night, closer to Melbourne, Jess tripped running from the RV camp playground back to where Cathy and I were setting up the RV for the night. Jess came zooming around a corner and ran right up to us and stood ramrod straight, like some private addressing an officer.

"I fell," she said in a high voice, "and I think it's bad, no, I'm sure it's bad, and so I haven't looked. I don't even want to look. I can't look. I was running and I tripped and I'm sure it's bad, but I can't look, so will you look? Because I can't. I think it's bad. Will you look?"

We looked. It was bad. She'd opened a good four-inch gash right over her kneecap, and it was embedded with bits of gravel the size of peppercorns. Blood was oozing everywhere.

We rounded Grace up, got straight into the RV, went to the camp's front desk, and found out that the nearest hospital was Frankston General, where we headed immediately. Cathy stayed with Grace, and once Jess and I had gotten inside the emergency theatre, the doctor—a Clive Owen look-alike named Jeff—gave Jess two options once he'd cleaned the wound and had a close look under the lights. It was ugly.

"Okay, girl," he said, putting a hand on her shoulder. "It's bad. But we can fix it. But you can either get a needle to freeze the area, and then I can pull the bits out. Or we can just clean it out, use lots of clean water, and pick the bits out that way. No needle. But it'll hurt."

"How big is the needle?" she said, her voice quivering.

He reached over and picked it up. It was plenty big. "I'm afraid I'd have to put the needle right in where you've opened up your leg, sweetheart. That's the only way I can get in there."

"I don't like needles," she said, squeezing my hand.

"I hate to say it, but it'll hurt both ways."

Jess looked over at me, her face pained. My heart was heaving for her. "I don't know what to do, Dad. What should I do?"

"You can do whatever you think is best, Jess. I think Doctor Jeff will do a good job, either way."

Doctor Jeff nodded. "Absolutely, I will. I promise."

"I know I don't like needles. I really don't like needles."

"Then why don't we just get it cleaned out," I said. "That'll be okay."

"Okay," she said. She took my hand and held on tight, squeezing hard. "Can I hold your hand?"

"I'll hold it the whole time, don't worry."

It was difficult to watch. Without anaesthetic, Doctor Jeff kept the area disinfected and liberally watered, picking the flaps of the wound open so that he could get his tweezers inside Jess's knee to find the bits of gravel. She wept, but didn't cry out, just gritted her teeth, and squeezed my hand harder and harder. Jess's body went stiff with the pain more than a few times. It took twenty minutes of poking and pulling and sticking metal instruments into the wound before he eventually stopped.

"Well, young lady," he said. "I think we've got it all out now. But I think you're going to have a bit of a scar there, I'm afraid."

"That's okay," she said in a weak voice.

"Well done, girl," he said. "Very brave."

Doctor Jeff bandaged the wound. Jess stood up and put her arm around my waist as she limped and I walked out to the waiting room to find Cathy and Grace. I put one arm around her and dragged my other forearm across my eyes. "Yes, you were brave," I said. "You really were."

*

It was all penguins, all the time, when we hit Phillip Island. As we lumbered through the roundabout intersections of Cowes, two hours south of Melbourne, all we could talk about was the Penguin Parade the island had become famous for. We'd read ahead, and had tickets for that evening's procession.

"I can't wait," said Jess, voice pitched high. "I've been waiting for this forever."

"More than forever," said Grace, head bobbing. "Forever plus infinity."

For decades tourists have been coming to see the cuddly little penguins, which breed only in southern Australian waters (their largest colony, at about two thousand birds, is at Summerland Beach on Phillip Island). A visitor centre and a small-scale viewing stadium have been constructed to allow thousands of visitors a night to flock, as it were, to see the birds. It sounds commercial and touristy, and it is, but the alternative to the visitor centre is worse. In the past, onlookers compromised the sensitive environmental area, walking across burrows, breaking down the delicate dune land, sometimes even creating fires with tossed-aside cigarettes, killing dozens of penguins in the process. The visitor centre seems the lesser evil.

That night, hundreds of us waited ninety minutes for the daylight to fade, at which point we listened to an eco-friendly lecture from the staff. We then sat for another twenty minutes before a lone little penguin finally washed up on the beach about forty metres from us. The crowd buzzed. The penguin stood, shook her head, stood for another five minutes, then waddled into the dunes. No other penguins emerged from the deep.

"Okay," I said to Jess and Grace, slapping my palms against my thighs. "That was spectacular. Let's hit the road."

Over the course of the next half hour, this same pattern was repeated, sometimes with one penguin, sometimes with five, so that by the end, maybe thirty or forty of the little gippers had come from the deep. Parade? It was more of a dribble.

But that all changed when we made our way back up the boardwalk. A number of penguins must have come ashore elsewhere, because there were dozens and dozens, maybe hundreds, waddling up the hills towards their burrows. The boardwalk, with its raised platform and diffuse lighting, was mere feet from the birds. They shuffled by, stopped, flapped their wings, pointed their beaks at us, waddled on, oblivious to our adoration. Despite the rather stage-managed necessity of it all, watching them make their way home for the night was a little bit of magic. So tiny, so vulnerable. It felt like a gift merely to be near them.

The animal theme continued later that day when we went to the Koala Conservation Centre on Phillip Island. Koalas are the anti-wombat, cute, cuddly, clearly not designed to nibble brake lines or disturb anyone's sleep, especially their own. The centre has erected a boardwalk about twenty feet above ground, allowing you to get close enough to watch them do what they do best, which, like teenagers, is sleep. Near the end of the boardwalk Jessica pointed up and there was the rarest of sights: a koala on the move. Its limbs were deliberately reaching from branch to branch, and after a ten-minute trek to move about five feet, it settled down, exhausted, and instantly dozed off. "They move so slow," said Jessica. "He's sure in no hurry."

It felt like a symbol of sorts: we were in no hurry to move on, either, although we'd have appreciated breakfast at the promised time the next morning at the B&B we were staying at in Cowes. The proprietor, who shall remain nameless, had passive-aggressiveness down to an art. She had asked us the night before what time we'd like breakfast.

"Well," I said. "We were hoping to get an early start tomorrow, and, of course, we've got kids who are usually up by about seven. So, why don't we say, eight?"

She shook her head. "Not going to happen."

"Excuse me?" I said. Up to that point in our trip it had seemed as if each and every Australian citizen had been issued a handbook entitled *How to Make Canadian Families Happy*. Hers had clearly not come in the mail.

"Nine, maybe," she said, staring at me flatly.

I looked around, unsure how to proceed. The walls were covered with exceptionally garish art, hers it turned out, the primary theme of which seemed to be penguins sprouting wings and flying away— a metaphor perhaps for her own wishes to escape the drudgery of serving breakfast to people at ungodly hours.

"Nine isn't going to work," I said, deciding to stand my ground. "We need to be on the road earlier than that."

She nodded, glared at me, then broke into a smile nearly as phony as a flying penguin. "Eight-thirty, then. See you in the morning." She turned on her heels and was gone.

The next morning we were seated at our table at 8:30, ready to eat and get moving. There was no sound from the kitchen or from anywhere else in her faux castle, other than the drumming of my fingers against the tabletop. Fifteen minutes passed, then another fifteen. Just as we were about to get up and leave, we heard noise from the kitchen, which encouraged us to stay. Ten minutes after that— forty minutes after she'd told us to be down for breakfast—she came out into the dining area and feigned surprise at seeing us. "Oh," she said. "Do you want to have breakfast, then?"

Cathy spoke right away so that I wouldn't. "Yes," she said. "We'll have breakfast and then we're going to push off, if that's okay."

"Oh, right, right. Okay."

Another fifteen minutes passed, and I said to our troop that if she didn't emerge in the next five minutes we were up and leaving. Our breakfast then somehow appeared, which we downed quickly. I told Cathy that I would take our luggage out to the RV and she could drop the room key off, because if I ran into our hostess I couldn't be held responsible for what I might say. I grabbed a couple of suitcases, left and walked straight into her as she was taking out some garbage. "Oh," she said blithely, "leaving already?"

*

After all we'd been through in the RV—the non-existent orientation, the luge-run back roads, the multiple middle-of-the-highway shrieking episodes, the numerous sickness episodes (which I have mostly spared you from)—it was naturally going to be the case that the closest we'd come to true disaster while actually driving it occurred in the most benign and unexpected of places. One thing I do know is that I wasn't half the driver of that RV that my dad was with the Big Red Stripe. He tooled that thing around, in and out of parking spots like he'd been doing it all his life, but whenever I backed out of a spot I had to get Cathy to get out and direct me. I was terrified of squashing a wombat. Or worse.

We were in an industrial park near the Melbourne airport looking for the offices of the RV company. I was rubbernecking looking for the sign, when Cathy shouted, "Curtis! Look out!" I'd veered off line and was heading straight for a tiny little car coming the other way. I veered away and didn't miss it by more than a couple of feet, but the other driver carried on imperviously, didn't swerve, didn't slow down, didn't even give me an angry gesture; just another example of the Australian ability to remain unfazed in any circumstances. You can't rattle these people. Not even when things seem to be going sideways.

Or perhaps I mean downwards.

We'd been looking forward to our dawn balloon ride in Melbourne. It seemed the perfect way to cap off our trip. I alluded to the notion earlier that the family vacation in our day and age, and perhaps even parenting in general, has started to take on too much of the culture of risk management. Safety first. Fair enough; it may sound romantic to court danger, but not when you have other lives in your hands, the lives of those who trust you absolutely. Still, there is also a danger in playing it safe, even if we might not see the results of overprotection until long after the fact. Essentially, we want to seek the new and adventurous, but temper that with a dose of common sense. It's not good for our children to enter adulthood without a sense of adventure and curiosity, but it's also not good for them to not *make it* to adulthood. This equation seemed one worth reflecting upon later that day, after our trip ballooned into something unplanned.

We were at our departure location in south Melbourne before the sun came up and watched in silent awe as the pilots inflated the giant, elegant balloons. As the city awoke, we got under way, drifting serenely over St. Kilda, past the Melbourne Cricket Ground. Melbourne is one of the world's great cities, and certainly one of the friendliest. It hadn't mattered where we'd gone, people treated us as if we were long-lost friends returned to the bosom of their company. It made a significant impression on Jess and Grace. I was pondering all this, the camaraderie of the city and how Jess and Grace seemed to love it here. It even occurred to me that Australia might be a fine place for an even longer family sojourn, a summer abroad, a school year if we could swing it. These were pleasant thoughts and I glanced over at Cathy, Jess, and Grace, all of whom were peering over the side of the wicker basket. Looking at them this way, the three of them lined up in a row, made me happy and proud, but this was interrupted by another thought, which was that all three of them were leaning out over the edge of the basket. We were a good thousand feet above the eastern edge of Melbourne's inner suburbs, yet none of us were harnessed in in any way. I pushed that notion aside and put my camera to my eye to take a photo of the three of them, but as I did I felt somewhere in the pit of my stomach that we were losing altitude. I took my eye away from the camera, and mentioned this sensation to our pilot. Let's call him Gunter.

"Ya," he said in a thick Germanic accent. "We see vat da wind is like lower down."

Gunter pointed to a patch of green a kilometre or two away, and said that that was our preferred landing spot. I put my camera back to my eye, focusing in on the downtown core, trying to make sure I got the MCG into the frame for one last picture.

I didn't get the shot.

I heard a rustling around in the basket. A couple of murmurs. I got that feeling in my gut again.

Then, without a warning of any kind, there was a panicky shout from Gunter, "Vee are going DOWN!"

All hell broke loose. We dropped like a giant sandbag. We hit the top of a gigantic eucalyptus tree, still easily a couple hundred feet off the ground. There was a great snapping of branches. Leaves and twigs filled the basket. A branch as thick as a chair leg snapped and the sharp end pierced the basket like a magician's sword through a box. We tilted over. Cathy literally sat on Jess and Grace to stop them from falling out, and I nearly toppled out into the tree since I'd been taking a picture and didn't see it coming. There was an elderly lady and her son in the basket with us and I lost sight of them; they'd gone to the floor of the basket. We stopped moving, the basket remained tilted at close to a ninety-degree angle, and then, slowly, the balloon righted itself, lifted off the tree, and carried on its way, silently, gracefully, as if the incident had not happened at all. Nobody said much, including our pilot. Then, looking over to the east, we saw one of our companion balloons hit a different tree a little lower down.

I looked over at Cathy. "What is going on?" she said. "Can you believe that just happened?" Grace was sitting in the bottom of the basket, trying to stay in, but Jess was standing at the edge of the basket, drinking in the adventure, as if it was all just a ride at the fairground. I looked back to Gunter and was about to say something along the lines of, "What the hell is going on in this goddamn balloon you quack pilot?" but I had my attention diverted. Jessica grabbed my arm and pointed at something. I looked in the direction she was pointing. A freeway. We were going to soon pass straight overtop of it. That was bad enough, given that we were now only about a hundred feet off the ground. But then I saw what she was really pointing at.

"Dad, I think we're heading for that thing."

It was a massive light standard, maybe a hundred and twenty feet high, the pointy parts of which were more or less at the height of the balloon's equator. I spent a frantic two seconds assessing whether we were in fact going that way. We were. And beneath the light standard was eight lanes of jam-packed rush-hour traffic doing 100 kmh on nothing but asphalt.

I turned to Gunter. "Gunter," I said, trying to jerk his attention away from his tanks and ropes and ballasts. "Gunter! That light pole," I said, trying to sound somewhat calm for the benefit of my children. I pointed at it. We couldn't have been more than fifteen seconds from hitting it. "We're heading for it."

Gunter swivelled around and took it in, narrowed his eyes, did a half-second calculation. "Oh dear! It vould be good to avoid dat," he barked. He slammed both gas taps into the full ON position, firing the burners into furious, hissing life, filling the balloon with as much hot air as he could manage in the ten seconds we had before hitting the tower. He leaned his full body weight into his single directional vent rope. Up we went and slightly to the left. We all did our best to lean away from the tower, but I knew in an instant that if we even touched that tower, if there was even one rip in the balloon, there were no trees to save our fall. It was straight down, straight into pounding traffic. As we drifted over the westbound lanes I could easily see into the cars, and what I saw were dozens of horrified expressions on the faces of drivers and passengers. They could tell what was about to happen.

Gunter was heaving and leaning into his rope. The tanks were furiously pumping flaming hot air into the balloon. I wanted to reach out and hang on to Jess. Cathy was near Grace. We silently drifted by the tower, none of us saying anything. When we passed it I could have easily reached out and touched it, since it was no more than eighteen inches away. That was how close we'd come to being on international newscasts. (And these accidents do happen; witness the tragic balloon accident in New Zealand in January 2012, in which eleven people died after their balloon hit a power line, burst into flames and plummeted to the earth.)

After we'd passed over the freeway, Gunter pointed to a tiny "park" about a hundred metres away. There were no other parks anywhere in sight. "Vee must land dare," he half-shouted, his eyes bulging, as he now wrenched both gas taps back into the full OFF position. Gems of perspiration glittered on his brow. "Get ready! Dare's going to be a bit of bump!"

He had a way with understatement. The "park" was in fact a steep hill, and the bottom edge of our basket rammed into the earth at an acute angle, so that we careened over and came to rest on our side. Cathy and Grace knocked heads, which left Grace in tears and Cathy with a bruise in the middle of her forehead that was still with her long after we'd returned to Canada. As we piled out of the basket we were dazed, giddy, high on the simple gift of life. Cathy couldn't look anyone in the eye because she was on the verge of a helpless incapacitating reactionary giggling fit. She was holding Grace's hand, who was weeping and moaning.

I turned to Jess. "Are you all right?" I asked. "Everything okay?"

"... *Okay*?!" she said. She smiled in that ecstatic, dizzy way only kids can. "That was awesome!"

Later that night, our last in Melbourne, as we four sat at dinner clinking glasses at the Italian Waiters Club restaurant, congratulating ourselves on being alive, we recounted for one another what had been the best part of our Australian adventure. Cathy went first. "I think it would have been Bendeelah, listening to the birds in the morning. Maybe the beach at Merimbula. One of those two places."

"For me," I said, "I think it's Melbourne."

Cathy and I turned to Jess and Grace. They exchanged a quick glance and said almost in unison, and almost with total predictability, "The balloon ride!!"

Strangely, no one picked driving an RV down Kangaroo Valley Road.

*

The multi-century graph charting the popular rise of the family vacation would look like a hockey stick—flat for most of our modern history, followed by a sudden upward movement in the last two generations. Within this short history of the family vacation, the RV has a solid footing. You can drive wherever you like, you can carry an enormous amount of gear, you don't get rained on, you don't have to put up tents. During the great flourishing of the family vacation in the generation after the Second World War, the RV became a permanent part of the vacation culture, and has remained there. But from its humble roots, it has adopted a stratified culture, not unlike so many other aspects of the family vacation (wherein ramshackle little lake cottages sit beside multi-million-dollar "cottages"). Many RVs have become symbols of luxury and status, an emblem of conspicuous consumption beyond all pretence of utilitarianism. I'm not bothered by that one way or the other; people can spend their money on whatever they want to spend it on. But to use the cottage analogy, if you were to burst in on a multi-million-dollar cottage and a multi-million-termite cottage, there'd be a good chance both would be filled with families. This does not appear to be the case with RV culture, at least as far as I can see. The huge, shiny fifty-foot, 1.5 mil rig tends to be the thing a couple buys once the kids are gone. I can only speculate why this might be: an expression of freedom, new disposable income with fewer mouths to feed, a wanderlust that can now be fulfilled. Most of the big shiny RVs I've seen on the road and parked on the expensive pads are filled with all manner of things, both corporeal and philosophical, but the one thing they don't often have is kids running around inside. The kids are usually crammed into a smaller RV or a trailer of some sort, which is fine. It suits families, that kind of travel. Various writers and tourism sites have posited that in the aftermath of 9/11, we are seeing less international family travel, and more RVing and camping, people staying closer to home, driving shorter distances. It's possible that this is the case, although anyone who regularly spends time in airports would dispute that. One certainty is that growing environmental realities will put pressure on cars and especially on RVs; the fuel consumption is heavy, particularly in light of the fact that RVs are so often carrying just two people.

As for the notion of adventure on a family vacation, I think it boils down to how that word is defined within your family. If you're travelling with your kids, and if they think it's exciting, and if they think it's some kind of new exploration, and if they're a bit nervous about it all (and especially if *you're* a bit nervous about it), then to me that qualifies as a family vacation adventure. The point being to expose them to things outside their comfort zone . . . but not too far outside your own. There's just so little left out there that truly qualifies as adventure or exploration anymore, that to meet some rigorous, unknowable standard would be a challenge for even the most hardy of solo travellers, let alone a family trying to keep track of Tamagotchis and special blankies. Being stuck in the driver's seat of an

RV, on the wrong side of the road, shifting with the wrong hand, with a sick kid in the hold and a hyperventilating wife beside me, negotiating vertical hairpin after vertical hairpin, was plenty adventurous enough for me. The balloon ride? Well, let's just say that not only will I never set foot in one of those things again, you're unlikely to ever find me so much as sitting in a wicker chair.

Every vacation I took with my family growing up was an adventure in one way or another, due to a kind of spirit that my parents had, a willingness to try anything and take us anywhere. If I had to find a way to sum it up, I'd say that they had no fear. I think we must have been somewhat famous in Dalhousie in northwest Calgary in the mid-seventies for the Big Red Stripe sitting in our backyard, if nothing else. It symbolized something about us as a family, something not just about our vacations, but our lives. It said, *We're willing to try anything.* It said, *We're less concerned with convention than we are with new experience.* It said, *Help, my name is Curtis and I'm being held hostage inside this family.*

I once read somewhere that the old Partridge Family bus, the real one from the show, suffered a less than noble end. After the show ended, the bus was auctioned off and then re-sold a number of times, until someone finally found it abandoned in a parking lot at a taco shop in East Los Angeles. Apparently, it was junked in 1987. I have sometimes wondered what became of the Big Red Stripe. I suspect it's long gone (like the man who drove it so well).

What I do know is that my parents sold the bus a few years after we got it, for two primary reasons. The first was that it was heated by a somewhat less than foolproof propane stove. That was bad enough, but what heightened the danger associated with the stove was that there were only bunk beds enough for four kids, which meant there were always two kids—and I seem to recall always being one of them—huddled around the propane stove every night. Parents sound asleep in the back. Four kids in bunks. And two kids more or less wrapped around a sputtering propane stove in an old school bus refitted by some guy my dad might or might not have known from childhood, who may or may not have actually had his mechanic's ticket. *Time for bed, kids. Lay down by the gas line.* My mother says they sold it because she wasn't comfortable having her children huddled around an old hissing propane stove. That makes sense . . . except that we did have it for nearly three years. Never mind.

The second, and I suspect the sole, reason we sold the bus was because my parents needed the money to finance another vacation. To Hawaii. Three weeks. Four islands. Nice hotels. Great beaches. And so, after three short years with the Stripe in our backyard, it was gone, sold. Hawaii was on. There was only one catch.

My parents went without us, leaving us in the care of our grand-parents.

I have still never been to Hawaii, but I can't say I begrudge my parents the trip. They took their children everywhere, and devoted their lives to us. Still, they were human, and everybody needs a break from their family every now and then. Even, or especially, the people responsible for it.

6

Variations, Permutations, and Implications

MY MATERNAL GRANDFATHER, Duff, was a bit of a bastard. He had grown up in tough times; too young to fight in the First World War and too old to get conscripted for the Second World War, experiencing the Depression, trying to find work in postwar western Canada. I'm not saying it wasn't a hard life, although in other ways he had it better than many. He and his wife—my lovely, kind, long-suffering, now sadly departed grandmother—raised four children and they never went without a roof over their head. Duff, a striking man who made you think of a bespectacled George C. Scott playing a prison warden, always managed to put food on the table and rye whiskey in his glass (*especially* the rye whiskey in his glass; I don't actually have any memories of Duff eating, so perhaps he survived on cigarettes and rye). But he was a blue-collar worker all his life, spending most of his working life doing a variety of jobs at the Edmonton Municipal Airport (an airport that will be phased out to make way for urban renewal). He worked in the machine shop, he helped out in the air hangars, and for many years, he ran the runway snowplow, which, in Edmonton, was no small job. Still, Duff had a difficult life in some respects, a life of more or less start-to-finish economic hardship, a life of possibly unfulfilled ambitions for a better career—I honestly don't know if Duff ever had greater aspirations for his life and career; it wasn't like we ever had any real heart-to-heart talks. He also suffered from an inability to express kindness (presuming that he may have occasionally had such internal emotional impulses). But despite the various apologies and explanations one could make for Duff's personality, it was still an irrefutable fact—and to us, his grandchildren, the reasons weren't really relevant anyway—that he was a mean-spirited, confrontational, moody, bitter, humourless man.

And he had a dark side, too.

All of this is a sort of prelude to say that I never quite understood why we spent so much time with my grandparents when I was growing up, although I never resented it in any way. It was just family, so we did it. Usually, we saw them on family vacations of varying lengths, since we moved away from Edmonton when I was four years old and we never again lived in the same city as my grandparents, on either side of the family. We used a considerable portion of our family holiday time over the years driving either to Edmonton or to Vancouver Island to visit them. If there was one common denominator to our family vacations—and to many families' vacations—it was that we spent many of them with extended family, sometimes making significant and/or difficult journeys in the process. It was about a three-hour drive from Calgary to Edmonton, which may not sound like much, but to do it over and again, with a car full of unruly children, often on icy roads in bad weather, was, I'm sure, not something my father found relaxing. I suppose it's possible that our regular trips to visit my grandparents (though we also stayed with aunts and uncles) were simply my mother's way of providing cover for her own mother; maybe she thought that if we were all there, then Duff would have someone else to focus on, some other target at which to direct his vitriol.

Duff was a bona fide character study, a novelist's dream. He was not a well-educated man, and didn't care much for books or music. His main outlet for entertainment and recreation was sports, but even that was compromised by his temper and negativity: One night, watching the Edmonton Oilers in the playoffs during their heydays of winning five Stanley Cups, Duff could no longer contain himself. He truly hated the Oilers, as he hated success in everything and everyone. He railed against Wayne Gretzky and the league and the referees, certain Gretzky's success was an inside job, a conspiracy, though for whose benefit he never said. His Gretzky hatred came to a head one year when the Oilers were in the middle of a particularly impressive playoff run; I'm guessing in the early to mid-eighties. We were all sitting in my grandparents' living room, in their house in north Edmonton, near the now-abandoned and apparently haunted Charles Camsell Hospital. Their house was a small post-WWII job, with a tiny kitchen and dining room, which didn't stop Grandma from having big family holiday dinners, which was the case on this Easter holiday. Everybody was up from Calgary for the holiday, and various aunts and uncles and cousins were also in attendance. The TV was going in the background as some of us watched it, while others sat talking or playing cribbage in the dining room, while still others were in the kitchen helping out with the after-dinner dishes. Most of the men, I'm ashamed to say, were sitting in the living room watching the hockey game and/or playing cards.

Duff was cheering for Calgary, not because he liked the Flames, but because every Oilers fan hated the Flames. There was, and still is, an intense rivalry between the two clubs (and the two cities) and Duff was loudly rooting for the Flames, if for no other reason than my grandma loved the Oilers and worshipped Wayne Gretzky. Duff regularly pointed out Gretzky's supposed flaws, which incensed Grandma, who not only saw him as a great hockey player, but as a fine young man, to boot. Duff often carried it further, regularly castigating Gretzky's eastern European heritage; every time the camera panned to the stands to point out Wayne's father, Walter, always smiling and cheering away, Duff would say, disgustedly, "Look at that dumb bohunk grinning like an idiot."

I didn't know what a "bohunk" was at first, though I knew it was not a compliment; I could only assume it was an aspersion against Ukrainians, who were plentiful in Edmonton. (The term is, in fact, thought to be derived from the commingling of "bohemian" and "Hungarian," but in Edmonton around Duff's time, it meant eastern Europeans in general, but particularly Ukrainians.) This was an epithet Duff would later use to describe the boyfriend of one of my aunts, Carol, who for a time dated a fellow named Gary Karpinski. Gary, a flamboyant fun-loving guy with a handlebar moustache and shirt always unbuttoned halfway to his navel, seemed to love Duff, for reasons that no one else could figure out. Duff responded by usually saying that Gary "wasn't half bad . . . for a bohunk." Carol eventually dropped him.

In any case, the Oilers were in tough against the Flames that year, and as I recall, Easter Sunday happened to fall on the same day that the Oilers were playing the Flames in the divisional final. It was clear that this was going to dictate who went to the Stanley Cup finals. The series was tied 3–3. It was a tense night in the house because there were so many people there from both Edmonton and Calgary, and, in a very real sense, it was a shame that it had come down to this; there was a feeling that these were the two best teams in the league, and here they were meeting well before the final.

It was an exciting game and there were many twists and turns in momentum and emotion. My dad was even getting amped up a bit, and that wasn't like him. My grandma, freed from having to wash dishes since she'd cooked, was watching along with her husband, son, sons-in-law, and about ten grandsons. I think a granddaughter or two might have also been watching. The Flames were actually leading the game 4–3 at one point, but the game finally began to turn towards the Oilers in the third period, which made my grandma happy, but which caused Duff to grimace and throw his hands in the air. Then the Oilers scored a goal that Gretzky played a part in, a goal that as I recall put them up 6–4. Gretzky made a pass to someone, then headed for the bench. As he hit the bench, his teammate scored. The living room exploded, as most of the people were Oilers fans. But for Duff it was all too much. He stood up and pointed at the TV.

"Goddammit! Look at that. That was the flukiest goddamn goal I've ever seen."

"Sit down," said my grandma.

Duff sat down, but became positively apoplectic a moment later when they announced the goal and Gretzky had received an assist. Duff shot back out of his chair.

"Jesus Christ, they gave that goddamn bohunk as assist and he wasn't even on the goddamn ice. What a racket! The league is fixed. It's fixed. They want Gretzky to win so bad, they're giving him points when he's not even on the ice. That stupid bohunk doesn't even deserve to be in the league."

It was too much for Grandma. Years of pent-up frustration emerged and she stood up to face Duff, though it wasn't much of a physical challenge, as he was at least ten inches taller than her.

"That's enough," she said. "I want to watch my hockey game, and I want to watch it in peace. I can't stand you in here all the time, going on and on about the Oilers and Gretzky. Get in the kitchen. You can listen to the game on the radio. And don't ever come in here again and watch hockey on TV when I'm watching it. I want to watch it in peace. Now get out of here."

Duff, stunningly, turned around and walked into the kitchen.

For years thereafter, I don't think he ever watched a hockey game again in the living room, certainly not when Grandma was in there. Many times, more than I can remember, I'd see Duff sitting at their small kitchen table, a tumbler of rye in one hand and a cigarette in the other, listening to the Oilers broadcast on a small table radio. I think he liked the solitude of it.

*

As if there weren't enough people around in our immediate family when I was growing up—eight of us at every meal, six kids scrapping for the best bits of food—it seemed that my mother and father believed in a variation of the family vacation that involved adding as many people as possible to the mix. These people were almost always relatives. This is an important offshoot of the family vacation, and in fact a style of family vacation that many other cultures view as the norm, either because they do everything with their extended family or because they all live together anyway. I generally hate to generalize but will do so here and say that Asian cultures seem to me to have a better track record of involving aging parents in ongoing family life. Not that I thought about it much growing up, although I could never really understand why we did so much travelling to visit relatives, primarily between Calgary and Edmonton. That was a three-hour drive, but we also made a few of those trips out to Vancouver Island, where Duff and Grandma lived for five years or so after Duff retired.

These variations on the family vacation were to me the familial equivalent of compound interest. The principal—our family—stayed the same, but every trip there was more. Just *more*. More crowded days, nights, meals, and sleeping quarters. More aunts and uncles. More cousins. More complications.

More Duff.

But here's the best thing about Duff, at least in terms of trying to understand the place the family vacation has in my life in particular and in society in general: I was blessed to have had him in my life. Because of Duff I have a selection of gifts that a loving grandfather could never have given me. To begin with, he gave me and my friends endless stories, stories that we still recount to this day, often to our own children, who listen with incredulity, as if we were reciting science fiction. *That kind of person simply does not exist*, they must think to themselves.

But the true gift Duff gave me, the gift that keeps on giving, was an outer edge to measure families by, to measure my family by, to measure my father by and to measure myself by. Watching him as I was growing up, on family vacation after family vacation, witnessing the misanthropic spell he threw over us all—because there was something magnetic about him, despite it all—I was able to use his behaviour, his personality, as part of a template I was creating about what it meant to be part of a family. Part of how one defined *family*, in fact. The words in the marriage vows, *for better or worse*, really ought to apply not just to sickness and health, good times and bad, but relatives, too. I never did get the chance to ask my own father, a man of measured diplomacy and understated, good-natured humour, what he thought of Duff, but I can imagine what the response would have been. I also wonder what my father thought the first time he came across Duff. My parents had a good marriage, and my father loved my mother until the day he died. He must have *really* loved my mother to have pursued her so diligently after meeting Duff and knowing who his father-in-law was going to be for the next forty or fifty years. For decades, I wondered why my grandmother married Duff in the first place, and when I was in my mid-forties I finally worked up the courage to ask her. She went all thoughtful for a moment or two, since she was pushing ninety by then, and said, "Well, he was a *very* handsome man when he was young."

I have no doubt that Duff played a role in shaping how my father chose to fill his role with his own children, because although my father had a temper that he sometimes let loose, there was never psychological damage, implied or overt, in his anger. I'm sure my father sat there, silently watching Duff, and thought to himself, "I'm not going to treat my children like that." And he didn't. And neither did my mother. But, again, this was partially Duff's gift to me, to all of us; harsh as it may sound, he showed us a way forward, which was not with him.

In my mind and memory, these realizations and moments are part and parcel of our family vacation history largely, I'm sure, because these times are almost always when we see our family as a unit and individual family members in the sharpest relief. On vacation with my mother's family, when we were with family only, I saw Duff clearly, usually side by side with my own father, and these were invaluable, on-the-ground lessons in how to go about building a family using love and trust, instead of bile and rage (though these were obviously things I absorbed rather than articulated, at least when I was younger).

The inverse example Duff set may have been invaluable, but it's still the stories that I love the most. I do sometimes try to think back and wonder what it must have been like to be Duff. I try to show some empathy to his memory, to understand him and therefore forgive him, though not much in the way of forgiveness is really required on my part; he never really did anything to me except abuse me verbally. It's more complicated for other family members, perhaps; I don't have a dog in that hunt.

*

Whether every family has a Duff or not, the extended family vacation—which the tourism industry calls either the "intergenerational trip" or "VFR" tourism (visiting friends and relatives)—is decidedly on the rise in the vacation culture. Writing in *Atmosphere* magazine in 2011, Isabelle Chagnon reported that American travel-marketing agencies are noticing a distinct rise in the formal planning of intergenerational trips. This is part of the trend of an overall rise in family vacations over the last fifteen years, as well as a charted rise in the number of trips grandparents are taking with their grandchildren; Chagnon reported that 28 percent of trips taken by grandparents today are with their grandchildren.

This trend will surely continue to grow, given that the baby boomers are now largely the grandparents for the current parenting generation. There are simply more grandparents out there right now, grandparents, we might add, who are used to having things their way. I can't imagine this won't lead to increasing intergenerational family travel that is, moreover, *driven* by the grandparenting tier, as opposed to the parenting tier. My read on trends such as this, in combination with increasing business in the cruise, all-inclusive, and theme park sectors, is that the tourism industry is beginning to cater to intergenerational family travel with a focus on comfort, safety, and convenience. Though this doesn't mean this will produce better, more meaningful family vacations, the logic is hard to refute; grandparents want to spend quality vacation time with their children and grandchildren, parents want to spend time with children and their own parents, and the children want to spend time with their friends and video games but don't have a say. This needs to be considered from all points of view: the grandparents want security, comfort, and togetherness, while the parents, who want to accommodate the older set *and* the younger set, want to ensure it's fun for all, but that no one breaks a hip. Hence the popularity of the cruise and the all-inclusive, which purport to cater to every vacationing strata (but which, I submit, perhaps cater precisely to none).

The *Atmosphere* article also touched on a key family vacation factor in much of the (rather sparse) literature on the subject: guilt. According to a survey conducted in 2010, 71 percent of adults polled said that one of the primary reasons for embarking on a vacation with children or grandchildren was a sense of guilt at having not spent more time with them on a day-in, day-out basis as the children were growing up (a guilt that apparently, once installed, is difficult to uninstall, given that grandparents are part of this phenomenon). The guilt Chagnon refers to echoes what most current researchers are finding: Neil Carr, writing in his 2011 book, *Children's and Families' Holiday Experiences*, found that this guilt also correlates with the fact that most parents are spending less time with their children than may have been the case in the past, and therefore see the family vacation as a chance to right that imbalance.

There are so many sources for this guilt it would be impossible to address all of them, but clearly the workload of the modern adult factors into the equation, and this guilt has led to an even larger concern—anxiety over the overall quality of parenting being delivered on a daily basis. "Given the pressures parents are increasingly under," writes Carr, "it may not be surprising to find that they are increasingly worrying about the nature of their parenting, the state of their family and whether they are actually 'good parents.'" One standard societal indicator of being a good parent, of course, is simply that of how much time you spend with your kids. And if we spend less time with them during "normal" periods than we feel we ought to (the guilt) then we inevitably assign a higher value to shared vacation time (the remedy). The connection between how we parent during our daily lives and the manner in which we choose to vacation is obviously deeply complicated, not least because the tourism industry plays on our anxieties by reinforcing the illusory notion of vacations being a balm for the stressed family, a straight path to familial fun and harmony, and therefore togetherness. The problem is that by viewing vacations as the remedy for what we might secretly fear we aren't providing during non-vacation times—parenting of both quantity and quality—we raise the expectations for the family vacation to unreasonable heights. It's got to be FUN. It's got to be MEANINGFUL. It's got to be GREAT. And if it's not, we tell ourselves (and the tourism industry covertly tells us) that we have failed as parents because not only do we not spend enough time with our kids at home, we can't even be happy with them on vacation, when no one has to worry about work or school or the dishes or vacuuming. *What's wrong with us?* we ask ourselves.

Yet this is a question we don't need to be posing to ourselves. It's a stress we simply do not need to take on, because it's largely created by societal expectations and the tourism industry. The suggestion that parents are not spending enough time with their children, and the parental guilt that goes along with it—to whatever degree it's true or not true—is clearly one of the tourism industry's primary promotional tools, even if it constitutes subversive emotional coercion. A good deal of research on the tourism industry has revealed that it directly and consciously seeks to exploit our parental guilt to encourage extensive family travel (since the tourism industry is, rather incredibly, only now starting to understand how huge a market the "family" is, whether that be the immediate family or the extended family). Parents get trapped, says Carr, in "a vicious circle that sees them encouraged to utilize potentially expensive holidays as a means of reaffirming family bonds and spending quality time with their children. This necessitates parents working long hours in order to afford the family holiday, in the process potentially cutting down the amount of time available for them to spend with their children, which reinforces the notion that they need to spend quality time with them in the holiday environment where they can escape all the day-to-day pressures on their time. The lack of quality time in the home environment and the allure of the holiday experience then almost become a self-fulfilling prophecy that is reinforced in a continuous feedback loop."

In other words, we're being guilted into an unsustainable family vacation pattern, wherein every successive vacation must be better than the last, and must also be more emotionally and/or symbolically significant than the last, since we know family time doesn't last forever and since that lack of family time is our fault, given that we're the ones off working all the time. And as alluded to earlier, this concept of guilt, valid or not, is intimately linked to the rise of the intergenerational family vacation, in which boomers now want to vacation with both their children *and* their children's children; surely this is, somewhere along the psychological chain, linked to the boomers' search to find out who they were in the seventies and eighties, to focus on what they needed. A generalization, perhaps, but one that contains at least a kernel of validity.

The other option, of course—the one that does not involve as much guilt—is to opt out, to recognize that the pursuit of a happy family via the tick-all-the-boxes or up-the-ante holiday is an invalid approach. The point, as I see it, is not to actively pursue the creation of a "happy family" (good luck with that) but a *connected* family. The family vacation, immediate or extended, brothers and sisters, intergenerational or FRV, is only potentially, but not assuredly, one of the many tools needed for the construction and/or maintenance of a connected and functioning family. This is the categorical lie that the tourism industry sells us—that a *happy* vacation will make us a *happy* family. Let's agree to just forget about using the word *happy*. A series of meaningful vacations, as well as the ones that are not even all that meaningful, will help make us a family which is, in the end, a collection of individuals with their own hopes and fears, likes and dislikes, admirable traits and character flaws, but also a family who know one another, relate to one another, and, fingers crossed, both love and like one another.

It's important to point out that none of what I'm saying is meant to be a plea, or a plan, for family cohesiveness. I'm all for it, obviously, but you can't mandate such things simply by stating you want it to happen, in the same way that you can't predict how your tomato plants are going to do every summer; all you can do is create decent conditions, water them when you're supposed to water them, bring them inside during a frost, and then hope they turn out. My parents never set out on a family vacation with the conscious notion that they were using the trips as a device or stimulant to create a "happy family." I suspect if they had a formal parenting and/or vacation strategy it revolved around an endless rotation of diversionary tactics. *If we keep them occupied with enough things, maybe they won't ruin our lives.* The goal of a family vacation is not to promote happiness, but to facilitate understanding, to engender insight, to create the lens through which we can see one another more clearly and understand who we are in relation to one another. If familial harmony results from that, all the better, but to make it a stated goal is to over-promise, which usually results in under-delivery. For everybody. Disasters and bad times are going to happen occasionally, anyway, no matter what, but the good news is that such moments are often the glue you use later on to build an idiosyncratic definition of your own family. Disasters make for the best stories decades down the road, anyway.

Sometimes, like Duff, those disasters are even related to you. I remember that the standard holidays were not the only times we'd have family vacations that involved Duff; he could always be counted on to stir things up even in the most seemingly innocuous of circumstances. It was his gift. One Thanksgiving there were more in attendance than the usual family throng. My mother had invited over various friends of ours, possibly because their own parents were out of town, I can't recall. Anyway, my friends Rich and his brother, Steve, had loaded up their plates with turkey, potatoes, gravy, Brussels sprouts, salad, rolls. There wasn't room at the dinner table, so we took our plates downstairs, to the TV room, a fairly standard turn of events, given that my mother often seemed to enjoy feeding half the neighbourhood on top of her own six children.

We were just tucking into our food when Duff appeared at the bottom of the stairs. I don't even know why he'd come downstairs. There'd have been a place for him at the dinner table. Maybe my grandma had exiled him to the basement. Steve had never met Duff before and was somewhat anxious about it, given everything Rich and I had told him. Steve had a huge forkful of food poised in front of his wide-open mouth at the precise second Duff gained the basement floor. The first thing he saw was Steve, someone he'd never met before, about to tuck into a plateful of food that he, Duff, did not yet have in front of him, though he was holding a glass of whiskey.

"Jesus Christ!" he hissed. "Look at you, stuffing your goddamn face. Jamming that food down your goddamn piehole." He pointed a quivering arthritic finger at Steve, which had the effect of making it look as if he were barely containing an explosive rage (which perhaps he was). "Filling your face," he continued, "AND YOU DON'T EVEN *LIVE* HERE!"

Steve's fork froze in front of his mouth. He kept his face oriented towards Duff—an intrinsic respect for one's elders, perhaps—but moved his eyes over to where Rich and I sat, looking for a clue as to how he ought to react to this insane elderly gentleman. I ignored him and put a forkful of turkey into my mouth. Rich started to laugh, though not too loudly, since he didn't want to draw Duff's ire; he knew Duff and had already passed through the Gillespie Family Friend rite of getting scorched by Duff. Steve must have stayed with his fork aloft for a good ten seconds before I finally spoke through a mouthful of food.

"Steve, this is my grandpa Duff. Duff, this is my friend Steve, Rich's brother."

Steve nodded at Duff, lowered his fork, and said hi.

"I don't give a goddamn who he is," said Duff. "Why isn't he eating at his own goddamn house?"

Steve cleared his throat, as if to speak. I'd have immediately stopped him from doing so if I hadn't already jammed more food into my mouth. "Curtis invited me over," Steve explained.

Duff turned his rheumy, rummy gaze to me. "Yeah, well, I didn't see this lazy good-for-nothing making the dinner. He's as bad as you." He turned and started to trudge upstairs, muttering as he went. "Goddamn lazy good-for-nothing sonsabitches stuffing your goddamn faces. Go eat at your own house, for Chrissakes."

*

Of course, sometimes your extended family follows you around on vacation. I doubt that the period movies of the Ivory/Merchant strain—*Howards End*, *The Remains of the Day*, *Pride and Prejudice*, and so on—have much insight to offer a person considering the nature of the family vacation in the early years of the twenty-first century, but they certainly affected me in one way, which is that the characters in those films always seemed to be going off on holiday, often as large and boisterous extended families, to one European city or another, though such destinations were often achieved by way of stopovers in Africa for a safari or India to see the Taj Mahal. Of course, part of the inherent comedy in such journeys was that the "normal" lives of these families were nothing but a holiday to begin with. For them, a European summer was not a break from a life of toil, but a departure from their standard life of leisure so as to experience a different form of leisure. The British TV miniseries *Downton Abbey*, set in the years before, during, and after the First World War, perfectly captures this gap between the haves and have-nots when one of the middle class, a lawyer named Matthew Crawley, says at one point to a related member of the aristocracy, Violet Crawley, the Dowager Countess of Grantham (played with perfect condescension by Maggie Smith), that he was working hard throughout the week, but that he hoped he wouldn't have to work "on the weekend." The Dowager Countess gives Matthew a look of pure incomprehension and then says to him, flatly, "What's a weekend?"

This brief and funny exchange nimbly captures the transition of the notion of leisure and the vacation through the early decades of the twentieth century. The working and middle classes in western societies were beginning to actually expect time off from a life of drudgery, and the elite were gradually coming to understand that those under their employ were soon going to demand such benefits. It would still be another decade or two after the time frame of *Downton Abbey* that such social change would become widespread, but this was the period of its germination. The family vacation may not have emerged as a middle-class phenomenon until, broadly speaking, the middle of the twentieth century, but what the wealthy British toffs of those period movies represented in this discussion, for me, anyway, was the family summer abroad. I'd watch these movies because I enjoyed the drama, the costumes, the tension inherent in watching characters trying to break free of stifling social mores and expectations, but I also remember watching them because I loved the idea, the *romance*, of living abroad for a summer. There was also always something romantic *and* reassuring in that it was often done with families in tow. And it was never a permanent move, because that entailed an entirely different set of expectations and plans. (This was in fact something our family did, when we spent a year living in

Scotland, through 2000 and 2001, an experience I wrote about in a book entitled *Playing Through*, though *Playing Through* was more a meditation on fatherhood, and on my father, than a travel book; my father had a stroke on the day Cathy and I were married, and he died a few days later. *Playing Through* was my attempt to understand what he meant to me as a father, and what it meant to *be* a father.)

But a family experience that always appealed to me was that of a summer abroad, not to pretend we were part of that elite of old, but more to place ourselves in a spot we knew we'd never live permanently, where we would be immersed in a foreign environment, a place where extended family would visit. It had to be a cultural centre, more an urban than rural experience. Shorter trips are chances to experience the new, the different; it's as if you're soaking up images. But to actually immerse ourselves elsewhere meant something different; it meant we'd be looking at ourselves in that environment, rather than just at the environment itself. The opportunity for family introspection, shared experience, family lore, was very attractive to me.

And so it had to be Paris. Paris is, of course, almost more symbol than reality. I know that once there I walked the streets, strolled park lanes, stopped in cafés, and all the while felt as if I was living a different life. Not a better life or a worse life, just a different life, though one still recognizably my own. A life in which I was, perhaps, a character in a movie, a darker, European existential drama. Whimsy and romance, perhaps, but what was telling is that I was never alone in these fantasies; my family was always with me. Part of the allure of Paris was certainly that I am a writer, and Paris is one of the world's greatest cities in which to be a writer. In Paris, you know that what you do is valued, that no one will bat an eyelash if you say you are going to go write in a coffee shop for the afternoon. A Parisian will nod respectfully and let you go about your business.

We decided to spend our summer in Paris when Jess was still young and Grace had not been born. It's difficult to make the case that it affected Jessica in any permanent ways, given that she turned three while we were there, but she does claim that her first memories are from Paris. But for Cathy and me it was about more than providing experiences and memories for our children (though I am certain it did that); it was about testing ourselves as parents, too, seeing if we were up to spending long periods of time in a foreign city with our children. It was about testing our own appetite for such adventure, with the complication of children . . . but without the exponentially greater complication of having children old enough to talk back.

*

There has been little written about the evolution of the family vacation practice of going abroad for an extended period. As I alluded to a few pages ago, there was a tradition of such "holidays" amongst the wealthy, but the only trickle-down effect—the only way it ever impacted the non-elite, that is—was that they usually took their servants with them. We certainly lived like servants that summer. Paris is an outrageously expensive city, and we'd rented a tiny flat on the fourth floor of a walk-up in the 5th arrondissement, a walk-up without an elevator. It had one bedroom, a kitchen with a slanted ceiling that I bumped my head on approximately thirty times a day, and a tiny bathroom with no shower and a deep square bathtub that was shaped like a walk-in rubbish bin.

Our daily ritual was that I wrote in the mornings and through the early afternoon, then we'd connect for a visit to the nearby park, have an early dinner, and then the three of us would hit the streets again, walking everywhere and anywhere, almost always without a destination, just turning corners because we felt like it. We walked and walked and walked. Jess did her best, but we always took the stroller, because she inevitably tired; she'd clamber about in the stroller and within minutes she'd be out.

One evening, we stopped by the original Shakespeare and Company bookstore on the banks of the Seine, not far from Notre Dame. We browsed for half an hour or so before a commotion broke out in the upper section of the shop. A man was yelling.

"I don't give a damn," he said. "I don't give a shit about your excuses. Out. Out, I said."

There was some muttering in response.

"I don't want to hear it. You're a lousy employee. You're probably stealing from me. You're a son of a bitch, and I don't care if you're writing the next *Ulysses*, get the hell out of my bookshop."

A few minutes later, a fellow about my own age, perhaps a couple years younger, shuffled down the narrow staircase and moped out the front door without looking at a soul. Cathy and I looked at one another. It wasn't until later that day that we learned George, the famous owner of the shop, allowed young writers to stay in his garret above the shop for free rent, so long as they were working on a piece of literature. We'd obviously happened in on a tempestuous moment, and about five minutes later it became clear that George himself was likely not the stable foundation in any of these relationships. He staggered downstairs, slurring his words a bit, holding the handrail. It wasn't until many years later that the Unabomber was arrested, but when he was, I remember thinking, "Boy, that guy looks like George from Shakespeare and Company." He sat down at the front till and railed on, to no one in particular, about how there wasn't anyone to trust anymore in this world, and that he was sick and tired of giving a damn.

We were getting the vibe that rises up in parents telling them that despite the entertainment value in witnessing a meltdown, one's children might be better off not risking involvement. We instinctively began to make for the door, me through the literature section, Cathy and Jess through the children's book section. Jess had on a yellow raincoat she wore often, sometimes with the hood up to protect her wild blond ringlets, although that only created a humidifier effect, which made them even more springy; perhaps it was the bright colour of the jacket that attracted George's attention, because as soon as Cathy and Jess moved, he turned his body towards them.

"Look, look, look!" he half-shouted. "A young reader. Delightful. Wonderful. I bet she wouldn't steal from me!!"

The man was bombed out of his gourd, and when I moved nearer to him, so as to be ready in case of, well, in case of what I didn't know, I could smell the whiskey on him. He couldn't have weighed more than a hundred and twenty pounds and he looked about ninety years old, so I didn't anticipate any difficulty if push came to uppercut, but still, I felt my palms get itchy and my weight go to the balls of my feet. The store was, and still is, I hope, made up of groaning bookshelves, the avenues between them barely big enough for two to squeeze by one another. There was no way for Cathy and Jess to get out except past George, who was still at the front till, but was now standing up watching Cathy and Jess advance towards him. There were a few other patrons in the store, and they'd stopped to watch, somewhat anxiously, I thought.

As they neared George, he broke into a giant smile. "Oh my God. Oh my Lord. Look at those curls. Have you ever seen anything like it?!"

Cathy kept advancing with Jess in her arms, wary, though Jess didn't seem in the least bothered. She'd recognized that someone was adoring her, and so what if he smelled funny. She unloaded her brightest smile for him.

"ADORABLE!" shouted George. He bolted out from behind his little kiosk and I stepped forward, but as he neared Cathy and Jess he turned sideways to squeeze past them, which he did in a hurry, and disappeared behind them. "Come with me, come with me," he was still shouting out, now from the farther reaches of the store where Cathy and Jess had just come from. Since there appeared to actually be no immediate threat of kidnapping or excessive child hugging, Cathy turned and followed him. I did the same. We found George in front of the children's section. He was busily rummaging through the stacks, muttering to himself as he did. "Let's see . . . let's see. She looks about three to me. Three. Hmmm." He was fingering books here and there, without ever really looking back to Cathy and Jess, but soon enough he'd settled on his choices, though what his criteria were is complete guesswork. He pulled the books out and breezed past all of us again, on his way to the front of the store, where he sat down at the till, pulled a pen out and finally looked up at our deeply puzzled faces.

"And what is this young lady's name?"

"Um . . . Jessica," I said.

Jessica was surveying it all with considerable skepticism, but rallied nicely when George signed the books, "To Jessica. From George," and handed them both to her.

"Really, that's so thoughtful, but it's quite unnecessary," said Cathy.

"Nonsense," George shot back. "So delightful to see a young reader." He was beaming with goodwill, but to me he looked ready to topple over from complete inebriation; I would learn, through many visits that summer, that this was his default state. Jess took the books and was so happy with them, and so happy to be the centre of attention, that it wasn't more than ten minutes later, as Cathy and I happily continued our browsing, that Jess was seated in George's lap, listening to him read to her. And although he may have been thoroughly hammered at the time, his memory was intact; he remembered Jessica every time we visited that summer. "My curly-haired little angel!" he'd cry as we came in the shop. He was a grizzled veteran, a bitter man in many ways, I'm sure, but there was a special part of him reserved for kindness, and I've always held him in esteem for that. We still have the *Curious George* books (how fitting) he gave Jess.

I was saddened to hear that George passed away late in 2011, at the age of ninety-eight. It is the kind of bookstore you don't see anymore, and he was the kind of owner that only existed once. Jessica to this day is an avid reader, and part of me has always thought that her summer in Paris had something to do with this, that her encounter with George imprinted books onto her still-forming psyche.

There are many things we could and did take away from our time with George, but I was filled with the belief that this was the kind of happenstance event that would never have occurred had we been rushing through Paris on a half-day guided tour (or staying in Cancún at an all-inclusive). Only through exposing our children to those things we can't control do we create the conditions for fortuitous events. Of course, there's always risk involved; sure, it worked out, but for all we knew George was urging us to the back of the bookstore where he kept the chloroform masks near the dungeon door.

It was also standing outside Shakespeare and Company one night, by myself, just out walking around, that I happened to glance up to a window in an adjoining building, some five stories up, and see a young, attractive, and completely, gloriously naked woman staring down at the street, gazing at me. At least, I like to think that she was looking at me, though in truth it was hard to tell exactly where her eyes were trained. I know where mine were trained.

Only in Paris.

This vision returned to me a couple weeks after that, when I was sitting outside the Café Mouffetard having a beer with Silvio. We'd met Silvio and his wife, Isabelle, and their son, Oscar, in the park near our house. This is one of the great advantages of the foreign interlude as family vacation; your children become your social lubricant. Jess became such a fast friend of Oscar's that Cathy and Isabelle struck up a friendly conversation as their children played. This led to an invitation to their apartment for dinner, which led to a return dinner.

Silvio was a handsome Franco-Italian man, fluent in French, Italian, and English, with a French wife. He was involved in the computer business and he seemed to have a lot of free time. We met for coffee or a beer more than a few times. I was only marginally more naive then than I am now, but I do still recall my sense of shock when, one afternoon, at about 4:30, as we sat at Café Mouffetard, chatting about nothing in particular, watching the Paris street life pass us by—which I could have done for days on end—Silvio glanced at his watch and said he had to go.

"Now?" I said. "For what, early dinner?"

He looked at me as if unsure whether I was pulling his leg. "No." He smiled.

"Oh . . . okay."

"It's nearly five," he said, by way of explanation.

I must have continued to express my befuddlement.

"Five o'clock," he said. "I have to go. I've got my *cinq à sept*."

"Your what?"

"My *cinq à sept*. You don't know this?"

I shook my head. He grinned.

"Every Parisian man has this. Well, many anyway. We finish work at 4:30. We go home at seven. In between we have our *cinq à sept* . . . we meet with our lovers."

"Excuse me?"

He smiled again. He stood up and began walking up the hill, away from our neighbourhood. "See you soon!"

*

Jessica's experience at Shakespeare and Company was not her only literary experience that summer. I'd met the owner of the only bookstore in Paris specializing in Canadian literature. It was a kind of haven, a small pocket of familiarity, both national and literary. My first book, a collection of short stories, had just come out the year before. Knowing this, the owner arranged a reading for me on Canada Day, July 1. It was quite an exciting moment for a young writer spending the summer in Paris. My first book, shacked up with my family in the city of Hemingway and Fitzgerald, Camus and Sartre, reading at an actual bookstore in the actual city of Paris, with (I hoped) actual people in attendance. It was the kind of thing the literary superstars of our world would be blasé about, but it was a big deal for me.

Cathy was under the weather and didn't attend, but our friends Rich and Mike were visiting at the time, and they came along as interested observers and Jessica's handlers. Jess, always a lovely child, was also quite curious and energetic. She loved playing with things, working with puzzles, fiddling with tricky little toys that she liked to take apart and put back together (not always successfully). She also liked to dress and undress herself, undoing the buttons, doing them up again, and so on. Nothing out of the ordinary about that, except that she also liked to do the same with her mother and father. She was often tugging at her mother's blouse, or, cutely, but somewhat embarrassingly if others were around, undoing my belt buckle and doing it back up. I guess she liked the solidity of it. I don't know. I didn't ask her, given that she was just three.

There were about thirty people in the small reading room in the basement of the bookstore, which was about twenty-seven more than I'd expected; part of my strategy to have Rick and Mike and Jessica come along was to have an audience in case no one else showed up. As it turned out, that might have been for the best.

About halfway through the reading, Jess somehow managed to wriggle free from where she was sitting with Rich. I'm not sure if she was being mischievous, conscious that her dad was standing up in a public place, or if she was just acting out of habit. Maybe Rich put her up to it. I like to think she was just being herself, comfortable in any environment, at ease in the world. This was what we want as parents, right? To have our children move through the world unafraid and with no hesitation, to be both confident and curious.

A little less confidence would have been a good thing. As I stood there reading away, Jess ambled to where I stood and put her arms around my legs from the side. The crowd thought this was cute, and a couple of the women in the audience cooed and smiled at both Jess and her adorable, and obviously incredibly gifted, father. Jess stood there long enough to absorb the adoration, and then she decided that my belt buckle needed to come undone. Without any warning, she reached up and began fumbling with the buckle. I stopped reading in the middle of a sentence. The women in the audience stopped cooing. There was an audible murmur of discomfort, but Jess seemed not to notice. She had my buckle halfway undone before I'd managed to put my book down.

"No, sweetie," I said, taking her hands off my belt buckle. I looked back up to the crowd and saw Rich and Mike failing to suppress their laughter. A couple of men in the crowd were laughing, but there wasn't much lighthearted laughter coming from the female side. Then I made the mistake of trying to get Jess to sit back down. "No, no, sweetie. Not here." Only after I spoke did I realize that my words could be taken various ways, none of them good. I saw one older woman put a hand to her mouth. Rich and Mike were no help at all, and their enjoyment of the reading had increased significantly in the last few minutes.

I finally managed to get Jess to cease and desist, but only by convincing her that she could stay up front with me if she sat still and didn't move. I tried to pick up where I'd left off, but the mood in the room had changed; most of the crowd were delighting in my embarrassment, while some were giving me suspicious looks. After another five minutes, I finished, then offered to answer some questions, of which there were none, although I was quite sure I'd be answering questions from a Parisian Family Services officer on the street outside as soon as it was all over. Later that night, over a bottle of wine, we had a great laugh about it all, and although I ought to have booted Rich and Mike out, we let them stay. Jess, for her part, had no idea what all the fuss was about.

Perhaps it was the general air of Paris that brought out the free spirit in little Jessica, because a couple weeks later we had Silvio, Isabelle, and Oscar over for dinner. The wine was flowing and the company was excellent, but about half an hour after dinner, the four adults noticed that our children had disappeared. Given that it was a small flat, there was only one place the two children could have gone. As our own conversation quieted, we heard Jess and Oscar laughing and giggling from the bedroom. They were only three years old, so there wasn't much they could get up to, but we all went and peeked inside. There they were, happy as clams, jumping up and down on the bed, laughing, pushing one another. And doing it all half-naked. Ah, Paris.

*

It was once the domain of the wealthy to visit the world's cultural treasures as part of the family experience, when travel was both less convenient and more expensive, but the family that makes a point of arranging their holiday around cultural exploits is much more com-

mon today, increasingly so. One of the many results of this development is, sadly, the degradation of many of the world's ancient archi-
tectural wonders and heritage sites. Angkor Wat, for instance, in
Cambodia, is under severe physical pressure due to the sheer numbers of visitors it must withstand. The same is true of sites throughout the world, from Mayan temples in Mexico and Guatemala, to the
Egyptian pyramids. This trend has led to crushing hordes of people
in the world's leading cultural institutions, from the Louvre to the
National Gallery to the MOMA, which means we're also increasingly
seeing middle-class families arranging summer holidays around educational and cultural opportunities (I'll address this a bit further on).

Of course, this kind of extended middle-class family travel was
impossible until relatively recently, but the family vacation has
evolved so much over the last half-century, that a solidly middle-class
family such as ours could actually dream of and make reality a sum-
mer-long family vacation in Paris. The predominant family vacation
half a century ago was the car trip across the country, but major
intercontinental travel was rare, for a variety of reasons. First, the
cost of getting to a distant foreign destination was prohibitive for
all but the very wealthy. Transatlantic air travel was not introduced
to the public until the mid-fifties, and even then it was many years
before the costs dropped enough for middle-class families to consider
going abroad together. The wealthy comprised a not-insignificant
demographic, of course, and their spending habits made them
worth catering to—and exotic foreign locations did just that—but
there was no mass global tourism until air travel allowed it. There
have been hundreds of books written on the phenomenon of modern tourism (though, as mentioned earlier, almost none on the family vacation), and most have noted that international tourism for the
masses came about through the increasing affluence of the westernized middle class and the advent of a transportation option (air

travel) that was quick and financially accessible, if not exactly cheap. Today, of course, air travel is prevalent and so reasonably priced, but so much quicker than ground travel, that even when it's more expensive than other modes of travel, the cost benefit is greater. The *Globe and Mail* ran a graphic feature in June 2011 comparing the costs for a family of four travelling from Calgary to Disneyland by car versus air, and from Calgary to Toronto, also comparing car to air travel. In both cases, it was slightly more expensive to fly than to drive, but in both cases, the travel took a matter of hours as opposed to five days' drive to Disneyland and seven days' to Toronto.

This presupposes, of course, that speed is of the essence. Air travel gets you there faster, but it disallows the accidental and inadvertent discovery, the unsuspected spot, the adventure you didn't know you were going to have. A variety of tourism mobility studies have shown that families driving to a destination are inclined to take detours; they don't go in straight lines, whereas once you're on that plane (or train, for that matter) you're going where it's going.

If the introduction of the automobile as a commonly available mode of transportation in the post–Second World War period revolutionized the family vacation, the onset of commercial air travel for the middle class moved the family vacation into the modern period. Roughly speaking, this would have happened in the late fifties and sixties, although it wasn't really until after the decline in auto travel, the oil embargo of the mid-seventies, and the advent of lower fares in the same decade that air travel came into play as a common family travel option. Up until that point, commercial air travel was, generally, used for business and singles travel. Rarely was a family of four found on a commercial flight in the 1950s. In fact, some writers have pointed out that not only was it not a particularly family-friendly mode of transportation before the seventies, it was not even all that *female*-friendly. As Anke Ortlepp wrote in "A Cultural History of Air Travel in Postwar America," in the decades between the 1940s and the 1980s, air travel was transformed from an elite way of travelling into a means of mass transportation, and that "elite" mostly meant white male businessmen. Ortlepp's research shows that "during the 1950s and 1960s, airlines tried to target a predominantly male traveling public," usually embodied in the industry's advertising as one of three figures: a *captain* (a uniformed figure of respect), a *businessman* (successful, but seeking relief from the corporate grind), and a *tourist* (men reuniting with old friends to fish or to go to Vegas with a girlfriend). These target markets for airlines in the fifties and early sixties in particular were almost exclusively white, single, successful men; one can hardly imagine a mother wanting to take her children on a flight such as those promised by Southwest Airlines, whose TV ads showed winking miniskirted stewardesses inviting passengers to "Fly Me."

The sea change in air travel—when it went from being an elite form of travel for white professional men to a middle-class family travel mode—came, as mentioned, roughly in the period around the late sixties and early seventies, with three primary factors instigating the change: the introduction of a wider array of flying classes, the emergence of the jumbo jet, and industry deregulation in 1978.

There are a dizzying number of flying classes today, but even as late as the early fifties, there was only one class: first. Later that decade, some airlines began opting out of the International Air Travel Association's policy of setting ticket prices, and were setting their own. These first lower fares were known as "Tourist" class, but even so, they were still prohibitively expensive, with one ticket often costing as much as it might have cost to buy a new car. "Economy" class was introduced in 1957, which reduced fares even further, though not even close to the degree that a middle-class family could afford four or more tickets. Air travel retained its upper-class tinge through the sixties, even though different fare structures were starting to come into play.

It wasn't until the introduction of the Boeing 747 in 1969, which went into commercial use in North America in 1970, that the possibility of air travel as mass middle-class option really emerged. It was partially this development, among a variety of other factors, that led to industry deregulation in 1978, after which air travel truly became part of the standard tool kit of family travel planning. There were now huge planes to carry masses of people and enough airlines competing with one another to offset collusion. Suddenly it was possible for families to go great distances, or to travel the same distances they would have in a car, but in a day as opposed to a week. And not just great distances, but great distances that, because it took so little time to get there, allowed for longer stays.

Longer stays allowed for longer visits from extended family, as we found out in Paris. Cathy's mother and sisters visited. Some of my siblings visited. And my mother and grandmother visited for two weeks. It was wonderful having them there, the kind of intergenerational family holiday experience that only comes along once in a lifetime, or my lifetime, anyway. Being abroad allowed us to see each other in new ways. I had always loved and appreciated my granny's spirit, but after what had been a lifetime of trial and decades of having to put up with Duff (who'd passed away by then), it was such a joy to see her tromp around Paris pushing eighty, enjoying herself immensely, almost as if she were starting her life anew, though, given that she was a lifelong smoker, we did worry about her health. Every day upon returning to our flat after many hours spent exploring Paris, she'd begin the ascent up the stairs, pause halfway for a cigarette, finally gain the top, flop onto a kitchen chair, and wheeze out, "Ginandtonic . . . ginandtonic."

*

The extended family vacation abroad is becoming more common, although, like ours, they are often combined with some sort of alternative working arrangement. If one of the adults has, for instance, a posting abroad for a period of some months, the entire family will go along. I know of many such circumstances, where a project in Australia or Africa will take a father or mother away for long enough that the family decides to make an experience out of it. The increased flexibility in working arrangements in the modern era has certainly facilitated this, facilitated the fantasy and the magic of the unfamiliar, which, in some ways, is the point, for both parent and child. As Orvar Löfgren wrote in *On Holiday*, "Vacationing has served as a laboratory for trying out new lifestyles . . . improving the art of daydreaming . . . defining the modern family . . . or perfecting the art of self-reflexivity . . . the history of holiday-making includes a constant process of learning and relearning."

Other writers have noted similar motivations. Tazim Jamal and Mike Robinson wrote in the introduction to *The Sage Handbook of Tourism Studies*, "From the late seventeenth century and well into the twentieth century, motivations such as curiosity education and social betterment took over as 'essential' travel evolved into discretionary, leisure travel, gradually moving from a pursuit of the social elite of the developed world, to a widespread activity of the developed world."

They also write, "At its heart tourism is constructed around a series of very personal and intimate experiences as tourists encounter new and different cultures," echoing what Kenneth Cushner wrote in *Beyond Tourism*: "Humans, as social beings, learn best in situations where the complexity of social reality is encountered, examined, and understood."

In other words, immersion matters. Lingering. Thinking. Daydreaming. To me, these things are as important in a foreign city as visiting a museum or an art gallery. Any family vacation is going to be meaningful in some way, because even if "nothing" happens it says something worth knowing about your family. Riding the swings and going down the slide at the playground in the 5th arrondissement, just outside our flat, was, I am sure, better not just for Jess (rather obviously, since she was only three), but for us, too. We came to know Paris in a way we never would have if we hadn't been there with Jessica. We met people and made friends through visiting the park, and this proved to be our entrance into Parisian culture. And it wasn't just one visit to the park that did it. It was being there day after day for a few weeks, seeing the same mothers and fathers, saying hello, striking up conversations. Hanging out in the park with children is surely one of the best forms of social interaction with strangers . . . though I don't recommend it if, in fact, you don't come equipped with children of your own.

We've told Grace the story of our summer in Paris and she has heard the stories of our year in Scotland, but she wasn't around for the first and was only a year old for the second. But both these times have entered family lore. We all tell the stories, but given that it was our first major family holiday, it certainly set an adventurous and exploratory tone for the years to come. It's hard to say precisely what effect it had on Jessica, since most of what she drew from it in shaping her personality was based on what we told her, as well as some photos (including one of her jumping half-naked on the bed with Oscar). She's been able to construct a version of herself that includes having summered in Paris, and having lived and gone to school in Scotland. The level of Parisian in-the-moment individual influence on her as a person is impossible to measure, but it's also impossible to imagine that something wasn't transferred to her person. What is certain is that it changed us as a family, even though we were not yet complete (to the degree that we had a notion of how many children we hoped to have). If travelling as a family creates opportunities for family members to see one another more clearly, and to see more clearly what it means to be part of a family, then our summer in Paris put things into focus.

*

My family reconnected on holiday in Jamaica in 2011 when we gathered there for my brother Conor's wedding. We hadn't vacationed together as a nuclear family for nearly three decades, but did so in Jamaica at an all-inclusive resort when Conor decided to end his embargo against marriage and tie the knot with his girlfriend, Melissa. This kind of intergenerational extended family vacation is, as mentioned earlier, becoming more common, but as Conor and Melissa's wedding illustrated, so too is the family vacation initiated by a celebration or rite of passage. A recent study showed that it's the "middle generation," the middle-aged parents, most often in charge of such trips (the "sandwich generation," with kids on one side and aging parents on the other). It's often events such as weddings, anniversaries, family reunions, birthdays, retirements, and graduations that are the cause for the intergenerational family vacation.

And so it seemed like a good idea for us to celebrate Conor and Melissa's wedding with them in Jamaica, although we did spring a surprise on them by telling him that none of us could make it and then showing up at the airport. Conor is usually fairly undemonstrative, but he looked surprised. And happy. I think.

Of course, our father wasn't there, having passed away nearly two decades earlier, and Bruce, the high-school teacher, wasn't able to take time away in the middle of term. But it was still six out of the original eight, which is a pretty fair representation, especially when it comes to partying, given that Janine, Matt, and Keith were along for the ride. Keith labelled himself an honorary Rastafarian the minute he arrived, no doubt heartened by the immediate availability of cold Red Stripe beer in the airport parking lot as we waited for our resort bus. Our driver regaled us with stories on the ride to Runaway Bay, telling us that no matter what happened in Jamaica, if it was complicated, or not complicated, if it was something that called for a resolution, or just a few seconds to stop and think about it, then it was, in every instance, "a situation."

"If you find yourself in a car accident, well, den dat's a situation. If you get to your hotel, and dere's no cold Red Stripe waiting for you in da minibar, well, den dat's a situation, too. But don't worry. Here in Jamaica, dere's always a solution for a situation. And if dere ain't," he grinned, "well den we got other tings to keep us occupied."

"Ya mon," boomed Keith from the middle of the bus.

"Ya MON!" echoed the driver, sensing a kindred spirit. Or a large tip.

In fact, upon learning that certain herbal medications are legal if you are part of the Rastafarian religion, I believe that Keith investigated the process one had to follow to be ordained a Rasta preacher. I'm not certain how far he's progressed down this holy path, but I'm sure he's applied himself to the research with the diligence and thoroughness we've come to expect of him in such situations. Last time I saw him his hair was still quite short, so perhaps he's abandoned his quest.

In any case, we soon arrived at the Gran Bahia Principe at Runaway Bay, an "all-inclusive" resort, which means you don't pay for any food or alcohol. This is rapidly becoming one of the more popular vacation options, and although it has typically been the purview of partying types and honeymooning or reconnecting couples, families are increasingly joining in the all-inclusivity of it all. Still, I was nervous; letting my family loose in such an environment was like setting jungle cats free in a fenced compound full of deer.

The all-inclusive is a strange beast, and one that I confess left me feeling conflicted. There is no denying that there is something appealing about not having to worry about *anything*. The food and alcohol are free (knowing, of course, that it's not "free" since you pay for it as part of your all-inclusive package). There are beaches, water sports, pools, gyms, more bars than patrons it sometimes seems. There are discos, karaoke bars, live concerts. There are snack shacks that serve surprisingly good burgers at three in the morning after you've been drinking and dancing all night, though I recognize that it might have tasted good only because I'd been drinking and dancing until three in the morning.

"Look at you," said my sister, Janine, grinning at me over her burger the first night we were out late. "Who'd have thought? I didn't think you had it in you to stay out this late and party."

"I'm doing it for the family," I said through a mouthful of burger. "I'm here to spend time with you and reconnect in a meaningful way so that we remain close as a family unit."

Janine stopped chewing and put a finger to her mouth as if about to vomit. Keith punched me in the shoulder, hard; it hurt. "That's the only reconnection we're going to have here."

The all-inclusive rests uneasily with many, often out of simple first-world shame: these resorts are frequently located in countries beset by poverty, such as Jamaica, Mexico, the Dominican Republic. We are always told that these resorts benefit the local population, but, still, it can't do the human soul good to indulge in luxury when you are surrounded by poverty. The wastefulness of these resorts is difficult to stomach, as it were. There is simply so much food produced that it can only be that a massive quantity of it goes to waste, as is the case with the alcohol (although that's not a staple . . . unless you're Duff). Overconsumption of food and alcohol is so encouraged that one feels gluttonous by the end of every day. Your habits get slack—you leave that half a banana on the table, you toss out half a beer to get a colder one, you dance until three in the morning because you actually begin to suspect one of your brothers has slipped a stimulant into that last Dirty Monkey before dinner.

The all-inclusive is, however, clearly beginning to cater more to families, a bit of full-circle irony given that its provenance was actually not hedonistic but socialist; it all began in the fifties with Club Med, which was created as a non-profit society by Gerard Blitz, a former Belgian water polo champ and prominent yoga practitioner. He opened his first club in Mallorca, Spain, and the whole thing was based on simplicity, activity, and fraternity. Although Club Med sought out single people and couples at the start, the company made a distinct marketing push for families in the sixties. It has expanded and contracted over time, but now family travel is a significant aspect of the Club Med business, as it is with most all-inclusive companies. The Sandals all-inclusive chain was the next big player on the block challenging Club Med, although it has never really gotten into the family affair. Today there are dozens of companies offering thousands of all-inclusive resorts around the world, from the bare-bones operations of the low-budget all-inclusives up to the outrageous luxury of a set-up like Turtle Island in Fiji, where there are twenty staff for every guest. The common denominator of the all-inclusive is that it's meant to provide some luxury, a respite, a place where you are released from life's cares and worries. Eat as much as you want, drink as much you want, play as much you want. You don't have to pay. You don't have to clean up. You don't have to drive. The weather is beautiful, the water is warm, the beaches are clean.

But if it's supposed to be worry-free luxury (one travel magazine I read said that "all-inclusive" ought to be a translation for "worry-free"), I'm not sure it works. There are other luxury and worry-free options; on our last trip through Southern California (when we made our most recent and, I suspect, final visit to Disneyland), we were fortunate enough to stay at the Grand Del Mar in San Diego, which, although not ostensibly a resort geared towards families, nevertheless seemed meant to host them, so thoroughly were the activities and services arranged. Nature tours, tennis courts, golf ranges, hiking trails, various swimming pools. I'd take two days at that hotel as a family before I'd take two weeks at an all-inclusive.

Still, there was a moment I realized how glad I was to be vacationing again with my original family; which meant, by the way, that I was not in accord with the probably tongue-in-cheek sentiments of Kathleen Deveny and Joan Raymond, who wrote in a 2008 *Newsweek* article, "There's only one thing wrong with family vacations: you have to bring your family." My moment of insight came whilst lounging in the pool bar, which is not a particularly telling detail, I suppose, given that you could have found us at pretty much any time of every day at the pool bar. It was the day after the wedding, about two in the afternoon, with the sun pounding down, the sky blue, the beer cold (which was useful to put against my throbbing temples given the hangover I was experiencing from the wedding party). At one point, I don't recall when, Janine's husband, Dave, switched us over to Dirty Monkeys, a drink that to this day I would have no idea how to make. All I know is that they tasted like Slurpees but hit like tequila shots. Standing there up to my midriff in the pool, laughing at stories Janine was telling about growing up the only girl in our family, nodding at stories Dave was telling of picking Janine up on dates and having to run the gauntlet of her five brothers ("Though I didn't worry about you, Matt, because you were still a little punk"), smiling at stories Matt told of how he did, in fact, know that he regularly got away with murder by blaming bad behaviour on his older brothers, I realized—going against every artistic and social and psychological and cultural piece of accepted wisdom about the damage a family is supposed to inflict on you as a child—that I actually *liked* my family.

Of course, I "love" my siblings because they are my family, but it was a moment of insight, as Matt brought me another drink and handed me his sunscreen ("Your face is red and bloating, bro'") how much I enjoyed hanging out with them. I don't see them all that often, I don't holiday with them on a regular basis, we don't feel the need to pretend we're best friends, but we're all comfortable with one another. Sitting in that pool bar at the Gran Bahia Principe, sipping a Dirty Monkey, a mojito, a Red Stripe, a margarita, I was struck by how my parents, partially through creating wonderfully memorable vacations for us as children, had laid a kind of foundation for us to enjoy one another's company as adults. It couldn't have been planned. But on the other hand, my parents *were* smart people.

Naturally, not every family, immediate or extended, gets the chance to reconnect in a pool bar in Jamaica under a scorching sun with free hooch at your fingertips, but if such a chance arises I recommend taking it. Be warned, however, because it could lead to dancing with strangers at two in the morning and receiving detailed, insistent, and wholly unsolicited advice from a younger brother on one's dancing style. After a couple of dances, Keith bundled me off to the side of the dance floor, half-yelling in my ear. "You've got to stop that!"

"Stop what?" I barked.

"That." He made a palsied motion of his right hand and twitched his head at the same time. "You look like a creepy old guy having a seizure. It's embarrassing to be related to you."

"No one knows we're related."

"Then it's embarrassing that people might think I know you. Anyway, watch me, and then just do what I do."

He made his way back onto the dance floor and executed a series of moves that I could only describe as primitive and suggestive. Striding like a primate, he shuffled back over to where I stood, grinning and shaking my head. "I hope you got an eyeful of that," he said proudly.

"You want *me* to do *that*?"

"I know," he said, sympathetically. "I don't expect you to be able to, either. But try. If you can do it, it'll work."

"Work? What do you mean, *work*?"

"It'll work. Women love the way I dance. It's a fact."

"You're married, remember. And so am I."

He smiled. "Yeah, we are . . . to women. Which means maybe your wife will want to dance with you after I teach you a few moves. Though I doubt it. Some things are beyond my powers."

We left Jamaica the next day, and it happened to be the day Japan was hit by the earthquake and tsunami that devastated the country. Matt had been living in Japan for close to ten years by that time, and although he lived, and still lives, in the south, he had many friends in the north. We sat around a good part of that morning worried for his friends but mostly thankful he happened to be in Jamaica with us. We left the resort in silence and the ride on the bus to the airport was less than festive. After sharing the plane back to Calgary, we split up and I stayed at the airport to catch a connector on to Edmonton. I said goodbye to Matt, wished him well on his journey home, and told him I hoped that everything was fine, and everyone safe, but that I wanted him back in Canada. "That's what Mom said, too," he said, smiling. Before everyone left the airport and left me to make the last leg home on my own, I thanked my mother for making the holiday happen, for getting us all together to share Conor and Melissa's wedding.

"You know what," I said. "That was a great time. I really enjoyed that, and really enjoyed hanging out with my family." It occurred to me later that that was the kind of thing I'd love to hear twenty years on from my own children. My inclination then would probably be to make too much of it and over-emote, but my mother played it cool, played it smart, much as she and my father had done for so many years, all of which was probably what had made our family vacations, and our family, possible in the first place.

"Me, too, hon'," she said. She gave me a kiss and then said good-bye.

7

The Future of the
Family Vacation

W HAT IS THE FUTURE of the family vacation? Perhaps all we can say with any degree of certainty is that in an age of increasingly splintered attention spans, cultural static, and general global uncertainty, the family vacation is perhaps more important, more valuable, and more *necessary* than ever, assuming, that is, that the family itself continues to be something we value. What the family vacation will look like is another matter. New technologies are already influencing the direction of the family vacation in ways both good and bad (and new technologies are in no way guaranteed to increase the ease of family and/or tourist travel; remember the Concorde). Technology has certainly given many workers the ability to be away from the office longer, which means more and more workers are able to take longer vacations with their families. The downside is that they are still connected to the office. The *Christian Science Monitor* recently reported that 23 percent of Americans regularly check and send voice mails and emails while on holiday. One wonders just how immersed in our family life we can truly be when the BlackBerry is always on and the phrase "I just have to take this call, I'll be right back" is as standard a holiday phrase as "Who wants ice cream?"

But it's not just adults whose family vacations are being impacted by technology, though it is we who are facilitating it, to use the modern parlance. With the introduction of video games and on-board entertainment systems in planes, trains, and automobiles, the travelling behaviour of children is being dramatically altered. On a recent long car trip Jess and Grace did what most kids do now on long car trips—they watched movies. I don't blame them; for years I read books on planes, whereas today I watch movies at least half the time. This pattern has meant that children don't read as much in the car, they don't interact with one another as much in the car, and they simply don't observe as much of their surroundings as they once did.

We've seen great changes in the nature of the family vacation in the last couple of generations, but the challenge now is not so much to move the family vacation forward, but to recognize and value it for the right reasons. This is not guaranteed. Already there is considerable research examining why we so often refuse to take our full vacation. One study showed that only 63 percent of American professionals use their vacation entitlement, which means less time spent with their families on vacation. Another study reported that one-third fewer American families are vacationing together than was the case in 1970. (And let me say here that Canadian data was often hard to locate.) But even if the workers of tomorrow can be convinced to take the vacations due to them, and use them to holiday with their families, what will those vacations look like? We're seeing distinct fluctuations in both traveller confidence and family makeup. Eco-friendly family travel is on the rise as environmental concerns grow. As terrorism threats multiply, we're seeing an increase in the security-conscious family vacation, and a decline in family travel to locations outside western industrialized cultures or without access to the tourism standards of the first world. There are more single-parent and blended families today, which has led to some long-overdue options, such as gay-only resorts and cruise lines, and even gay-family cruises and all-inclusives, pioneered by Rosie O'Donnell, no less. New transportation modes or fuels may very well shift the expression of the family vacation, though it's hard to imagine there ever being as massive a cultural shift as that of the post–Second World War era when the planets aligned to offer a burgeoning middle class accessible transport in the automobile, routes to follow in the new Interstate Highway system, and places to go in the newly popular National Park system.

The future may bring about changes of a more recessive nature. If oil continues to rise in price and drop in environmental reputation, and if no alternative energy form replaces it, automobile and air travel could substantially decline. Another major, if seldom talked about, factor in the bleaching of the family vacation is that of liability issues. North America, and the United States in particular, has become highly litigious over the course of the last generation, and this development has created a lawsuit chill that often goes unnoticed. A friend recently told me of going back to the lake where he and his family vacationed for decades. Some of his best memories were in the tiny little town on the lakeshore, running around free as birds, going to the store and, most vividly, playing in the mom-and-pop amusement park, with its cheesy rides and hokey displays. One of these "rides" was a set of twelve or so trampolines, lined up in rows of three, with bits of padding here and there, coil springs sticking out at weird angles, and strips of concrete separating every tramp. They'd bounce for hours in the hot summer sun, having simple, plain, but probably dangerous fun, often involving contests to see who could leap the farthest from tramp to tramp, flying around like little Cirque du Soleil gymnasts. My friend went back to this small town last summer, passing through on his way back to their original cabin, and he saw that the mom-and-pop trampoline outfit had disappeared. He stopped in the local grocery and asked what had happened to it, why it was gone.

"Been gone for years," said the woman at the till.

"How come?" he asked.

"Lawyers."

One word said it all. The point being not so much that these kinds of experiences led to injuries, though they could have, but that as the litigious nature of society gathered critical mass, small outfits could no longer afford the insurance needed to stay in operation.

"You used to be able to just cross the street and go out in one of the canoes they had sitting on the beach, too," my friend told me. "It was first come, first served. They'd just let us kids go. Good luck finding that today unless an adult signs a million forms."

Another friend told me of the family vacations they used to take in the late seventies when they'd pile into the family station wagon and drive from Edmonton to Trail, B.C., to visit grandparents. Upon arriving, the kids would sprint from the car to the beach and then fan out into town, unsupervised; this pattern was repeated daily for the two weeks they were there. "They were such great times," she recalled. "And our parents seemed happy, too, just so long as we all showed up at the end of the day." (The less happy, but still vivid, memory she has of those holidays was of being forced to play Dodge Rock on the beach with her older brothers, a game that seemed to be separated into two parts; her with the Dodge and them with the Rock.) So much of the existing research, as well as my own unstructured research, tells us that for many adults looking back to the vacations of their childhoods, particularly their summer vacations, one of their most cherished memories was the freedom they felt. Today, there is approximately a 00.00 percent chance that a passel of children would be allowed to roam a town largely unsupervised for two weeks without either the police or social services descending on the parents. Having said that, there is about the same statistical likelihood that we parents would *let* our children roam a town on their own for two weeks, given how we've been conditioned by the media and society to believe that that would be a gross dereliction of parental duty that would place our children directly in the path of some unspeakable harm or violence. (This example also raises the point that there is safety in numbers, to a degree, and families of generations past were typically larger than today's; it's entirely possible that what I recall as considerable freedom as a child on holiday was simply that my parents were ignoring me because they were busy putting out fires, sometimes literally, created by my younger siblings.)

Safety versus experience has always been an equation we have had to solve for ourselves, in life as much as in the family vacation, and of course there's no law that says one can only be had at the exclusion of the other. But there seems no denying that our culture has drifted, fraction by fraction, justification by justification, towards valuing safety over experience in terms of what we expose our children to. One of my favourite holiday photos from growing up is that of us children lined up on the precipice of a gorge. There is no railing behind us, only a serious drop-off of the certain-death variety. The photo is taken from above, which suggests to me that my parents were standing higher up the ledge or perhaps near a railing from which they'd ushered us down for the photo. It's a superb picture, and we all look happy and carefree despite the fact that two steps backwards for any us would have been game over (which was perhaps part of my parents' plan, I don't know). But that photo also helps me to understand how difficult it has become for parents to know where to stand, both literally and figuratively: Do I look at that photo and smile, and laugh at the memories, and allow myself to relive so much of what we experienced, and realize how lucky we were to have parents who threw caution to the wind and took chances? Absolutely. Would I put my own children on the ledge to get such a great photo? Probably not. The parental state of mind that allowed for that photo, that didn't even hesitate, has probably passed into history, whether we like it or not, and that saddens me.

So many factors—fear, guilt, liability, terrorism, over-control, inconvenience, expense, technological addiction, environmental-ism—are leading to what feels like a retreat in some family vacation quarters. Already we are seeing a rise in the notion of the "staycation" or "fake-cation," the family vacation that is taken in one's hometown, even in one's own backyard. Simplicity and frugality are often the reasons advocated for these holidays, although security concerns over terrorism and the hassle of air travel are no doubt lurking in the background of such decisions. Given the rise of home entertainment systems, as well as leisure options available in most metropolitan areas, its advocates feel they make a strong case for the staycation, but I find the notion dispiriting. The point of a family vacation is to remove yourself from the trappings of your daily existence, to see yourself and your family outside your standard definition of self and unit; clarity often emerges only with distance. To me, a staycation is not a fresh meal, but a stale old bun wrapped in a new bag. Still, who knows what technology will bring. With the advent of in-home 3-D perhaps the "virtual" family vacation is just around the corner.

The baby boomers' demographic dominance is also significant to the family vacation in a variety of ways. This group (roughly, people born between 1946 and 1964) put more of an emphasis on their own relationships than their parents did, which is not such a bad thing, of course, though it has led to challenges to the family vacation. Not only did the baby boom generation tend to put more emphasis on their relationships, they also put more emphasis on themselves as individuals, particularly as they began to assert their demographic and cultural predominance. Libraries full of books have been written on our relatively recent quest for self-fulfillment, our need to find out who we really are, to unlock our inner potential and be the best we can be. Of course, much of it is nonsense, but that doesn't mean it isn't seductive nonsense. Who amongst us doesn't want to be better, do better, make more, understand more, *see* more? *What is holding us back?* this movement asked. It had to be an external agent, because clearly it couldn't have had anything to do with our own shortcomings. The barriers to the full realization of our personal potential were the boss, wife, parents, siblings, government, faith, lack of faith, or, among any number of other things, being weighed down by children. We have been told by a new generation of experts that the way to unlock all that potential is to really focus on who we are, what we're capable of, to go on retreats, to take courses, to read books, to attend seminars, to really get inside of ourselves and roam around for a spell. Who on earth could have time for a family vacation with all *that* going on?

Yet to me one of the attractions of the family vacation is that it takes us *outside* of ourselves, it takes us beyond the fences we normally surround ourselves with: work, home, friends, bills, neighbourhood. We are alone only with what's essential about us as a family. We can see past those huge time silos that fill up every day with the simple raising of a family (and raising a family of *any* size is not easy, as every parent knows). On vacation, all there is is one another. That's why those families most at ease with one another—despite any surface appearances—are often the ones who vacation together and enjoy it. This is almost certainly the novelist in me talking, but if you think you have the perfect family yet your vacations are always fraught and tense, my guess is there's something misfiring down in the engine room. Well, it's not a guess; of course there is.

We are what we were raised to become. I was raised in a very crowded house. I was raised in a house in which my parents sometimes lost their temper and administered corporal punishment. I was raised in a house in which extended relatives frequently imported their own brands of oddity. I was raised in a house where my parents got sick of me ignoring their requests to clean my corner of the basement—my "room"—and took action; I came home from working as a busboy at Blackbeard's surf and turf restaurant at 2 a.m. that summer night to find every single possession of mine in the backyard—clothes, sports equipment, books, records, April Wine poster. Even my bed. The door was locked. I had to knock on the basement window near Conor's corner of the basement to get him up to let me in. I was raised in a house in which my mother called a family meeting when I was about fourteen and said she'd had it, that she couldn't take it anymore, that she was tired of cooking and cleaning for a horde that didn't appreciate it and she damn well wasn't going to do it anymore; starting the next day I did my own laundry and ate a lot of Kraft Dinner.

But, and this is the *but* that counts, I was raised in a house that was anchored by the fact that my parents loved their children and raised us with good humour and an absence of psychological and emotional abuse. It was all straight up. Which is why I believe our family vacations were fun and memorable in a positive sense—we got along. Who knows, maybe our home life was a nightmare, and I'm just remembering a couple of good vacations. I don't think so. And because we got along, those vacations, caught in time, highlighted, have informed my understanding of what our family was like. This is fundamentally what is of value in the family vacation, one of its truly significant functions—they serve as symbols of the larger project.

I wrote earlier that family vacations are a key element in the project "family." Not the family project, because that implies one thing, but the project "family," since that's really a never-ending endeavour. Working together on this project, which is what you're doing when you're on a vacation together as a family, helps develop a shared set of understandings, a baseline knowledge of that family as a unit, of how we relate to one another, of how we move together through time. We bank a shared roster of stories. We create a history project without ever calling it that, a history project that through understanding our past helps us understand and successfully negotiate our present.

There is now research being conducted around family narratives, focusing on how shared experience that is translated into shared narrative aids children in figuring out who they are as individuals and as family members. The research team of Bohanek, Marin, Fivush, and Duke, in a 2006 *Family Process* journal paper entitled "Family Narrative Interaction and Children's Sense of Self," looked at such shared experiences recast as family narrative (nearly 85 percent of the sample group used family holidays or visits to relatives as positive examples). They found that narratives of past experience, told and retold, are "the way in which we make sense of ourselves and our experiences," and that families "using a coordinated narrative interaction style teach their children that they are part of a unified, cohesive family whose members understand and work through positive and negative experiences together." Narratives, they write, "provide understanding, evaluation, and perspective on the events of our lives. Through narrative interactions about the shared past, parents help shape children's understanding of who they were, who they are now, and presumably who they will be in the future, both as individuals and as members of the family," which means, they add, that "the role of family narratives may be particularly critical for children's developing sense of self."

At some level, we are the stories we tell about ourselves, and a family is the stories it tells about itself. To have stories to tell, there must be events to stock those stories. The family vacation is a kind of accessible time capsule, something we can catalogue and refer to. It's there to remind us, and represent for us, what our family was like. And what a family *is*. That's not always going to be positive, sadly, but that doesn't mean the family vacation isn't any less powerful a symbol. So much happens in a family's life as it grows and evolves that it's hard to keep track of it all. But on vacation it seems easier to keep a record. We're together. Alone with each other. You could say, and some will, that it's a false environment, as if a family vacation isn't an accurate reflection of a family because it's all fun and games and a separation from the norms of daily life. But to me that's precisely what makes it both an ideal memory-making tool for families as well as (often many years later in the retelling) a window to look through, or look *back* through, to see and reflect upon what you were as a family and are now as a family. Not only *are* we the stories we tell about ourselves, we *become* the stories we tell.

On holiday, it's just the family, nothing else. There are none of the interruptions that prevent us from spending time together at home. Soccer, hockey, dance, piano, work, babysitting, socializing, gymnastics, school, volunteering, friends. Yet on vacation a family is together *all* the time. That's when the sharpness of understanding and insight can be found. That can't be a bad thing, even if the occasional illusion is punctured (which may be an adventure in itself, if not of the physical variety).

Insight comes in many forms, or at least we hope it does. Part of the appeal (or perhaps *curiosity* is the better word) to test even the lightest of boundaries for "adventure" travel with one's family lies in that it allows you to not just think about but put into action elements of providing experience for your children as opposed to providing them with security. Today's family vacation is more or less a constant tug-of-war between the two impulses. This matters because it will have a say in the family dynamic you create (families with parents who are too controlling—*they never leave us alone, they don't trust us*—versus those who are permissive—*they don't even care what we do, they never watch or join in what we're doing*). It will certainly be a factor in what type of adults your children grow up to be. I mean this to be a statement free of moral implication, because too much emphasis on either extreme will not benefit our children. And it's unlikely to lead to the best family vacations. You say you want them to experience life to the fullest? Fine, but it's still going to scar them emotionally or injure them physically, or both, if you don't mitigate the danger to reasonable levels. "Oh, come on," you tell ten-year-old Sally. "You don't need a life jacket when you're solo sea kayaking. Do you think the Salish Indians wore life jackets when they fished here a century ago? Just get out there with the whales and see what happens. We're here to live like they lived. Don't worry, Mom and I will be taking the video from shore."

Conversely, too much of an emphasis on security will almost surely dampen the appetite for exploration. A childhood full of nothing but unilateral parental decisions calling for two weeks every summer at the Slim Dudes Weight Reduction Camp followed by a week every winter with Mom, Dad, sis, and the nanny on a Disney cruise will quite possibly create a child—and then an adult—with no investigative spirit, let alone an enthusiasm for even the smallest doses of risk.

You might very well guess which side of the equation I come down, though I don't come down as hard as you might think on the adventurous side. I do worry we sometimes place too much emphasis on creating "peak experiences" for our children, transferring our hopes, fears, and desires onto them as we inevitably do. The natural extension of this is putting too much confidence in our own appetite for adventure and risk, and dragging the kids along with us. Sometimes we just need to read them, gauge them, let them tell us.

Funnily enough, although I am certainly an advocate of as much adventure as possible on a family vacation, I don't think I'm the most adventurous person in our family. I might not even be second. Or third. Cathy has an adventurous spirit, and although she isn't one for stupid risks, she doesn't frighten easily (except when I'm driving an RV on a luge run). Jess and Grace are both up for pretty much whatever we throw at them. Me, on the other hand? Well, whenever we're hiking, I'm the one telling the girls to stay away from the edge. When we're in crowded foreign cities, I'm the one who gets a bit panicky if I lose sight of them.

Is that fear? I suppose it is.

But what I'm more afraid of is going too far in the other direction, of overprotecting, of Cathy and me sacrificing their experiences to ensure as little risk as possible. Yes, we want the lazy lakeshore days. But sometimes we need to be doing the things our children define as an adventure. And if it's adventurous to them, if it gets their hearts pitter-pattering, if it scares them even just a little, then it's adventurous enough to use that word.

*

A fundamental point worth reiterating is that when it comes to the family vacation, it almost doesn't matter what you do, so long as you do something, which, to me, means *going* somewhere. Removal from the everyday is key. I was reminded of this in reading an essay by David Mamet entitled, "A Family Vacation," which was anthologized in a collection called *Bad Trip*. In this essay, Mamet admits that few things repelled and terrified him more than the prospect of a family vacation. But when his daughter turns three his wife goes to work on him about a family vacation. He eventually runs out of excuses and the vacation planning begins, which brings up all sorts of anxiety in him. Being an intellectual Jew, he says, means there are immediately two strikes against the prospect of a family vacation being even remotely fun. Jews, he says, have a long cultural memory involving trips with the family . . . tracing back to the Babylonian exile. Essentially, if you were on the move with your family it meant something bad had happened, something bad was probably going to happen en route, and there was every likelihood that something bad was going to happen when you got there. "My parents and the parents of my friends were one short generation removed from The Pale Settlement in Russo-Poland," wrote Mamet, "and to *their* parents the shortest trip away from home offered real possibilities of real trouble: difficulty of obtaining food acceptable to their religious laws, of confusion as to local customs, of persecution and murder itself." He agrees to go, but plans to weasel out of it when the time comes, except that his wife outsmarts him. He tries to undermine the process by focusing on his work on the plane, by trying to find things wrong with the Caribbean resort, by hoping a hurricane sticks around. But then magical little moments weaken his resistance. A football lands—plop—on the water outside his hotel window. Then the football opens its wings: it was a pelican diving for fish. The sound of the undertow pulling stones out to sea is surprising and more complex than he'd expected.

Gradually, as he relaxes to the best of his ability, aided by considerable deep sleep, he begins to warm to the whole concept. His daughter lures him onto the beach to make "flour," which consists of pouring sand into a palm leaf. "I was surprised to find it just as enjoyable as (and certainly more productive than) a business lunch at the Russian Tea Room," he notes. He bounces on a trampoline with his daughter for "a couple of hours every day," he goes water skiing, he skinny-dips. Later, he comes to an insight about why it *worked*, why for the first time in his life he'd been able to actually take and enjoy a vacation: it was the simplicity.

"We are Urban people," he writes, "and the Urban solution to most any problem is to do more: to find something new to eat in order to lose weight; to add a sound in order to relax; to upgrade your living arrangements in order to be comfortable; to buy more, to eat more, to do more business. Here, on the island, we had nothing to do [and] we found rather than achieving peace by the addition of a *new idea* (quality time, marital togetherness, responsibility), we naturally removed the noise and distractions of a too-busy life and so had no *need* of a new idea. We found that a more basic idea sufficed: the unity of the family."

Of course, the assumed irony of all this is that Mamet—who I sense is a workaholic because if he's not he has no right being that talented and productive—probably got back home and fell into the old patterns. But the takeaway of Mamet's piece, at least for me, regardless of whatever patterns he returned to, was that he arrived at lovely and simple insights about the nature of family unity, but that these were insights he hadn't yet arrived at during the first three years of his daughter's life in the city as part of their urban-people lifestyle. It took removing himself and his family from their daily constraints for him to arrive at these insights. It took a family vacation.

So simple, yes, but we live in an increasingly complex world, and one can't help wondering if the family vacation as a staple of middle-class life will subside with the rise of the aforementioned environmental movement, technological dominance, and the threat of global terrorism? Or will such factors actually bring about an even greater desire for family unity, for trusting and believing in and wanting to know those you are growing up with? Will parenting styles adapt to accommodate the onslaught of information and technology that will surely continue to assault the attention spans of our children (not to mention us parents)? Can parents find ways amidst this rampant modernity to not just drop the pace at home and therefore on vacations, but to make that something our increasingly sophisticated children will buy into? Or can we, alternatively, find ways to turn the overwhelming tidal sweep of electronic change to our advantage? Can we make our vacations fast and wired, and still create story, shared event, history? Certainly, there's a new breed of families who travel together and create blogs or websites of their adventures. The children do the updating. Mom and Dad weigh in with their observations. Photos are shared. In this way, the family vacation does become a project they share.

That particular example is part of the broader culture's apparent need to document its experience, which is both a good and potentially bad thing for the family vacation. Using the family vacation as overt "material" in the creation of electronic records is a value-neutral activity to me; it could be a wonderful way to create family narratives and capture some history, but what will it do to how we use our memories? We have memories for a reason—so that we can forget things, then misremember them, then ask someone else what happened, then come up with a story we might all agree on. Or not. That's okay, too. Maybe even better. In any case, the electronic record of a family vacation is clearly a wave of the future, which can be good so long as the tail does not wag the dog. Digitally recording our every experience has other implications. Ironic distance is the default stance of our culture, and there's no reason to expect the family vacation to remain immune from this. Irony is invaluable armour against the commercialization and shallowness of our society, but it's also armour that deflects empathy and that too often labels emotion as sentiment.

Other trends, such as the rise of the intergenerational family vacation, seem poised to skew the family vacation towards a safer and more easily digestible experience, given the reasonable precautions that have to be taken with older travellers. This is tied to the rise in the cruise industry and the all-inclusive industry; it's safe, knowable, secure, predictable. As are the staycation, the Edu-Cation, the guided camp. A trend I find worrying indeed is the new push from some educational theorists to eradicate the summer vacation altogether, the rationale being that it's an outmoded scheduling format (based on what was once an agrarian culture; the kids needed to help with the farming in the summer). The thinking is that children lose much of their knowledge over the summer and have to relearn things in the fall. The proposed changes will see school taking place year-round, with shorter breaks more often throughout the year as opposed to the one big break. To begin with, the academic evidence is not conclusive, but even if it were, it does not take into account that while having summers off might create slightly less academically perfect students, it might be encouraging greater creativity. The problem with having shorter breaks throughout the year is that it will inevitably begin to feel as if school is a year-round proposition. If the longest break any child ever gets is two weeks, there can be no doubt that there will be homework, assignments, and parental pressure during those two weeks. Kids need time to be kids, and the research on creativity and "boredom" discussed earlier demonstrates that it's essential for children to develop creative solutions through having "nothing to do." But what if we, as adults, in our infinite wisdom, make sure that they always have something to do? Like school for twelve months a year? We may turn out more mathematicians and engineers, but perhaps not as many painters and philosophers.

The needle does seem to be pointing in the direction of conservative and/or constricted family vacations gaining ascendance. But how can we be sure? Despite its obvious prevalence as a cultural institution, the family vacation remains an understudied and only partially understood phenomenon. Why should this be? Perhaps the lack of study and research and writing on the family vacation, as alluded to in the introduction, has to do with the fact that it's one of the new kids on the academic and cultural block. Perhaps the family vacation's sentimental overtones or its relation to the perceived "shallowness" of tourism and leisure have hindered our best writers and thinkers from taking it up more often. But I also sometimes wonder if it isn't a different kind of problem, if it doesn't have something to do with how my generation has both altered and interpreted the family vacation. Or, even more fundamentally, how it has altered the concept of parenting, since the family vacation is nothing if not an expression of parenting styles.

I admit it often feels to me as though today's family vacation (and, I suppose, by extension, today's parenting) has become something of a preventive exercise rather than an exploratory undertaking. Certainly, the speed and information overload of our culture, and the increasing personal exposure of our children through technology, does not predispose any of us to breezy, laissez-faire parenting; we have to put up *some* fences. But the preponderance of manuals, books, guides, television shows, Internet sites, and just the whole damn culture chiding us, practically paralyzing us, doesn't help either. We are told in so many ways how to not make mistakes—for fear of irreparably damaging our poor little young ones—that we too often make the biggest mistake of all, which is to play defence, not offence. It often appears that being a parent in today's world has become about what *not* to do, about what to avoid, about creating a culture of risk management. This has inevitably spilled over into the family vacation.

I wonder what effect all this will have on our children, on the memory bank they carry with them as they leave childhood. Our past is an aquifer, a subterranean river that empties into our conscious memory pool, keeps it fresh, full, vivid. It needs to brim over, this memory pool, to tip into the present moment and hydrate our imagination. Under overprotected lives, without childhood adventure *and* misadventure, the aquifer trickles, the level of the memory pool drops. If our past cannot continue to adequately replenish our memory we face lives of diminished context, lives yoked to the immediate, the present, the decontextualized. The managed childhood is not wrong—it *must* be managed, at some level—but childhood needs some risk, some hazard.

It's particularly controversial to say that mistakes often form us to a higher degree than their prevention (if we survive them, that is). These are the situations in which memory blooms, where it finds contrast, definition. "Safety first" may be sound parenting, but it does not always supply the optimal conditions for the accumulation of memory and the formation of character. The family vacation and its usually survivable disasters, its wrong turns, right turns, traumas, and overall unpredictability (when we allow and accept that unpredictability) present the ideal circumstances under which families can form bonds . . . and, of course, sometimes break them. Every family is a construct, a collection of often radically different beings. They may get along when everything's fine. But things don't always go smoothly in life or on the family vacation, and although that's not necessarily a bad thing, it seems as if our culture is intent on removing *any* possibility of the kind of mishap or adventure that a family can experience together, the kind of adventure that might, in fact, actually conspire to unite them. It's what families are made of.

I need to add that this book is not meant as a plea for family togetherness, at least not as defined by the cozy picture of the traditional nuclear family used by the media and the tourism industry. Some of the most well-adjusted families I know are blended or single-parent families; I mean, you can't always get it right the first time. Susan Sessions Rugh reported that only 24 percent of all U.S. households are "married with children," and only 30 percent of those who vacationed with a family member fit into a traditional nuclear family. This means the "family" is changing, and so is the family vacation. If you are an adult and you are holidaying with a child you're related to, that's a family vacation as far as I'm concerned. In fact, the inherent values we hope to both find and strengthen on a family vacation—to create strong bonds, to stock the memory pool, to build the traditions and continuity that lead to the construction of personal and familial identity—can all be just as powerful and meaningful with a divorced mom and her two girls, or a gay couple with their adopted son, or any combination you can think of, as with a standard "nuclear family." If people who define their joint relationship as "family" are on holiday together, that's a family vacation.

Of course, a fantastically exotic family vacation will not cure what ails any troubled family, and a lousy, rainy, boring family vacation will not ruin a strong family. No family is perfect given that families are, as a general rule, stocked with human beings; the same principle implying that no family vacation will ever be perfect. Sometimes I wonder if we shouldn't make William of Occam the patron saint of the family vacation (instead of Franz Kafka, who I perhaps ill advisedly touted in the introduction). William of Occam was the fourteenth-century English logician and Franciscan friar who stated, *"Entia non sunt multiplicanda praeter necessitatem,"* or for those of you who, like myself and every other person I have ever known, do not speak Latin, "Entities must not be multiplied beyond necessity."

This is familiarly referred to as Occam's Razor. If you apply Occam's Razor, what you are really saying is, don't make things more complicated than they need to be. Such as the family vacation. On the path of the overhyped vacation lies many a broken parental heart. The simplest approach is usually the best starting point. The family vacation is about the troop, not the target.

But we must believe, first and foremost, that the family vacation is worth pursuing in the way that best serves the family, because we believe our family lives are something worth cultivating, interpreting, and understanding. We have to believe in *that* project first. If we do, then the family vacation becomes a little bit easier to create. Naturally, interpreting and understanding something may not always lead to the happiest conclusions, but then at least you'll have the insight into what made your family tick . . . or ticked you off.

The twenty-first-century family vacation faces so many challenges, but on the bright side, being awash in information as we are does mean that there is enough information out there to get a pretty good sense of what's worth avoiding. We have an ease of travel like never before, and the tourism industry is operating at a higher standard than ever. Families have enormous economic clout in the tourism industry and this means the travelling family is a prized unit.

This also means, unfortunately, that the family will continually be shunted into the FAMILY box. The tourism industry will do what it can to direct families to destinations and experiences that are "suited" to families, for the stated purpose of making it more convenient to travel with kids. The real purpose, of course, is to make it easier for the tourism industry to cope with those kids, to sand away the edges of services required, and to maximize profit. You can't blame the tourism industry for doing this: it's like criticizing a lion for killing an antelope—it's what they *do*. But it's our job as families to define what's in the box. My sense is that parents are in a fight to preserve what is best and unique and messy and unpredictable about the family vacation, a fight to preserve its integrity—meaning, simply, that we continue to value it and pursue it and define it as we like and as best suits our individual families. Who is the "fight" against? This is not a simple question to answer, because we are up against an opponent that may not even view itself in those terms. Broadly speaking, however, I'm referring to the corporate interests of the globalized tourism industry. Money and profit are not the enemy, but rather the homogenizing of experience which the industry pursues in the name of efficiencies (which, okay, means money and profit). We're in a struggle to preserve our own ability to shape our family vacations. I'm not into predicting Orwellian dystopias, but it increasingly appears that the more cautious we become as parents planning family vacations, the more we support an industry becoming ever more centralized, standardized, structured, and, naturally, risk averse (because avoidable risk threatens profit). Perhaps such concerns are a touch far-fetched for some, too much of a generalization, but the channelling of our experience is a reality. Increased control and the shaping of our options is a logical extension of that.

However, this is decidedly not an advice book. Do this and *that* will happen. Act this way and your children will act *that* way. It doesn't work like that, as anyone with children knows. But I did work for many years in the social services, and still volunteer for various community service organizations, and what I see are families under increasing pressure, despite the rise in overall wealth and health in western society. The reasons for this are too numerous to record here, and hundreds of books have been written on the subject, but it's real and it's there: raising a family has never been easy, and it's even harder now, given the relentless pressures we face of twenty-four-hour-a-day media bombardment, the pressures of both parents feeling as if they need to have meaningful careers, the pressure children are under at larger schools with greater competition for university spots, and the wash of the media forever telling all of us we need to be something other than what we already are.

But some of this is pressure we put on ourselves as parents. Why do we do this? To raise perfect children? Good luck with that. There is no perfect family vacation, either. Instead, each family vacation is a brick in a wall you're building together. It's about creating relationships, establishing patterns for your family to communicate, learning how to be together as a unit—things that will stand us all in pretty good stead as children leave home. It's about creating the conditions for the development of vivid memories, shared stories, a history that helps us form the basis of our movement throughout time as a family. All we're really trying to do is give our children a few tools to help them forge and keep reliable relationships when they hit the road . . . at which point we'll begin the process of badgering them to call us every now and then, reminding them that we gave them tools to forge and keep reliable relationships so they could use them on their parents.

If there is one thing this book is advocating, to the degree that it's advocating anything, it's that the family vacation is a meal best served at an informal table. With no set menu. And maybe no cutlery. In some ways, it's about accepting everything that's *imperfect* about the family, and ourselves, and the vacations we take. It's no surprise that the stories that live on the longest and which contribute the most to family lore are the ones where something goes awry. And yet for some reason we keep trying to remove every possibility of such stories finding life.

I often think of that trip to Mexico my family took in 1973, eight of us jammed into a station wagon for six weeks. It was a crazy notion, the kind of quixotic trip almost no parent would take with their kids nowadays. What were they thinking?! Well, they weren't thinking; that's the point. They were too busy living. There was no orchestrated approach to child-rearing, and they were not afraid to make mistakes. There were no books, manuals, guides, DVDs. They didn't manage our childhoods so much as open the cages and let the animals run the zoo. My parents made a profound impact on me by not trying to make a profound impact on me. One of the ways they did this was through our family vacations. Loading up the car and driving to Mexico City and back was but one example of many. The memories are endless. In fact, even my first memory is related to a family vacation.

I have various images drift in and out of my brain when I think back to my early childhood and try to recall my first memory, but the one thing I can state categorically is that the first memory I am *sure of* also happens to be my first memory of being on a trip with my family. It was 1965 and I was four years old. Having moved from Edmonton to Calgary earlier that year so that my father could start his glass and trim business, we were now back in Edmonton visiting Duff and Grandma. It was a three-hour car trip, which was still a long and exciting journey for us. I remember it was night when we arrived. Summertime. I was sitting in the rear jump seats of our first station wagon, the progenitor of the Vista Cruiser we took to Mexico. This station wagon also had the rear jump seats that opened to face one another. Even though I wasn't yet five years old, we needed all the seats, as I was already the oldest of four children.

It was late. I was tired. I wanted to lie down but there was no room in the tiny jump seat, so I decided I would put the seat down and stretch out along the back hold. This was back in the days before seat belts, of course.

But the seat wouldn't fold down. I pulled on it. I yanked on it. I jiggled it. Nothing. I assumed there was a catch somewhere, and, unable to find one on the surface, my four-year-old brain deduced that it was hidden somewhere between the seat cushion and the back cushion. I shoved my right hand in the seam between the two cushions and began groping around in the darkness, prying here and there with a finger or two while simultaneously continuing to apply downward pressure to the fold-down back cushion. My fingers were probing various metallic bits. Something gave, a latch freed up, and the back cushion collapsed sharply onto the seat cushion with my arm still trapped between them. I felt a sharp tugging somewhere on my right hand. It hurt. A lot. I pulled my hand out from between the cushions to find that the entire tip of my middle finger, nail and all from the third knuckle up, was gone. I recall blood spurting out of it like a new oil gusher, though that can't be the way it really looked. I broke into screams and shrieks, yelping with pain and shock.

"Shut up back there," my dad yelled from the front.

I kept shrieking. "Arrrgghhhh!! My finger. Arrrghhhhhhhh!! My finger!"

My mother turned around. "Now, you listen to me back there, all of you. Just pipe down."

"My finger," I said. "My finger!" I held it up so they could see. Blood was everywhere.

"Mom!" said one of my brothers, probably Bruce. "Curt cut his finger off!"

My mom turned around, saw the gore, and lost it. "Gerry, he's cut his finger off. Oh my God! Oh my God!! He's cut his finger right off? Where's his finger? Gerry, get to the hospital."

I spent that night in the Royal Alexandra Hospital (which was also where I was born). They would have tried to sew my fingertip back on, but my dad couldn't find it in the dark between the seats. They had to stitch it up and let it heal over. It looks today pretty much what it looked like that night: three-quarters of a finger.

Three weeks later, back in Calgary, my dad was cleaning the car out and he found my fingertip down between the seat cushions. It had shrivelled up, hollowed out, and turned a bit greenish-black, but with the nail perfectly intact it was clearly recognizable as a chunk of finger. It was the suburban boy's digital equivalent of a shrunken pygmy head. I kept it in a little pill jar and took it to show and tell on the second day of grade one a few weeks later. The stitches still hadn't healed, so I was able to graphically connect the story and the prop. When I rattled the fingertip around like a stone in a jar, some girl in the first row of the class started to cry. It was a powerful talisman I had at my disposal for a couple of years until I accidentally left the lid off the jar one day when I went to school. I never saw my fingertip again, and although there was no hard evidence to link the two events, our cat began to suffer digestive tract problems around the same time.

If that was my first memory, and my first memory of being on a family vacation, it was an event of a more recent vintage, and with considerably less blood and gore, that reminded me of a central insight into the family vacation. A couple of years ago we were at Slide Rock State Park just north of Sedona, Arizona, on a road trip, a late-fall family vacation, a journey of a few thousand kilometres, one direction taking about a week, with stops in Bozeman, Idaho Falls, Zion Canyon, Las Vegas, Sedona, and finally down into Phoenix and Scottsdale. Cathy did a bit of planning and identified a few sights we wanted to make sure we got to, but we also left a fair bit of room just for driving, stopping, poking around. We saw buffalo in Yellowstone Park. We stood on a glass walkway three thousand feet above the floor of the Grand Canyon. We promised the girls a few hours in one of the world's largest outdoor pools at the MGM Grand in Las Vegas, only to arrive, check in, get changed, find the pool through the maze of casinos, set foot in the water and be instantly hauled out by frantic lifeguards due to that moment's arrival of the first thunderstorm Vegas had had in three years. The pool remained closed, and we never did get to set foot back in it.

And now we were in Sedona.

We'd stopped at Slide Rock on an offhand recommendation; we hadn't planned on it, hadn't scoped it out, hadn't really built any portion of our trip around it, and had almost passed it over completely because it was raining so hard the night before that we contemplated skipping Sedona altogether and pushing on into Phoenix. But we stayed overnight, and went to Slide Rock in the morning. Before going in, I tested the water and when I pulled my foot out it had gone blue from the arctic temperature.

"Aiihh!" I said. "That's wickedly cold."

Grace saw an opportunity. "Dad?"

"What?"

"That water's super cold, right?"

"Uh, yeah."

"So you're chicken to go in?"

"No. I'll go in. But Mom's going first."

Cathy shot me a look, but didn't say no.

"But you're too chicken to jump in?"

"I'm not sure that's how I'd put it."

"I'm not chicken. I'll jump."

"No, you won't, you're too scared. You're chicken, too."

"I bet I could dive right in the deep pool. I won't even dip a toe in. I don't care how cold it is."

"That'd be brave," I said. "But I doubt you could do it."

She thought about that. "If I dive in," she continued, "will you give me ten dollars?"

There are some things you just can't budget for on a family vacation. I laughed and was on the verge of saying yes.

"Okay, okay," she said, misreading my hesitation. "How about five dollars?"

Cathy did go first, and although it took a while she finally managed to immerse most of her torso into the frigid waters of Oak Creek, shrieking like a banshee. Jess and Grace got in behind her, and I brought up the rear. The ice-cold shock of it took my breath away. The girls began schussing. I followed after them. The surface of the creek bed under the water was slick and smooth, red rock worn over the millennia into the sensual curves of a perfect gliding slide. We let the current carry us down the slippery chute until we were finally deposited into a deep pool with water so clear every tiny pebble was visible ten feet under the surface. Our hoots and whoops echoed like hyena calls off the high red walls. We were in the moment, laughing, freezing, daring, leaping, all of us exactly where we wanted to be.

It occurred to me later, after we'd dried off and were back on the road, what it is, finally, that makes family vacations work when they work and what sinks them when they don't. The family vacation is at once vastly complex while also being deceptively simple. It's partly about where we're going and how we're getting there. It's partly about how well we've managed expectation and how successful we've been at quelling our desire to control the outcome. It's partly about how well we've planned and what activities are arranged. Yes, it's about all of these things and so much more. But mostly it's about remembering who we're with.

Acknowledgements

I'd like to thank the many people who assisted me directly or indirectly in the writing of this book. There were many scholars and writers whose work I benefited from, and I hope that I reflected their work properly while also reflecting my gratitude for their efforts. There are many magazine editors who have sent me on assignment over the years, often with my family, including those at *Western Living*, *Travel Etc.*, *Westworld*, *Canadian Geographic Travel*, and *Up!* I would most particularly like to thank Ilana Weitzman, my long-time editor at *enRoute*, the Air Canada in-flight magazine. Ilana is a fine editor, a good friend, and an intelligent sounding board; I owe her a great deal. For their feedback, insight and encouragement, I am indebted to my agent Anne McDermid, and to Janice Zawerbny at Thomas Allen and Patrick Crean, formerly of Thomas Allen. I'd also like to thank the various granting bodies that supported the writing of this book: the Canada Council for the Arts, the Edmonton Arts Council, and the Alberta Foundation for the Arts. Thanks, too, to the Banff Centre for the Arts for the use of the Leighton

Studios (my lucky charm). I also greatly appreciate my sister-in-law, Patty Condon, allowing me the use of her house in Fernie, British Columbia, as an occasional writing retreat.

One person I owe a considerable debt to is my friend Bruce Grierson for his sleuthing, his wisdom, his humour, his sympathetic ear. He will scoff at this, but I might not have written this book without his insights and encouragement. I have already thanked my mother in the opening pages of the book, but I'll thank her again, along with my sadly deceased father, for the endless memories and fun and laughs—and sometimes the emergencies and trauma—of our family vacations . . . and our family, period. I have always enjoyed the company of my brothers and sister, and their families, and I want to thank them for their spirit and good humour. I'd also like to thank my in-laws, Bob and Marg Condon, for creating such a fine family, all of whom vacation regularly with us. It's always fun and always welcome.

Lastly, I want to thank Cathy, Jessica, and Grace, my fellow travellers in the world, in life, in spirit. The journey would be pointless without you.